THE VICTORIA AND SIDNEY RAILWAY

1892-1919

Waiting For The Train - Sidney Station

by Darryl E. Muralt

PUBLISHED BY THE B.C. RAILWAY HISTORICAL ASSOCIATION

with assistance from the B.C. Heritage Trust

3

ISBN 0-9692511-1-4
Copywright © by the B.C. Railway Historical Association,
Box 8114, V.C.P.O.,
Victoria, B.C.   V8W 3R8

Typeset by Trade Typesetting, Victoria.
Production co-ordination by Currie's Forestgraphics Ltd.
Printed and bound in Canada by Hignell Printing Limited.

Dedication

1900 - 1992

To the memory of Walter Bate, the last surviving employee of the railway. Walter was always eager to pass along his recollections of the old "Cordwood Limited".

Preface

Perhaps not unnaturally, the preface, which comes first in the order of this book, is the last thing that gets written. I don't know if that's a quirk peculiar to myself, or whether other writers work in the same, seemingly backwards, order. This is my third book and the writing and research embodied in it was enjoyed to an even greater extent than with the two works which preceded it. Perhaps I needed to finish up by coming back to the beginning so that in some way I could assure myself that the work was at last finished and the process had come full circle.

The number of individual tasks associated with writing a book are too numerous to elaborate on here and one often wonders why he writes or whether the project will ever end. But, this third time around, I am aware of a more compelling reason for setting this story down than I was with my two previous works.

There has been much political unrest in Canada of late and when I examine the reasons for the claim of "distinct society" status for one province in this Dominion, I am aware that the features that make that society distinct are not only its unique language, but its long, well-chronicled history and the vibrancy of its cultural and literary tradition. There are many positive aspects to this which we in the West should emulate and, indeed, many of us have.

Here in Western Canada we are just beginning to discover and set down the details of what really is a rich and varied history and culture. In spite of the efforts of many historians over the years, there is still much to be done and no serious historian should ever fear for lack of employment opportunities. Every nation (and province) needs a cultural and mythological identity of its own and that only comes about when we get in touch with our roots as a people.

British Columbia is a rich province, as well endowed with historic and cultural assets as is any other part of the country. The trouble with us here, is that not enough of our diverse history has been set down yet. Now, more than ever, we need a past with traditions, just as we always have, but perhaps the need is more urgent than before because we are in danger of getting lost in the inflow of culture from our southern neighbour. Indeed, many say that we're just really Americans of another type anyway.

I don't agree, and I hope that this work will make some small contribution to the realization that the local Greater Victoria and Vancouver Island area has many great Canadian stories just waiting to be discovered and told.

The story of the Victoria and Sidney Railway has already been chronicled once in the wonderful *Cordwood Limited*, written by George Hearn and David Wilkie, first printed in 1967, and reprinted by the British Columbia Railway Historical Association on at least a half-dozen occasions.

As the centennial of the Victoria and Sidney Railway in 1992 approached, our Association discussed the possibility of updating the *Cordwood Limited* but, in fairness to the original authors, it did not seem right to trifle with what has become a popular and enduring local classic. That publication became the inspiration for an entirely new work which has taken most of the past two and one half years to research and write.

I've been very fortunate to have access to information and technology that the original researchers and writers never had, and, I can only say that it has given me a great personal respect for the magnitude of the task which was undertaken by them in researching the original 1967 work. Today there are microfilm reader-printers, xerox machines, and mini-cassette recorders to aid the researcher and the ubiquitous computer to put it all together. Without these advances, the task of getting out the Victoria and Sidney story as it is told here would still be in process.

The task of the serious historian is a difficult one and quite different from the writer of popular fiction or even non-fiction. The problem is that while he must strive for objectivity and all the other requirements of historiography, he sees the story only through his own eyes and prejudices. As a professional transportation manager, I feel comfortable with part of the task, but I know that my view of the Victoria and Sidney Railway story is probably influenced by my own particular interests and biases. However, sometimes an awareness of our own limitations can be a helpful factor in striving just that much harder to be objective.

In the case of this story, I've tried not to judge others in any personal way. I make this reference with the late Captain Albert Sears of the *S.S. Iroquois* in mind. He made a mistake and suffered for it. Others have recently dealt harshly with him in print, but I find little hard evidence to support the statements made about him. How just was Captain Sears' punishment was not for me to decide. I only report what I believe to have happened from the evidence available to me.

Finally, with due respect to those who have grown up accustomed to using the metric system of measurement, I must apologize for retaining the Imperial system of feet and miles as I feel that the repetitious use of bracketed metric equivalents seriously impairs the continuity of the text. To bypass this problem and to retain historical data in its original form, the text uses only those values appropriate to the period of time under review. The number of instances where this will create a problem for those used to metric should be very minimal.

Researching and writing this history of the Victoria and Sidney Railway has been a sometimes daunting, but always pleasurable task. If the reader enjoys his role in this exercise even half as much as I have, I will feel justified in having completed this work. This is not my story or history, it is **our** history - I hope you'll find it as interesting as I do.

Acknowledgements

Although an author may long work at the task of perfecting his work, no book is every truly the effort of a single person. Over the past two years or more I have enjoyed the support and assistance of many people whose contributions have been invaluable.

As always, I want to thank Joan Barton and the staff of the Provincial Legislative Library for tolerating my presence and rendering so much assistance over the years.

A special appreciation is due my colleagues in the British Columbia Railway Historical Association who have spent long hours in reviewing the manuscript and providing valuable input and inspiration. They include Paul Crozier-Smith, David Wilkie, R. Ken Bradley, Donald MacLachlan, Don Van Akker, and especially Hugh Fraser who helped in the research as well as the editing process. The late George Hearn and David Wilkie, co-authors of the *Cordwood Limited*, were always a special inspiration to me in this project - they have been a hard act to follow.

The staffs of the Provincial and Delta Archives also assisted with photographs and information which is gratefully acknowledged.

A special thanks is due to Moran Brethour, of the Saanich Pioneers' Society, who gave every co-operation and much useful information about the Saanich Peninsula and the Brethour family in particular. Moran also contributed valuable map information which is found in the text and appendices of this book. Thanks also to the regular Monday morning Pioneers' Society members who work so hard and so co-operatively to preserve the history of the Saanich Peninsula.

Valuable advice and assistance has been given by my fellow researchers Robert D. Turner, Bob Spearing and Frank Clapp. Chark Nipp and Al Lompart at the Surveyor General office were most helpful in locating and copying pertinent railway survey maps. George Williamson, of Nanaimo, did the wonderful cover illustration that adds so much to the overall image of the book and I hope that I will have the pleasure of working with him again.

I also had the good fortune to spend some pleasant hours in three interviews with the late Walter Bate, the last surviving employee of the Victoria and Sidney Railway, who only recently passed away. Walter helped to plug some gaps in the information that no one else could have and he is sadly missed.

My final appreciation goes to my longtime friend and colleague Gordon Currie who has so ably taken the book from manuscript through the editorial and design stages. Gordon has gone the extra mile in producing fine maps, drawings and artwork and it was a pleasure to work with him.

If there is anyone that I have left out, it is by erroneous oversight and not deliberate omission. The number of people who gave advice and encouragement was many and space prohibits their inclusion here.

Lastly, but most importantly, I must express appreciation to my long-suffering wife who was so often without me while I pursued some item of research information or spent long hours in front of my word processor. It's hard living with a writer, especially one who is so compulsive about his work.

Darryl E. Muralt
April 1992

Table of Contents

LIST OF MAPS

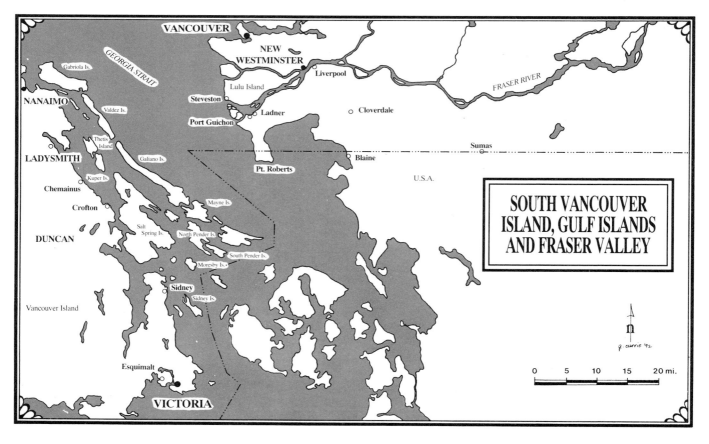

INTRODUCTION

Within the overall picture of railway development on the west coast of Canada around the turn of the last century, the Victoria and Sidney Railway was a small nondescript shortline. It began as an independent enterprise, but emerged as part of a scheme to make British Columbia a corner of the corporate empire of James J. "Big Jim" Hill, an ambitious expatriate Canadian railway magnate. Ultimately, it became the unwanted stepchild of Hill's American transcontinental, the Great Northern Railway.

Even as shortlines go, the V&S was definitely short. From mudsill to stringer, and from the Sidney Wharf to the Market Station in Victoria, it never aggregated much more than 16 miles. Its importance lay not in the achievement or failure of some grand scheme of commercial exploitation or conquest, but in its simple utility as a carrier of people and goods between the Saanich Peninsula and Victoria, and later by steamer connection with the Gulf Islands, Nanaimo and the lower B.C. Mainland.

After losing its independent status and becoming an arm of the Great Northern Railway in 1902, the V&S remained, at heart, a shortline railroad in the classic mould and therein lies its appeal to the railfan and historian.

The principal commodity over the V&S line for much of its operating life was cordwood, to fuel the stoves and furnaces of Victoria. The trains of the little line soon earned the sobriquet, "The Cordwood Limited." Throughout the years, the farmers of Saanich and district transported their goods to markets in Victoria over its rusting 50-pound rails. On summer weekends there were numerous excursions over the line by church groups, fishermen, hunters, rusticators and plain garden-variety tourists.

Chief among the memories of the Victoria and Sidney Railway was its chronic tardiness and frequent deviation from advertised schedules. (The wait for the connecting steamboat service often caused delays). In spite of this and other occasional difficulties, the V&S became a necessary evil for many on their way to and from Victoria and for some it was, if nothing else, the line they liked to complain about the most. For others it was the butt of many a "slow train" joke. Local contemporary writer Clive Phillipps-Wolley dubbed it "the Creeping Paralysis."

However, absence makes the heart grow fonder and the passage of years has been kind. Though few vestigial traces remain, the V&S occupies a revered place in the history of the Saanich Peninsula. There are a dwindling few, who yet savour the memory of a childhood trip over its sinuous rails but, with the passage of time, their ranks are thinning.

The sight of the typical Victoria and Sidney locomotive moving its mixed freight and passenger train along the meandering right-of-way, crosshead deep in meadow grass, emerging from a thicket in the woods near Bear Hill, or running on the highline west of Elk Lake, must have been memorable for the fortunate few who witnessed it. The Victoria and Sidney was no highspeed, flatland mainline; it was just a rural, backwoods, workaday railroad making an accommodation with time and topography as it wound its way from Sidney to Victoria and return.

There is much more to the V&S story than just its locomotives, cars, and a few miles of rails. Early in the history of common carrier railways on Vancouver Island there had been the dream of a combined rail and ferry link from Victoria to an associated mainland line running east to a connection with the transcontinental railroad. The Saanich Peninsula line would also be a connecting route between Victoria and the many settlers then establishing themselves in the outlying Gulf Islands, north of the Saanich Peninsula.

The V&S was at first built simply as a railway operation, but by 1895 it had connections with a small inter-island steamer service. After it won the Gulf Islands mail contract in early 1900, the company set up its own maritime subsidiary, the Sidney and Nanaimo Transportation Company (S&NT). The S&NT connected the Victoria and Sidney Railway with the Islands of the southern Gulf of Georgia and ran as far north as Nanaimo. It was the Railway's first venture in the maritime trade but by no means its last.

By 1901, plans were also in place for a rail and passenger connection between Sidney and the Great Northern Railway on the Lower Mainland of British Columbia. This resulted in the formation of the Victoria Terminal Railway and Ferry Company (VTR&F) and the construction and operation of a rail and passenger ferry to Liverpool, on the south shore of the Fraser River, opposite New Westminster. Later, to shorten the water route, the VTR&F built a terminus at Port Guichon, west of Ladner, and from that point a rail connection eastward to Cloverdale. The VTR&F actually became the parent of the old Victoria and Sidney company, but the latter continued to exist as a separate corporate entity since the V&S held a provincial (British Columbia) charter, while the Victoria Terminal Railway and Ferry Company a federal (Canadian) charter.

During 1902, the Sidney and Nanaimo Transportation Company expanded its ferry service in the Gulf Islands to serve the new smelter town of Crofton and to provide a daily service to Nanaimo. The new Victoria Terminal Railway and Ferry Company inaugurated its run between Sidney and the Lower Mainland in May of 1903.

The VTR&F, through its management, had close connections with the Great Northern Railway of James J. Hill. In October of 1902, the Great Northern acquired control of the two smaller companies through purchase of outstanding stock, however they continued to maintain separate corporate identities. (At times, the names of the two railways were combined and published in joint passenger schedules as the "Victoria Terminal and Sidney Railway".)

What began as a positive step, within part of Hill's grandiose plan to invade Canadian territory, soon became an unwanted "bust". The Great Northern gave the Victoria and Sidney line little encouragement or support over most of the next 17 years until the line's formal closure in 1919. There were slow trains, accidents, shipwrecks, and the arrival of competition in the form of electric interurban and steam railways. There were also protracted squabbles with the City of Victoria and the Provincial Government of British Columbia. Both levels of government had guaranteed the bond interest to help fund the construction of the Victoria and Sidney Railway.

Even after all this, the line into Sidney wasn't ready to die. It was essential to the survival of that town's local industry and a short portion of the V&S line remained in use after 1919 between the town and a connection with the nearby Canadian National Railway. This operation continued until the shutdown of the Sidney Sawmill and the last rusting rails were then removed. Thereafter, only the abandoned grade, the memories and a few faded photographs remained.

The Victoria and Sidney Railway was not in the class of the great and memorable transcontinentals, but it played a useful and necessary role in the growth and development of a small isolated region, the Saanich Peninsula north of Victoria, and was an important connecting link with civilization for the scattered inhabitants of the Gulf Islands and beyond. It was the archetypal Canadian short line railroad. It had about it, in precise microcosm, all the great and tangible realities and glories of the high iron in the years when the locomotive engineer was among the heroes of many red-blooded young men.

So sit back in your plush seat on the Cordwood Limited. The train is just pulling out. Join us now for a trip along the best 17-odd miles of railroad to be found anywhere between Victoria and Sidney.

"All aboard!"

1

GENESIS

Birth of
a Dream

As a condition of British Columbia's entry into Confederation, in 1871, the Government of Canada promised Vancouver Islanders an "Island Railway" as part of its new transcontinental rail system. Most local communities of any size vied for recognition and each saw themselves as the only logical Island terminus. For several years (prior to the awarding of the contract, for construction of the Island Railway from Esquimalt to Nanaimo, on August 16, 1883), both Victoria and Nanaimo agitated vigorously to be selected as the Island's main railway centre.

During October of 1879, a champion also emerged for the agricultural community of Saanich. Mr. A. Bunster, formerly the local Member of the Provincial Parliament (MPP), outlined a plan whereby the northern end of the Saanich Peninsula would become the Island terminal point for a ferry system between the Canadian Pacific Railway (then, yet to be built to the lower British Columbia mainland) and Vancouver Island.

If Bunster's scheme had matured, the north end of the Saanich Peninsula would have been connected with Victoria by a short line of railway, and from there an extension would have run further up-Island. This idea, no doubt, made great sense to Bunster's former constituents. But, in the coal mining community of Nanaimo, it aroused little enthusiasm and the *Nanaimo Free Press* of October 23, 1879, was quick to condemn the ex-MPP from Saanich:

Left:
Before the coming of the railway, the solitude of the forest was interrupted by only a few roads and a network of trails. On a beautiful day in the 1880s the unknown photographer couldn't resist a picture of the primeval forest at a place in Saanich called "Cape Horn."

"The scheme proposed by Mr. Bunster on Thursday night last, of making the north end of Saanich Peninsula a terminal point in the Canadian Pacific Railway, the more it is studied and digested the more impractical and unfeasible it appears. The idea no doubt was that vessels from Burrard Inlet, the Mainland terminus, would land freight and passengers at the head of the Saanich Peninsula and from thence be transported to Victoria, not Esquimalt, by an abortion of the Island Railway properly now known as 'Saanich Shunting.' A comparison of the sea route from Burrard Inlet to Nanaimo, with the route between the former port and the Saanich Peninsula may not be inopportune at the present juncture. The distance to Nanaimo from Burrard Inlet is about 33 miles, in a direct line across the open Gulf of Georgia, and can be traversed with safety every hour in the year for with the establishment of the proper signals at Point Atkinson Lighthouse (Burrard Inlet) and Entrance Island Lighthouse (Nanaimo),this route could be traversed with safety at full speed in the densest fog ever known to envelop the blue waters of the Gulf of Georgia. The entrance from the Gulf to Nanaimo is fully five miles wide and can be entered by the Great Eastern if necessary in all weathers and at all stages of the tide...Can the same be said of the route necessary to connect Burrard Inlet with Saanich? Every mariner will answer with a stentorian No! In the first place the distance is about double. The first 30 miles of navigation is by the Gulf of Georgia and is almost similar to the navigation across the Gulf to this port. So far so good, but as Mark Twain would say 'Now come the rub.' From the Gulf to Saanich several fair weather and small steamboat routes present themselves, viz: through Porlier Pass and around Trincomali and Swanson Channel or on the inside of Salt Spring Island and through the Sansum Narrows. Another route is by way of Active Pass and Swanson Channel. Either of these routes would provide extra safe navigation for large steamships in fair and clear weather and with favourable tides. The ship channel around East Point affords the most open channel, but a large steamship would be liable to delay, besides having to pass so close to the American islands, that they would be at the mercy of hostile batteries in case of a war between Great Britain and the United States. As a route for a ferry therefore there can be no comparison between the clear and open route between Burrard Inlet and Nanaimo and the intricate navigation necessary to reach Saanich. Independent of the advantages of a ferry to Nanaimo as compared to one to Saanich, Vancouver Island, by the 'Carnarvon terms,' has been promised an Island Railway and not a 'Saanich Shunting'..."

Arthur Bunster, M.P.P.

In ensuing years, Nanaimo would get its Island Railway connection first, but the dream of a railway link between Victoria and the north end of the sparsely populated Saanich Peninsula would be revived again, and again, and finally become reality. Some ideas, whether fraught with difficulties of marine navigation or not, are bound to happen when their utility to the general public is finally recognized. Within a decade, the idea of a Saanich Peninsula railway line and a Mainland ferry connection was revived. This time, the sponsor of the measure would be none other than the Honourable Amor De Cosmos. He was the former Premier of British Columbia and federal Member of Parliament for Victoria.

De Cosmos first suggested the scheme in 1886, and after three years of formulating plans and submissions to government, the Provincial Legislature granted a charter for his railway plan. It was to be called the Victoria, Saanich and New Westminster Railway. The promoters then requested that the City of Victoria guarantee 4% interest on $500,000 worth of first mortgage bonds for undertaking the railway construction. However, the details of the railway plan were unfavourable from the City's viewpoint - the Mainland portion of the line was to be much longer than the Island section and apparently no Mainland community was to provide any similar financial support. Consequently, in October 1891, while the by-law was up for second reading, it was turned thumbs down by a vote of six to three.

Amor De Cosmos, former Premier of British Columbia and M.P. for Victoria at Ottawa.

In the meantime, developments in Saanich and elsewhere were pointing towards the inevitable construction of a railway line through the Saanich Peninsula. The Victoria and Sidney Railway was incorporated, by other parties, on April 23, 1892. Its charter entitled it to "construct and operate telegraph and telephone lines along the line of the said railway; also to construct wharves, docks, elevators, dock-yards, ships and piers, warehouses, etc."[1]

The initial objective was mostly local in scope, intended primarily to provide the farmers of the Peninsula and the owners of the newly surveyed townsite of Sidney

The Victoria and Sidney Railway

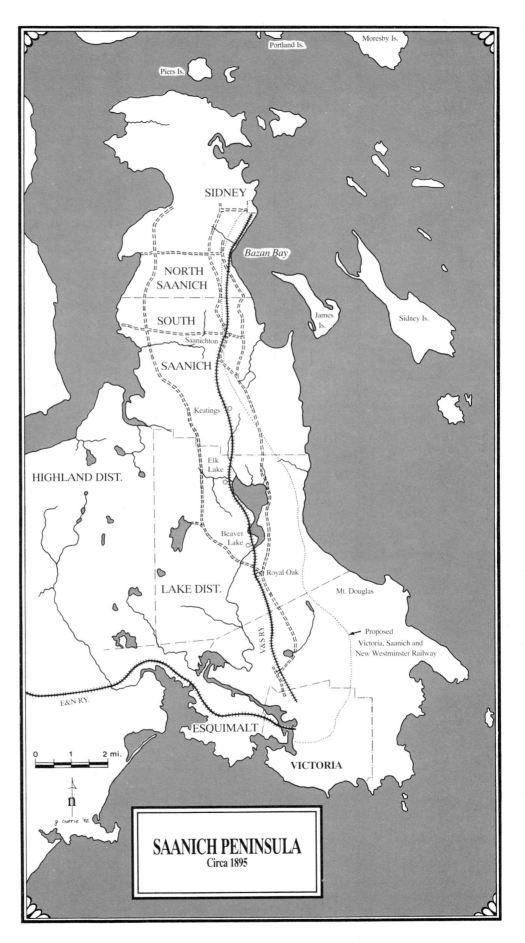

Moresby Is.

Portland Is.

Piers Is.

SIDNEY

Bazan Bay

NORTH
SAANICH

SOUTH

Saanichton

SAANICH

James
Is.

Sidney Is.

Keatings

Elk
Lake

HIGHLAND DIST.

Beaver
Lake

Royal Oak

Mt. Douglas

LAKE DIST.

Proposed
Victoria, Saanich and
New Westminster Railway

V&S RY.

E&N RY.

ESQUIMALT

0   1   2 mi.

g. currie '92

n

VICTORIA

SAANICH PENINSULA
Circa 1895

with a means of access to the markets of the city of Victoria, sixteen miles to the south. While the privileges granted the new corporation seemed rather grandiose, they were typical railway charter conditions of the period. They allowed the new company to enter into associated lines of endeavour should they wish to do so.

The provisional directors of the new corporation were the Brethour brothers, Julius and Henry, of Sidney, and Robert Irving, of Victoria. They asked the City of Victoria to pass a by-law guaranteeing 3% interest on First Mortgage bonds for a period of twenty five years. The Province of British Columbia was also asked to act as a guarantor, in the amount of 2%. The City was also requested to exempt from taxation all rights-of-way and railroad property within the city limits during construction and for a period of ten years thereafter.

The Railway Assistance By-Law

The Victoria and Sidney Railway Assistance By-Law was presented to Victoria's City Council on May 20th, 1892. It passed second reading and was refined during the last week of June. It incorporated several amendments, all moved by Alderman Munn,: (1) That a ten dollar per day fine would be imposed on the contractor for each Oriental employed on the construction; (2) That a $100 fine per day would be imposed on the contractor for each day that the construction was carried on prior to October 1, 1892, or beyond a scheduled completion date of September 1, 1894; (3) That the Victoria and Sidney Railway Company need only submit plans to City Council for works located within the city limits or on city owned properties. (This would include the city's water supply area at Elk and Beaver Lakes.); and (4) That the railway would be required to operate at least one steam powered train per day over the entire line, Sundays excepted.[2]

This by-law was much more acceptable to the electors of Victoria than the old De Cosmos sponsored interest guarantee by-law, especially after Victoria ratepayers received assurance that the new rail line, less than 20 miles in length, would substantially reduce the cost of fuelwood in the city by providing for cheaper shipment. Alderman Munn suggested a saving of $20,000 dollars per year was to be expected - more than twice the annual interest to be guaranteed. Several of the aldermen felt that owing to heavy unemployment in the Victoria area some form of public works should be started and the project seemed to fill the bill admirably. The new rail line would also facilitate improved transportation between the Gulf Islands and Victoria through connection with a proposed steamboat service. The by-law was ratified by public vote on July 20, 1892, by a ratio of almost three to one, with 685 for the by-law and 234 opposed.

In spite of the general acceptance of this new railway scheme by the citizens of Victoria and the Saanich Peninsula, there were those, even two years later, who were not elated, even less so at the prospect of subsidizing yet another railway. On March 10, 1894, the *Province* newspaper, of Victoria, would critique another proposed Saanich Peninsula-Lower Mainland railway scheme, with direct reference to the previously approved V&S subsidy:

"A meeting was held at the City Hall, Victoria, on Tuesday last, to discuss the subject of Government assistance being granted to the Delta Railway. Mr. Alderman Munn was voted to the chair, and after a good deal of discussion a resolution was passed requesting the Government to lend every possible aid to the undertaking. Having subsidized the Victoria and Sidney Railway, which to the most casual observer could only be looked on as part of a greater scheme, it becomes necessary that its complement should be supported. It is to be regretted, however, that in the first instance the whole scheme was not

Julius, Sam and Henry Brethour. Julius and Henry were initiators of the Victoria and Sidney Railway scheme and principal early backers with liberal grants of land.

submitted to the people. It is an underhanded way of doing things which we cannot at all approve of.

"The public would have been well advised if they had opposed the Sidney Railway scheme tooth and nail, until its further developments were explained. And it behooves us all to keep an eye on this new scheme and to see to it that no such jobbery takes place as was the case with the V.&S. Railway."

A week later, on March 17, 1894, the *Province* would have even more to say in hindsight to the Victoria and Sidney Railway interest approval:

A LEAP IN THE DARK

"Public meetings have been held and a great deal of correspondence written urging the Government to afford assistance to the scheme of which the Victoria and Sidney Railway forms a part. If our memory serves us, when the Peninsula Railway scheme was first put before the public nothing whatever was said about its' being a part of a larger undertaking, nor do we remember to have seen in any of the local journals a warning to the public to look before they leapt. A guarantee on the interest of half a million dollars was asked for to make a railway to Saanich, and that was enough for Victorians and for the farmers of Saanich. One party was going to have half a million dollars spent on its neighbourhood, the other was going to have a railway built to its doors. That was sufficient. The one party did not get its one half million, but only about three-fifths of that sum, with which however it appeared to be satisfied, and the only opposition to the affair came, if we mistake not, from certain persons who did not share in the spoil that arose out of the difference between half a million and three hundred thousand dollars. But that is an old story, and is not the point we want to make here, which is that before the public allows its money to be voted for any purpose, let it be assured in doing so that the viable object is the end of the matter, let it take care that when money is so spent it does not turn out that a great deal more is required to make the first expenditure profitable.

"At present the Victoria and Sidney Railway is an instance of isolated and expensive folly. It cannot possibly pay as it is, and the only possible reason for its existence is as a part of, or as a connecting link with some other scheme. That scheme obviously is a connection by means of a steamer with some railway system on the Mainland. Having gone thus far, the country must go further and complete the work, and it must take care that the well being and future prosperity of the undertaking are not harassed or even menaced by any combination for its downfall and destruction that may be arrived at by its two rivals, the C.P.R. and C.P.N."

The rivals mentioned above, the Canadian Pacific Railway and the Canadian Pacific Navigation Company, were the major players in the railway and steamboat businesses in those days on the B.C. Coast. The comments in the *Province* show that even two years after the City gave its approval to guarantee interest on the Victoria and Sidney Railway bond issue, some still had serious reservations about such guarantees for the construction of a railway - any railway! Future developments were to prove them justified in their position.

Notwithstanding these kinds of reservations, most Victoria and Saanich residents, and the Provincial Government as well, were solidly behind the idea of a railway line along the Saanich Peninsula from Victoria to Sidney.

While the Victoria and Sidney Railway Assistance By-Law was pending approval during the early summer of 1892, the Brethours and Irving had considered its passage almost a *fait accompli*. They had continued with their plans for the Victoria and Sidney Railway through the interim, by attracting to the new townsite of Sidney a sawmill they hoped would provide much needed economic stability. The railway, the sawmill and the Sidney townsite were part of a greater development plan for the Saanich Peninsula that would see its forest and agricultural products transported to the markets of Victoria, and in the case of lumber shipments, even overseas. If these objectives were not ambitious enough, the company could always expand outward towards the Gulf Islands and the British Columbia Mainland as Bunster and De Cosmos had originally envisioned.

The Brethours and Irving Make Plans

The promoters of the Sidney townsite attracted the lumber industry with generous concessions of waterfront land from three of the five local Brethour family farms. There was also a willing and industrious local labour force and easy access to the almost limitless stands of timber which could be brought to the fine harbour at Sidney from anywhere along the Coast. There was already a dock at Sidney where the steamer *Isabel*, the chief means of marine transport up the east coast of the Island, made her regular calls, and plenty of deep, sheltered water for a mill booming ground.

The company established to take up this challenging commercial opportunity was the Toronto and British Columbia Lumber Company. It was incorporated on June 2, 1892, almost seven weeks before ratification of the Victoria and Sidney interest guarantee by-law, after obvious assurances by the Brethours and Irving that the by-law was little more than a formality. One can only speculate what might have happened if the by-law had failed and the Victoria and Sidney Railway scheme had collapsed like its predecessor, the Victoria, Saanich and New Westminster Railway.

Fortunately, the Toronto and British Columbia Lumber Company, a well financed firm with backing from Ontario, could safely proceed with its plan to open a new industry at Sidney that would ship to Victoria, western Canadian and foreign markets. The principals in the firm were John White, a recently defeated Liberal Member of Parliament from Ontario, and T.J. Hammill. Other investors included Messrs. John, Strathy and Davidson, of Toronto and Barrie, Ontario. While these gentlemen were perfecting their plans, the survey commenced and preparations for construction of the Victoria and Sidney Railway were getting under way.

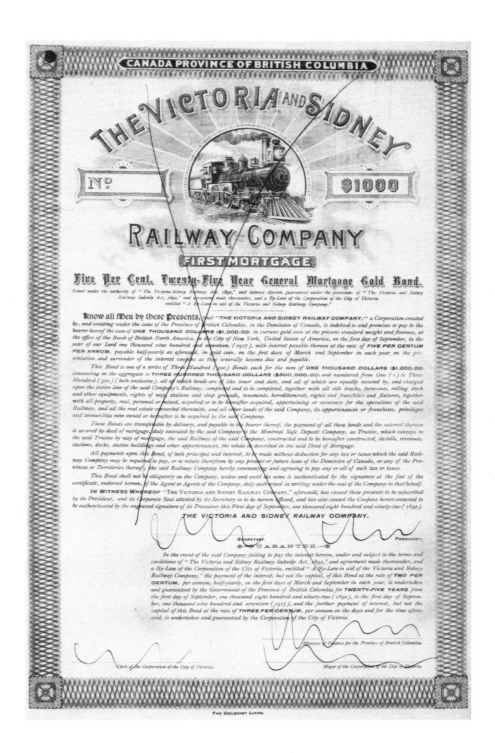

A sample $1,000 share in the stock of the Victoria and Sidney Railway. Like much of the rest of the share capital, it was never paid up.

Within a week of the by-law ratification, a survey party was in the field under the supervision of John Hamilton Gray, C.E., who was an experienced railway engineer and son of one of the Fathers of Confederation. He had been Resident Engineer on construction of the northern section of the Esquimalt and Nanaimo Railway. Following completion of that, he conducted a survey for a proposed extension of the Island Railway line north to Seymour Narrows. Next, he moved on to the construction of the Shuswap and Okanagan Railway in the British Columbia interior before returning to Vancouver Island.

After landing from the steamer *Isabel*, Gray's survey party began its work at Sidney and proceeded south towards Victoria at the rate of a mile and a half per day. The survey party stayed in private homes and inns along the way. On August 1st they stayed at the Prairie Inn at Saanichton, and on the night of August 5, 1892, they registered at the Royal Oak Hotel, on the northern outskirts of Victoria.

The names of Gray, Chief Engineer of the V&S survey, W.H. Going, W.H. Lynn, Jas. Fraser and driver H. Harbell are still clearly legible in the old hotel register. The Royal Oak Hotel was for many years a favourite watering spot for travellers going to and from Victoria. Passing trains frequently stopped at the nearby station for passengers, or to pick up or set out cars on the adjacent Royal Oak Creamery spur. Local legend states that when the Victoria and Sidney Railway train was stalled on the Royal Oak hill, because of slippery rails or a heavy load, passengers would walk up to the Hotel for a drink while they waited for the train to catch up.

The survey considered several routes into the City of Victoria. Seriously contemplated was a route passing Cedar Hill (now Mount Douglas) and entering town along the route which became Shelbourne Street. This was close to, but east, of the route later followed by the Canadian Northern Pacific Railway along the east side of the Saanich Peninsula and west of Blenkinsop Road. This projected route would have been an easier line to build but it missed most of the few settled areas on the Peninsula. The route finally chosen was meant to pass through the communities of Royal Oak and Saanichton. It faced gradients at several points of from one to two percent, and the most infamous of these was the steep hill approaching Royal Oak from the south.

The original route chosen by John Hamilton Gray began at the intersection of First Street and Beacon Avenue in Sidney (Station 0.00)* and ran south to Victoria, ending at a station site near the junction of Market Street and Saanich Road (Station 847.15).

In slightly more detail, according to the original plot, the line ran south from its initial point, through the farms of Julius Brethour and C.H. Reay, then past Bazan Bay at Mile 2 before swinging upgrade and inland to the southwest towards Saanichton, just past Mile 3. Between Miles 4 and 5, the survey passed through the properties of Henry Croft and A. McKenzie then swung south through heavily timbered, rolling benchland between Miles 6 and 7. The line passed to the west of Sandhill Creek and crossed that stream on the property of William Rippon, near Mile 8. At Mile 9 it touched the west shore of Elk Lake, where there was to be a passing track, then ran south through the city water supply area, crossed a small bay on what is now Beaver Lake and dropped down towards Royal Oak at Mile 12.

For reasons to be explained later, the line was relocated, necessitating a rock cut, on the west side of Elk Lake. This was to be one of the most spectacular points on the railway. Subsequently, there were a number of westward relocations farther to the south in the area between Glanford Avenue, at Mile 13, and Mile 15 where the tracks crossed the Saanich Road (as the continuation of Douglas Street north of Hillside was known at that time). Closer to Victoria, there was another relocation eastward, between Miles 15 and 16, to a new terminal site at Hillside Avenue and Alpha (now called Nanaimo) Street.

The Railway Survey

Engineer John Hamilton Gray.

The Chosen Route and Relocations

* The term "station" is used in engineering and surveying and describes the division of the survey into stations of 100 feet, plus fractions of 100 feet. i.e. Station 847+15 means that the end point is 847x100+15 feet. This results in an aggregate length of 84,715 feet, 16.04 miles, or 25.812 kilometers.

Above:

A younger Julius Brethour posed for this formal portrait, probably in the mid 1880s. Brethour was a pioneer farmer, prospector and mine owner, and took a leading role in local politics.

Above Right:

The farm of John Brethour as portrayed by an itinerant painter who perhaps earned a day or two of room and board for his effort.

The First Annual
General Meeting

Victoria businessman Peter Dunlevy was the first President of the Victoria and Sidney Railway.

There were still other relocations to be made, one being just south of Sidney, between Miles 0 and 2 towards the shoreline of Bazan Bay (the original was inland to avoid bridging the delta of Lagoon Creek). Between Miles 2 and 4 the line was relocated slightly to the west. (See maps for details of relocations.) The company did not file plans for these relocations until December 13, 1893. The initial railway survey was finished by the beginning of October 1892, and with the completion of a few other formalities the work of construction was free to begin. (For details of Gray's survey, see Appendix A.)

The Victoria and Sidney Railway Company held its first annual general meeting at 28 1/2 Broad Street, Victoria, on September 1, 1892. The first slate of officers included Peter C. Dunlevy, President; Maynard H. Cowan, Vice-President and Treasurer; Robert Irving as Secretary and Julius Brethour and W.J. Macaulay as Directors.[3] The company was capitalized at $1,250,000 in 1,250 shares of $1,000. Each of the Directors held ten shares and the Saanich Land Company held the remaining 1,200 shares. The officers of the Land Company were much the same: Dunlevy as President; Cowan as Vice-President; and E.G. Tilton as Secretary-Treasurer, with H.C. Macaulay, Percy Wollaston, Robert Irving and Julius Brethour as Directors. These seven men each held one share of this company which in effect appeared to be a holding company controlling the V&S.

The next order of business for the new Board of Directors was to arrange financing for the railway, but it appears that the Directors commenced the work of clearing the right-of-way on September 2, 1892, using their own funds. The Victoria and Sidney Railway was finally about to become a physical reality and there was cause for optimism in the newly plotted town of Sidney, and in Victoria. It seemed that only good fortune would smile on the efforts of the small but dedicated band of aspiring railway builders.

With the 5% interest on the $300,000 bond issue guaranteed jointly by the city of Victoria and the Province of British Columbia, the Board of Directors were successful in raising bond financing through a New York agency. They also attempted to find investment capital in London, England. However, financial terms were much more favourable in the U.S. market and funding was arranged there, at the end of November 1892.

Ironically, while the bond financing was arranged in the U.S., all of the investors in the new railway, with the exception of McGill College (which held $50,000 worth of bonds), were British. The sum of $270,598.36 realized by the bond sale was credited to the Victoria and Sidney Railway Bond Account at the Bank of British Columbia. On February 28, 1893, the first cheque was drawn on this account for the sum of $17,448, of which $13,150 was required for terminal facilities and wharf at Sidney, $4,148 for surveys and $150 for legal expenses.

The Sidney Sawmill

In the spring of 1892, the Sidney townsite was nothing more than a tract of farmland and forest overlooking a small bay along the shoreline south of Shoal Bay. A visitor there would have noted the sparkling white beach, a fine deepwater bay and the surreal image of Mount Baker rising up out of the haze to the east, along with other peaks of the mighty Cascades tumbling away to right and left in a sea of mountains.

Close at hand, the tree-clad islands of the Gulf lay scattered across the blue waters of the inland sea. By December of 1892, the town of Sidney boasted the Sidney House, a comfortable hostelry; a commodious wharf where the steamer *Isabel* stopped on her way north; a general store; butcher and blacksmith's shops; a scattering of new dwellings, and finally the newly built steam sawmill of the Toronto and British Columbia Lumber Company.

The driving force behind the mill operation was John White. On August 25, 1892, he set the first two men to work on clearing the millsite with brushhook and spade. The initial mill building was to be 36 by 170 feet and by September 20th construction work was under way. This mill was intended to be only a temporary structure, with a capacity of 50,000 board-feet per day, where the timbers would be cut for the erection of an even larger mill of 250,000 board-foot capacity. Superintendence of mill construction was in the hands of Mr. Mark Hewitt, an experienced Ontario millman.

John White sent T.J. Hammill east, in June of 1892, allowing plenty of time to purchase the mill equipment, but delays in delivery put off the opening of the plant until the end of the year. In the meantime, the work of clearing the railway right-of-way to Victoria was continuing. Although the winter was exceptionally wet, about fifteen miles had been cleared by the end of November.

Right:

Between Sidney and Saanichton, the survey location was revised as shown. Originally, the surveyors avoided the mouth of Lagoon Creek. The adopted location ran straight along the shoreline of Bazan Bay.

The Victoria and Sidney Railway let tenders for railway construction in March of 1893. Bids came in from three prospective contractors: Henry Croft's bid of $304,000; Alexander McBean's bid of $289,000; and T.W. Paterson's bid of $285,000.

The contract went to Thomas Wilson Paterson, who agreed to build the Victoria and Sidney line for $15,333.33 per mile (see Appendix B for contract). The company also gave him concessions for the purchase of stock in the new railway.

Railway Grade Construction Begins

This is the only known image of the original Prairie Tavern.

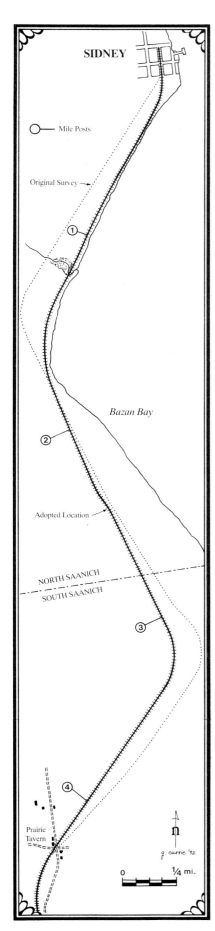

Thomas Wilson Paterson, successful bidder for construction of the V&S Railway, was an experienced railway contractor.

Paterson was an old hand in the railway construction game. Born near Kilmarnock, Scotland, in 1851, he came to Canada at an early age and settled with his parents in Ontario. Thomas entered the railway building field and soon demonstrated a flair for leadership, becoming a successful contractor. He worked on the construction of the narrow gauge Toronto, Grey and Bruce Railway and on other lines in the province of Ontario. Later, he won a contract and was superintendent in charge of enlarging the Welland Canal between Lakes Erie and Ontario.

Thomas Paterson's first work in British Columbia was on a contract for the construction of a fifty mile section of the Esquimalt and Nanaimo Railway between Shawnigan Lake and Nanaimo in 1885. Next, Paterson contracted to build the first five miles of the street railway line on Fort, Government and Douglas Streets in Victoria. Then he was a contractor on the Shuswap and Okanagan Railway line in the interior of B.C.

Paterson held other credentials. He was engaged in the lumber business, at Port Moody and Alberni, and later went into ranching. Not only was he a competent manager and contractor, he knew and had worked with John Hamilton Gray, the surveyor and engineer of the V&S line. Paterson seemed to be successful at everything he undertook and when he bid and won the V&S contract it was certain that the work would be done well and on schedule. Paterson was probably the most experienced contractor of the three bidders for the railway construction, but at least one of the others had illustrious credentials as well.

Henry Croft was an experienced civil and mining engineer who had been an inspecting engineer for the government of New South Wales, Australia. After coming to Canada, Croft commanded a survey party on the exploration of routes for a proposed extension of the Island Railway north of Nanaimo. If he had won the V&S contract, it was likely Croft would also have done a capable job. He would later gain fame as the man behind the fabulously rich Lenora Mine on Mount Sicker, near Duncan. Although he was not successful in his bid to build the railway, he nevertheless must have profited from the sale of right-of-way land to the Victoria and Sidney which crossed his Saanich property. The qualifications of the third bidder, McBean, are unknown.

With his successful bid for the construction contract and the stock concession, Thomas Paterson bought into the Saanich Land Company and eventually replaced Mr. E.G. Tilton as Secretary. Construction work was soon under way and the company submitted plans to the City of Victoria on April 20, 1893, showing the new line of railway running through the city watershed area at Elk and Beaver Lakes.

The City of Victoria was co-operating with the construction of the new railway that was expected to be of great benefit to the local populace. But, as a guarantor of a portion of the interest on the railway bonds, they wanted the line to be constructed in accordance with accepted engineering practice. Council accordingly sent out City Engineer C.A. Wilmot to check on construction operations.

Wilmot found that while construction specifications called for embankments twelve feet wide at grade level and fourteen feet wide in cuts, the embankments and cuts, as built, were somewhat narrower than these standard engineering specifications. Also, the crossties were only seven feet long, as opposed to a standard dimension of eight feet. The rail was lighter than usual for a railway of this type, weighing only 50-pounds per yard. (Perhaps Paterson intended building the line with shorter ties and then replacing them with ties of the usual size later.)

In spite of these deficiencies, Engineer Wilmot speculated in his report on May 11th, that Paterson could build the line for an estimated cost of $297,950, exclusive of right-of-way costs. The city council debated Wilmot's findings at length but did nothing about them, apparently not wanting to interfere with early completion of the railway project. Within a short time they would be giving much greater attention to the railway construction activities, as it approached their watershed area.

Actual grading of the right-of-way began at Sidney in early spring. By mid-summer some 180 men were employed on the project and the line had been graded to the north end of Elk Lake.

The railway construction scene would have fascinated any observer. Grade clearers working with axes and saws followed the line of surveyor's stakes to clear the right-of-way. Other labourers followed, roughing out the grade with shovels. Heavy grading work utilized horsepowered scrapers and dump carts to move the earth and rock for construction of the subgrade. Final grading and levelling was mainly hand work. The crews accomplished heavy rock work and stump removal with the judicious use of black powder.

As the construction gangs made their way along the west shore of Elk Lake, in August of 1893, a rumour reached Victoria that the company had deviated from the survey plan filed with the Victoria Land Registry Office earlier in the year. The rumour proved unfounded but created grave concern with city council who were extremely sensitive of any threat to the city's Elk and Beaver Lakes water supply. At that time the city obtained its water from Elk Lake through a pipeline at the south

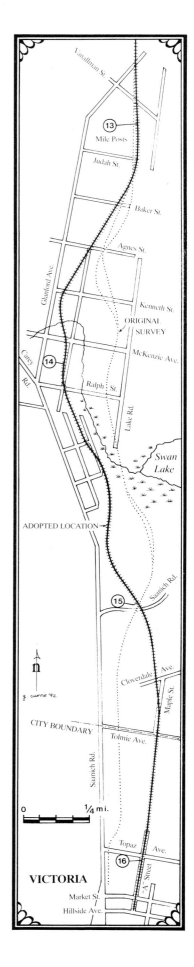

Left:
This map shows the original survey approaching Victoria and the final adopted location of the railway (December, 1893).

end of adjoining Beaver Lake and aldermen feared that a serious threat of contamination would be caused by trains crossing parts of Beaver Lake near the water supply intake. The council sent out Mayor Beaven and City Engineer Wilmot to investigate.

They found a line of stakes crossing a swamp in Section 49, south of Beaver Lake, and beyond this a clearing which indicated the intended course of the graders who were steadily approaching from the north. The mayor and city engineer then took a boat up to the west side of Elk Lake and landed at a point within Section 61. There they found some piles driven, in the line of a trestle, that would cross a small bay on the west side of the lake. (See map of grade relocation at Elk and Beaver Lakes.)

Although the course of the grade and trestle location was in accordance with the plan filed in Victoria, this proposed 350-foot trestle in Section 61 and another larger 750-foot structure crossing Beaver Lake in Section 50, were considered a danger to the city water supply - the grade, as located, would also interfere with planned future enlargements of the water basin. An immediate request was made to President Peter Dunlevy of the Victoria and Sidney Railway to relocate the line farther westward.

The V&S quickly agreed, even though the company had powers of expropriation, if necessary, to use the route filed earlier. The grading crew was laid off while the surveyors relocated the route. The result was a grade between Miles 10 and 11 that subsequently caused operating hardships for the railway, which now had another new summit to cross just five feet lower than the highest point elsewhere on the line. The approach to this summit was through rock cuts.

The relocated southbound grade now had to approach the summit on twisting nine degree curves that were the sharpest on the line. It traversed a sidehill of wet, spongy ground that would be an operating problem causing many derailments over the years, trains having to approach this grade at high speed in order to clear the summit.

Towards Royal Oak, a mile farther on, the grade dropped steeply downhill and continued in the direction of Victoria, finally ending near Glanford Avenue. Thus, the approach to Royal Oak from Victoria was up this steep hill and likewise required a highspeed run by the locomotive. Sometimes more than one attempt was necessary, and in later years heavy freight trains were helped up the grade by a "pusher" engine from Victoria. The latter would cut off at the top of the Royal Oak hill and then return to town.

The Elk and Beaver Lakes section of the line required constant filling and levelling. The V&S built a rock quarry spur, eastward from the mainline at Mile 11.2, to obtain fill material to build up the soft ground approaching the lake area from the south. Other ballast pit spurs were located farther north, along the line at Mile 5.1 and just south of Sidney on the beach at Bazan Bay, near Mile 1.

Rails and Equipment Arrive

The first rails for the Victoria and Sidney Railway arrived at Sidney on the ship *Rathdown* on September 11, 1893. On board this British vessel was hardware for 18 miles of track, consisting of 6,426 rails weighing 50 pounds per yard, 14,160 fishplates, 48 cases of spikes, and three tons of No.9 telegraph wire with 500 insulators and brackets. Tracklaying could finally begin.

The first locomotive for the Victoria and Sidney Railway was a fine new 2-6-0 or "Mogul" type machine built by the Canadian Locomotive Company of Kingston, Ontario. She weighed only 40 tons and arrived by barge in Sidney on October 3rd, a spur track having been laid from First Street to the beach south of the townsite. This fine little machine was the builder's engine construction number 445, and was equipped with 16"x24" cylinders and driving wheels 50 inches in diameter. These were relatively small drivers, but well suited for the 2% grades on the line north from Victoria.

The No.1 was well adapted to her role on the V&S but the No.2, a secondhand locomotive that had been built as the Canadian Locomotive Company's entry at the

American Centennial Exhibition, at Philadelphia in 1876, was not. On her return from Philadelphia, the Kingston and Pembroke Railway of Ontario purchased the No.2, a 4-4-0 or "American Standard" type engine. She ran on the "Kick and Push" until moving west to work on Canadian Pacific Railway construction projects in the Kootenay area of British Columbia.

The No.2, or "Deuce", was not the best type of engine for the V&S job, but the price must have been right and the company needed a second locomotive. The No.2's cylinders were the same size as the No.1's but her wheels were much larger in diameter, making her very slippery on steep grades. Passenger service began with two 56-foot passenger cars, one a first-class coach and the other a combination baggage-smoker. They were built by the Crossen Car Manufacturing Company of Coburg, Ontario.

The company completed its initial equipment roster with 18 flatcars, thirty-three feet in length with a capacity of 20 tons; two handcars and two velocipedes. Three of the flatcars were converted to makeshift boxcars. With this roster of equipment the grading and tracklaying progressed towards the line's southern terminus at Victoria. During the final stages of construction throughout the winter of 1893-94, the No.1 performed in work train service, carrying ties, rails and gravel for ballasting the line southward between Sidney and the station yards at Victoria.

The Victoria and Sidney reached the northern city limits of Victoria, one mile from the intended southern terminus, in January of 1894. It was unable to proceed beyond that point because of a dispute with Elford and Smith, the operators of a brickyard in the area now mostly occupied by the Mayfair Shopping Centre.

This dispute took some time to resolve and the V&S decided to establish a temporary railway terminus at Tolmie Avenue, where passengers could transfer to the nearby cars of the National Electric and Tramway Company, the predecessor of the British Columbia Electric Railway Company, and then proceed into Victoria. The Victoria and Sidney was nearing completion and, at last, the dream of a railway line between the capital city and the Saanich Peninsula hinterland was coming true.

The southbound passenger train awaits the "highball" at Sidney in this 1894 view from the very early days of railway operations. Engineer Dave Hasker peers from the cab with Julius Brethour standing below. Conductor Andy Forbes stands farther back alongside the locomotive's tender.

Although the first official run over the Victoria and Sidney Railway would not take place until later in the year, there was a first, unofficial run over the line on May 12, 1894, from Victoria to Saanichton. The Victoria *Daily Colonist* published an account of this trip the next day:

> "A number of pleasure loving citizens took advantage of the first train over the Victoria and Sidney Railroad to attend the annual ball of the North and South Saanich Agricultural Association, held last night. The train left Tolmie Avenue about seven o'clock in the evening, making the run in good shape. The ball was a very successful affair, and ranks well with past similar ones held by this association. The weather proving all that could be desired added materially to the pleasure and comfort of the visitors. The various committees had their work well in hand and the comfort of all guests was made the matter of careful and successful solicitation."

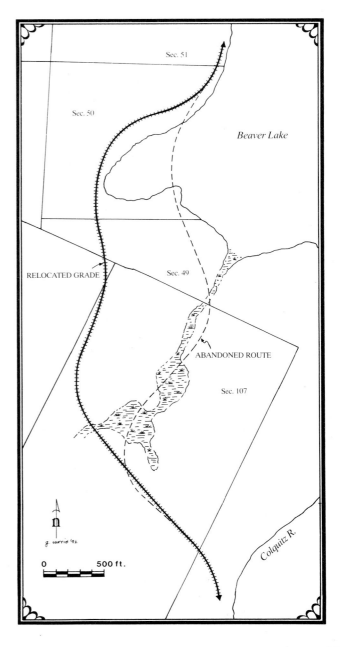

The Beaver Lake Relocation of 1893. The adopted grade is now a popular hiking trail in Beaver Lake Park. The abandoned route, which had been graded, is still visible in places in the underbrush.

Thus, the first, unofficial run had been a success. The V&S repeated it the very next day, with the train going all the way to Sidney and return for President Van Horne of the Canadian Pacific Railway, who happened to be in Victoria during an annual inspection of CPR holdings in western Canada. The party of dignitaries also included Vice-President Shaughnessy, of the CPR, Colonel Sir Casimir Gzowski, Thomas Skinner, of London, England, C.C. Chipman, Commissioner of the Hudson's Bay Company, and General Superintendent H. Abbott, of the CPR Pacific Division.

These distinguished gentlemen, on the invitation of Messrs. Paterson, Irving and Gray, left their comfortable accommodations at the Driard Hotel in Victoria at one o'clock in the afternoon and proceeded to the V&S Station. From there, the Railway whisked them to Sidney in the short space of 26 minutes, the engine at times reaching a speed of "37 miles an hour," as reported in the *Victoria Daily Times* of that date. The party was returned to their Victoria starting point by 2:45 p.m.

The Van Horne visit quite naturally fed rumours of an imminent CPR takeover of the line. This had already been suggested in some quarters. It would have been at least a partial fulfillment of the old "Saanich Shunter" dream of 1879, if true. When asked about it, at the Driard later in the day, Van Horne was quick to put the rumour to rest: "Simply for pleasure, I assure you. I always like to study geography when I'm travelling, and never miss a chance. The road's alright - a good road, but the CPR has no designs upon it that I know of. We haven't any intention of establishing a ferry connection between Sidney and the Mainland at present."[4]

After much speculation, and with continuing delay over the still unsettled right-of-way dispute in the brickyard area, the Company finally scheduled what is considered to be the first "official" run over the line from Victoria to Sidney and return on June 2, 1894. On the invitation of the V&S Directors, the locomotive and trainload of guests, gaily decorated with bunting and flowers, departed the station at Tolmie Avenue at 1:30 in the afternoon, making the run out to Sidney within the space of a half hour. On arrival there, the party adjourned to the local park reserve, which was thrown open for them and a sumptuous repast was spread for the enjoyment of all. The afternoon continued, with dancing on a spacious platform specially built for that purpose, and concluded with boating and other amusements.

Everyone had a wonderful time and it was a tired but satisfied party that boarded the cars for the run back to Victoria at 9:00 p.m. On their return to the Capital City, special streetcars, sent out to the temporary terminus, picked up the party and took them on into town. The Victoria and Sidney Railway was a dream realized for the widely dispersed population of Saanich and an anticipated boon to the city of Victoria. In spite of this, there were several more months of difficulties to overcome before the scheduled operation of trains could begin. Meanwhile, other developments of importance were taking place in the new community of Sidney.

The premier industry of the new peninsula town, the Sidney Sawmill, was put up for sale in September 1894, after less than two years in the hands of John White and his Ontario investors. The reasons for this sale are not entirely clear. The mill had been managed by James J. White, the nephew of John White. (James would later be V&S Station agent at Sidney for many years.) It was a success from an operational standpoint but there was a more competitive lumber market than had initially been anticipated.

The Sidney Sawmill Changes Hands

The British Columbia lumber trade in those early years, following the completion of the Canadian Pacific Railway into Port Moody, in 1885, was divided between the markets of the Canadian prairies and overseas. The overseas or maritime trade was relatively small and in the hands of a very few companies that had established export trade connections. Mills along the CPR Mainline in the eastern part of the province dominated the Prairie lumber trade. This left the Sidney mill dependent on local markets in Saanich and Victoria. Since Victoria already had several local mills and the new railway was not yet in regular operation, trade must have been very difficult indeed for the fledgling lumber company.

In an interview with R.D. Harvey, Q.C., many years later, James White would admit that his only experience in the lumber trade before coming to Sidney consisted of having watched a seasonal log drive on a local stream in his native Ontario.[5] What the Sidney Sawmill needed, in order to get properly started, was a manager who was totally familiar with the difficulties of the local lumber trade. The man who took over the mill operation at Sidney was Ewan Morrison of the Rock Bay Lumber Yard in Victoria, a former partner in the Shawnigan Lake Lumber Company, a pioneer Vancouver Island mill firm.

Morrison would give the Sidney Mill his best effort, but the operation was to face stiff competition for many years. It passed through the hands of several successive owners who operated it with varying degrees of success. However, with Morrison in charge it appeared that the mill had a chance of making it in the local lumber trade just as soon as rail connection was open to Victoria. The anticipated lumber traffic would be an important revenue source for the mill and for the new railway as well.

However, the Victoria and Sidney Railway was still having problems of its own in the fall of 1894, with the continuing brickyard right-of-way dispute on the very doorstep of its Victoria terminus.

The Line Opened for Service

Elford and Smith, the owners of the brickyard in the way of the new line, were not about to let the railway company off easily. Their price for settling the right-of-way dispute hinged not only on the $780 they wanted for the 25-foot wide strip of land the railway company would expropriate; they also claimed for the loss of a strip of land seventy feet wide which the constructed V&S line would cut off.

The V&S paid $780 for the expropriation, but to bypass the outstanding issue they opted for the construction of a long railway bridge over the brickyard so that the operator's claybeds could be utilized on both sides of the new track. This 750-foot railway trestle, while it did provide extra income for the lumber mill at Sidney, delayed the opening of the Victoria and Sidney Railway into its Victoria terminus by yet another few months.

Work continued through the winter of 1894-95, with the railway finally reaching the new station facilities at Hillside Avenue after crossing another trestle, 700 feet long, located on an ascending grade to bring it up to street level. This provided easy access from Hillside to the trains and was a great convenience in the handling of baggage. After the dreams of the Island Railway days, the "Saanich Shunting" of the 1870s and the Victoria, Saanich and New Westminster Railway scheme of Amor De Cosmos in the '80s and early '90s, a full railway link connecting Victoria and Sidney was in place.

It seemed almost anti-climactic, in March of 1895, when Thomas Paterson notified President Dunlevy of the V&S that the railway was at long last completed - and at a cost of only $315,938.20, somewhat over the $297,950 originally predicted by City Engineer Wilmot. This was not unreasonable considering the unforeseen cost of bridging the brickyard.

The formal handover of the line from Paterson to the Victoria and Sidney Railway took place on April 1, 1895, and the company commenced operations with two scheduled trains in each direction per day between Victoria and Sidney. Trains left Victoria at 7 a.m. and 4 p.m. on weekdays while on Sundays the afternoon trip left at 2 p.m. Return trips left Sidney at 9 a.m. and 5:30 p.m. Scheduled time for each trip was fifty minutes and the round trip fare was a mere fifty cents.

VICTORIA AND SIDNEY R'Y

Trains will run between Victoria and Sidney daily as follows:

Leave Victoria 7 a.m., 4 p.m.
Leave Sidney 8:15 a.m., 5:15 p.m.
SATURDAYS AND SUNDAYS.
Leave Victoria 7 a.m., 2 p.m.
Leave Sidney 8:15 a.m., 5:15 p.m.

T. W. PATERSON, Manager.

2

THE EARLY YEARS, 1895-1899

Thomas
Paterson
in Charge

During the construction of the railway line and throughout the formative period of 1894-95, Thomas Paterson had managed both the construction work and railway operations. Now that the line was about to enter formal scheduled service, the Directors realized that they were facing the problem of finding a permanent manager. Perhaps not unnaturally, they finally settled on none other than - the "old reliable" one, T.W. Paterson. If anyone was going to make money on this deal it would be Paterson himself. Not only did his salary of $250 per month amount to one third of the total company payroll, he also held the contract to supply cordwood fuel for the locomotives, at $1.70 per cord delivered to trackside.

Paterson built the Victoria and Sidney Railway with a view to economy and although it was somewhat less substantial than some of the Canadian mainline railways in strict engineering terms, it was certainly adequately constructed and equipped to provide the twice daily scheduled service between Victoria and Sidney. At this juncture a review of the railway's facilities is in order.

Although Station Zero on the original plot of the railway was at First Street and Beacon Avenue in Sidney, the completed railway actually ran northward for several hundred yards, into the Toronto and British Columbia Lumber Company's mill yard on the Sidney waterfront. The actual railway yard at Sidney was a three track affair, stretching from First and Beacon southward for several hundred yards in the direction of the Victoria terminus. At the lower end of the yard a single track diverged to a turntable and a single-stall enginehouse. Nearby, was a water tank that serviced the locomotives.

The Sidney Station was 24 by 60 feet in size with a wide overhanging roof which provided shelter to wooden platforms outside. The five-foot wide platform along the west side extended beyond the ends of the building, paralleling the railway track that ran northward towards Beacon Avenue. At arrival and departure times, the station was the busiest place in all of Sidney.

Just south of the main rail yard another spur line ran off northeasterly to the railroad and ferry dock on the waterfront. This was where locomotives and cars were delivered and freight landed from passing steamers. There was also a short spur line running down to the beach just south of Sidney, where sand and gravel was removed for use as track ballast and fill. This gravel was also used for the construction of concrete sidewalks in Victoria for many years and Bob Douglas, a local teamster, took the product of this seaside pit into Sidney for local use there.

Left:
The Sidney Station was one of two principal stations on the line. It served the V&S for 25 years. Later used as a Scout Hall, it was eventually donated to a now-defunct tourist railway near Victoria. The timetable insert is from 1896.

Immediately east of the station area, the company established a splendid park and picnic area that was to be the destination of summer railway excursions and picnic parties for many years. The park contained a large dancing pavilion that was the pride of the local community and the nearby lawns were a favourite meeting and trysting place for local youngfolk. This completed the early railway facilities at Sidney. In later years the trackage at the town would be augmented from time to time as new industries came into the area or when the Sidney sawmill operation expanded or altered its facilities.

The first timetable issued by the railway showed, besides stops at the terminal stations at Victoria and Sidney, intermediate station halts at Royal Oak, Elk Lake and Saanichton, where there were passing tracks or sidings. The siding and station stop at Keatings was not listed at this time, but was constructed at a later date. South of Saanichton and Bear Hill, the major wooding-up point for the locomotives on the line was at Elk Lake, which also had a water tower to service the locomotives.

The V&S located its only major station structure between Sidney and Victoria at Royal Oak, where a hotel, creamery and other local businesses contributed substantial traffic to the new line. In addition to these carded stops, the trains would stop at a number of wayside points or crossings along the line when flagged down by passengers. The way stations in most cases consisted merely of either an open platform or one with a shanty to shelter passengers from the inclement weather. Besides the sidings listed above, there was a spur leading into the creamery at Royal Oak for the pick up and set out of cars and, later on, a spur line ran eastward from the mainline to a lumber yard just south of Royal Oak. The Royal Oak siding was located on level ground, upgrade from the station and hotel. In later years helper engines, sent out from Victoria to assist heavy trains up the Royal Oak hill, were cut off at this siding and then returned to town.

Southward from Royal Oak, the next regular station stop was the Victoria terminal itself, where there was a railway yard and a large station building 240 feet long with 50 feet of frontage on Hillside Avenue. The Victoria station contained a waiting room, office and baggage room. A two stall enginehouse stood just north of Topaz Avenue and a turntable and freighthouse were located just south of that street, on the west side of the main line. A water tank for locomotive service stood nearby. These facilities comprised the physical plant of the Victoria and Sidney Railway at the opening of scheduled service in 1895, and although the company would add to its buildings and equipment over the years, the V&S line would always be characterized by physical sparseness, the informality of its schedules and downhome manner of operation, but above all - by the friendliness and hospitality of the train crews.

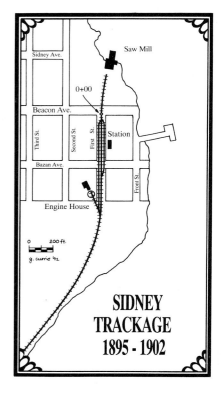

SIDNEY TRACKAGE 1895 - 1902

The Victoria and Sidney Railway employed eleven trainmen at the commencement of scheduled service: The first conductor on the line was Andrew F. Forbes; brakemen included George Parsons, Herman Shade, F.J. Andrews, A.K. Jones, Thomas Brownley, and F. Carpenter; engineers were D.M. Hasker, George Walton (also a fireman), and John Walton (fireman and wiper). C. Irvine was listed as a wiper.[1] These men, and the crew members who joined them later, were well remembered by local residents for many years after the demise of the proud little line in 1919, and many were leading citizens in their community. They, along with section gangs, shop and station staff, and an army of woodcutters, were the ones who gave life to the little railway and kept the diminutive trains running in all weather for the 24 years after the line's opening in 1895.

First Train Operating Personnel

As mentioned, the initial scheduled operations on the V&S began with two carded trains in each direction daily. The railway also connected with a local steamer service at Sidney for transport of passengers and freight to and from the Gulf Islands.

The Royal Oak Hotel was one of the principal "watering holes" on the Saanich Peninsula. Passengers would often stop for a cool drink while the "Cordwood Limited" made attempts at the steep grade on the Royal Oak Hill, catching it again when it reached the Royal Oak Station.

First Summer in Steam

The first summer of service on the V&S line set the pattern of operations for following years - twice daily on weekdays, morning and evening, the little locomotives trundled their trains out from Victoria to Sidney and return. On summer weekends, or special occasions, extra trains were added to the regular schedule as required, to accommodate all the traffic presented. On June 6, 1895, the *Victoria Daily Times* chronicled an early railway and steamboat excursion to Sidney and the Gulf Islands:

> "A correspondent who has been making a trip of the Saanich District and among the Islands, reports that in those regions the indications are that this season's crop will be plentiful. The hay crop promises to be abundant. The fruit crop, now commencing with strawberries, gives an excellent prospect. He remarks that the town of Sidney is progressing, with the exception of temporary stoppages of the steam sawmill there, which formerly gave employment to a large number of employees. With the summer season the town will be lively with Victorians and picnickers who find it makes a pleasant, inexpensive outing. Several residences are under contract for erection, and a number have been completed and nicely painted, which gives the town a clean, tidy appearance. The construction of the Victoria and Sidney Railway has given the town a permanent position..."

The article went on to describe the scheduled runs of the steamer *Mary Hare* in detail. This convenient combination of railroad and steamboat was a partial realization of the old "Saanich Shunter" dream of the 1870s and an indication of even greater things in the future.

That first summer in steam along the Saanich Peninsula line of the Victoria and Sidney must have been memorable to those fortunate ones who witnessed it. One can imagine the proud little No.1 locomotive struggling to climb the hill northward from Swan Lake to Royal Oak. From a wayside vantage point, the railway would have assumed an almost toylike quality, winding its way through the rural background of meadow and undulating hillside, its tiny engine puffing mightily as it assaulted the long upgrade. As it approached the station at Royal Oak it would blow for the crossing, a tall plume of steam issuing from its shiny brass whistle. The little mixed train of the Victoria and Sidney Railway had arrived at last and in its passing it achieved an almost legendary status in the history of Victoria and the Saanich Peninsula.

That first summer continued with a round of excursions along the line, with people stopping off at all points between Victoria and Sidney and some even destined beyond, for the Gulf Islands. On June 6, 1895, the *Victoria Daily Times* gave an account of a typical summer weekend excursion over the V&S that is rich in the nostalgia of those days, when people delighted in the simple pleasures of life and especially in the company of each other among the beautiful fen and farmlands of the Saanich Peninsula or on the waters of the Gulf of Georgia. In commenting on the inter-island run of the *Mary Hare* the *Times* correspondent loudly praised the little steamer and her crew:

> "...The 'Mary Hare' is a trim, staunch steamer under command of Captain Hare, an experienced navigator. The cabin is handsomely fitted up and capable of accommodating excursions. On the return trip on the 5th instant from Ganges Harbour, the chief port of Salt Spring Island, the cargo consisted of wool, sheep and lambs, calves, hides, butter, eggs and strawberries which were transferred direct from the wharf to a freight car switched on the morning train for Victoria, reached the city before noon, and were placed in the consignee's hands with the greatest expedition. This makes Sidney a port of considerable importance and it has already become a favourite 'outing' for Victorians as being convenient of access, varied in scenery and inexpensive to reach..."

Only two days later on June 8, 1895, the *Times'* "northern correspondent" described another trip along the Victoria and Sidney line:

> "...The trip from Victoria to Sidney is varied and pleasant. Leaving the station at Hillside Avenue, the lofty, rocky bluffs - Mount Tolmie and Mount Douglas - rising from fertile, well cultivated fields, are on the right with 'Big Saanich' on the left. Skirting through roads and clearances along the Lake District, almost due north, the train passes within sight of Beaver and Elk Lakes, whence the supply of our city water is obtained. Saanichton Station is soon reached, the centre of the Saanich District, celebrated for its fine farms and productive orchards, which extend at intervals along the length of the whole peninsula beyond the railway terminus at Sidney...
>
> "At Sidney a spacious grove, containing lofty trees, on rising ground along the seashore, has been reserved by the company, and the surface levelled for the accommodation of excursion parties. Seats and swings are improvised at different places, and in a central, shady spot a floor has been laid and enclosed for those who wish to 'shake the light fantastic toe.' The view eastward is magnificent, reaching across to the mainland and including Mount Baker, immediately opposite. On the evening of the third instant the view of the extinct crater from Sidney was sublime. At that time it happened that there was a clear space of sky over the mountain, which was entirely covered by snow, whilst the nearer portion of the mainland, Islands and channels were shaded by clouds. The panorama, with the immense silvery cone in the background, was exquisite, and the view lasted until sunset...Northward the scenery is romantic, embracing the high bluff, Cape Keppel, southern point of Salt Spring Island; also portions of Pender, Prevost and Galiano Islands. Amongst this enchanted scenery the steamer 'Mary Hare,' commanded by Captain Hare, a 'Master Mariner,' makes daily trips in connection with the railway at Sidney."

VICTORIA & SYDNEY R'Y
TIME TABLE.

GOING NORTH.

Stations.	Train No.	a m / p m	Mon Tues Wed Thur Fri	Saturday	Sunday
Victoria Lv	1	a m	7:00	7:00	9:00
	3	p m	4:00	2:00	2:00
Royal Oak	1	a m	7:14	7:14	9:14
	3	p m	4:14	2:14	2:14
Elk Lake	1	a m	7:23	7:28	9:23
	3	p m	4:23	2:23	2:23
Saanichton	1	a m	7:35	7:35	9:35
	3	p m	4:35	2:35	2:35
Sidney ... ... Ar	1	a m	7:48	7:48	9:48
	3	p m	4:48	2:48	2:48

GOING SOUTH.

Stations.	Train No.	a m / p m	Mon Tues Wed Thur Fri	Saturday	Sunday
Sidney Lv	2	a m	8:15	8:15	10:15
	4	p m	5:15	5:15	5:00
Saanichton	2	a m	8:28	8:28	10:28
	4	p m	5:28	5:28	5:13
Elk Lake	2	a m	8:40	8:40	10:40
	4	p m	5:40	5:40	5:25
Royal Oak	2	a m	8:54	8:54	10:54
	4	p m	5:54	5:54	5:39
Victoria ... ... Ar	2	a m	9:08	9:08	11:08
	4	p m	6:08	6:08	5:50

Satisfactory arrangements will be made with parties desiring to charter trains, special cars or steamer for picnic or other excursions.

Close connection made at Sidney with steamer Mary Hare for Salt Spring and other Island ports.

T. W. PATERSON,
General Manager.

**This timetable was
published in 1895.**

**This 1890s view from
Saanich Road looking east
towards Mount Douglas
encompasses the
prosperous farm of R.P.
Rithet. See pages 40-41 for
view from opposite side of
the road at same location.**

Looking back on these events, with the benefit of hindsight, seems only to magnify the nostalgic beauty of these pastoral scenes in the mind of the reader. That first full summer of operation, one can only surmise that the train service and the *Mary Hare* generated great excitement among the travelling public. The residents of Victoria, Saanich and even farther afield knew that they lived in an age of transportation miracles. The line was bringing the city within easy reach of all but the most remote residents of Saanich and the Gulf Islands.

By mid-June of 1895, the railway was almost overrun with a rush of excursion traffic and although there were shipments of agricultural products, lumber and cordwood, and general freight as well, the passenger business was the major money earner for the V&S. It was winning accolades from an appreciative public.

One lucrative source of passenger revenue were the picnic excursions to Sidney by various church groups and on June 11th the *Times* again commented:

> "...Already numerous excursions have been arranged. The Sisters of St. Ann have secured trains for next Saturday, when a picnic will be held at Sidney under their auspices. The annual Sunday school picnic of the Centennial Methodist Church is set for July 1st, and this also will be held at Sidney."

Again on June 27th, the same paper chronicled the adventures of a party of excursionists from Victoria area schools, who met the children of Sidney in the Railway's picnic grounds where they celebrated with a picnic and sporting events. On July 3rd, there was an excursion of Methodists and on August 9th it was a red letter day for a party from Vancouver who travelled to Victoria on the little train.

A half-dozen streetcars met the excursionists on Douglas Street opposite the Victoria station and whisked them into the city. However, the waiting streetcars were not as full as anticipated on that day because many of the impressed visitors decided instead to remain at Sidney where they spent their time in the park or inspecting the new town.

The excursions continued each weekend and the *Times'* correspondent described yet another exciting trip over the line in its issue of August 2nd:

> "Leaving the Victoria and Sidney Railway at Saanichton Station the traveller lands in the centre of a splendid farming district. There are only a few buildings in the neighbourhood of the railway station, namely two well kept hotels - the 'Rural House,' by J.J. Gray, and the 'Prairie Tavern' by John Camp. The post office is kept in a wing of the residence of Mr. Frederick Turgoose, farmer and stock raiser. The extensive barns and outhouses required for the accommodation of the crops and stock of the Turgoose farm make quite an imposing appearance; but their appearance does not harmonize well with the style of the 'Rural House,' with its double verandas,
>
> flights of steps and lace window curtains...A grocery store and blacksmith's shop may be said to complete the principal buildings of the hamlet. An Episcopal Church has been erected a few hundred yards southward from the commodious station, for which, no local agent has been appointed. No doubt this will soon be attended to as trade is steadily increasing.
>
> "The extensive farm and commodious farmsteading with orchards on the rising ground belonging to Mr. John Sr. first attract the stranger's attention. The farm is crossed by the Railway, passing on to Sidney with the valley keeping level with the track for a long distance. This valley connects with another which crossing the Turgoose farm joins the farm of Mr. George Fox, who in partnership with an English gentle-man recently purchased that valuable estate. Starting from the Prairie Tavern and taking the Crossroad, after passing another ascent another wide and rich valley appears in view. This

valley extends over two miles and along with its gentle sloping sidehills furnishes ground enough for half a dozen farms which are all occupied by well-to-do farmers - Messrs. Simpson, Thompson, Marcotte, Hagen, etc. When your correspondent passed along the Crossroad (August 19) three reaping and binding machines were at work in the neighbouring fields. Those 'broad acres' dotted as they were with long rows of stocks and fringed with orchards in full bearing, presented a charming panorama - an encouraging picture of the wealth and progress of the Saanich farmers..."

In the glow of the foregoing congratulatory journalism it is almost hard to believe that anyone could be less than satisfied with the Victoria and Sidney Railway. But some were and on November 2, 1895, the *Province* newspaper of Victoria published its first letter of complaint against the railway by a disgruntled passenger:

First Service Complaints

THE SIDNEY RAILWAY

"To The Editor:- What do you say to the following as an instance of railway management? My wife and I who were anxious to attend the performance of 'Dorcas' on Monday night, arrived at the Thomas's crossing of the Sidney Railway at a quarter past five that afternoon being the advertised time for the departure of the train for Victoria. There we waited until five minutes past seven when quite by accident as it appeared the train turned up. It took us in the direction we didn't want to go, back to Sidney as a matter of fact, but movement of any sort was a relief after so long a period of inaction, and we accepted it as an earnest of good faith on the part of the train. We only waited a quarter of an hour at Sidney and finally fetched up at Victoria about eight minutes to nine, instead of six o'clock, almost three hours behind time. We reached the theatre, for we had to dress in town, just about ten and were probably amongst the fashionable arrivals. We thoroughly enjoyed a third of a delightful evening, but nothing we saw in that extremely amusing piece 'Dorcas' struck me as being quite so funny as the management of the Sidney Railway.
Saanich, B.C.   W.M. le P.T."

The editor of the *Province* could not possibly let this letter pass without comment and had the following to say:

"Our correspondent W.M. le P.T. whose letter we publish today quotes an instance of the way in which the Sidney Railway is managed and asks us what we think of it. We think that the company in question is animated by a spirit of emulation which (always from the railway's point of view) does it infinite credit. It evidently sees no reason why the CPR and E&N should continue to enjoy undisturbed a monopoly in the matter of disregarding the convenience and requirements of the public. It is neither so large nor so formidable as either of its competitors in this respect but it is relatively strong to the extent of a $6,000 yearly bonus from the city treasury and it unquestionably intends to make its presence felt. These are days of railway records and we are not sure that the Sidney line in the matter of unpunctuality hasn't beaten them all. As a delay of three hours is to a run of 18 miles so is a delay of 500 hours to a run of 3,000 miles. Now 500 hours represents within a fraction of three weeks and we do not recollect having seen any announcement posted in a CPR station to the effect that the westbound train was 21 days behind time, accidents barred in both cases."

One might have hoped that the letters above were the end of the matter for the time being, but they would be disappointed. Only two weeks later, on November 16, 1895, there was another letter to the editor with commentary on the operations of the Saanich Peninsula line:

VICTORIA AND SIDNEY RAILWAY

"To The Editor:- I was glad to read in your issue of the 2nd instant a letter from W.M.le P.T. and also your remarks respecting the extremely irregular train service which those using the Victoria and Sidney have had just grounds to complain of for some considerable time, causing myself and many others who have relied on the timetables of the Company the greatest inconvenience. The Victoria and Sidney Railway should undoubtedly be of the greatest service to the residents in Saanich, an important factor in the development of the peninsula and would, I am satisfied, provided it considers the convenience of its passengers, receive the support it merits from those interested in the district, and I hope the Manager, whose courtesy and that of his staff has always been most commendable, will endeavour to run trains which can be relied upon to reach their destination within a reasonable time of those specified on their advertised timetables.
R.H. Breeds   North Saanich, B.C."

In spite of the irregularity of the scheduled operations on the Victoria and Sidney Railway, even at this very early date in its history, the little line tried hard to provide a better service. In hindsight, it seems that the reason for many of the delays was probably the frequent necessity for the train to wait at Sidney for the arrival of the connecting steamer service from the Gulf Islands. The joint schedule of the Victoria and Sidney Railway listed the connecting steamer service of the *Mary Hare* and it was an ambitious one. There were no modern navigation aids in the Islands and the vagaries of weather and tide would often interfere with the schedule.

The career of the *Mary Hare* was to be a short one, and when it was over, the schedules of the V&S line, for a while at least, were probably much more punctually obeyed.

In December of 1895, the V&S obtained the contract to carry the mails to Royal Oak, Keating (Young's P.O.), Saanichton and Sidney, six times per week for $400.64 per annum (a contract they held until operations ceased). Prior to this the mail had been carried by stage once a week from 1877 to 1887, and twice a week thereafter, over the few, and often muddy, narrow dirt roads that penetrated the Peninsula.

That the Victoria and Sidney Railway was providing a valuable and necessary service to the residents of Victoria, Saanich and Sidney was undeniable. Unfortunately, from a strict financial standpoint, the line was much less than a success. In its first year of operation to June 30, 1896, the company logged 11,520 train miles, carried 15,052 passengers and 4,573 tons of freight. But when the final financial result was in, there was a net loss of $4,321.56. [1]

The staunch *Mary Hare* was a coasting steamer, and although we have several descriptions or her, no picture is known to have survived. From the information given earlier in this piece we know that she was a relatively small vessel by today's standards, but probably much larger and more seaworthy than the small boats owned by the numerous settlers on the Saanich Peninsula and in the Gulf Islands at the time.

The Loss of the *Mary Hare*

Residents of the Gulf Islands, who were until then serviced only by the weekly trips of the steamer *Isabel*, warmly welcomed the arrival of the *Mary Hare* on a more frequent schedule. On Tuesday, June 18, 1895, the *Victoria Daily Times* chronicled a visit of the little steamer to Galiano Island:

GALIANO ISLAND

The Welcome Visit of the
'Mary Hare'

"Galiano Island, June 17.-It is with great pleasure that the Islanders welcome the arrival of the accommodating little steamer 'Mary Hare' and her gracious master. No matter how small her consignment of freight is for the Island she will always land it at the wharf, and thereby often save the settlers from pulling out against a strong tide to meet her. It is to be hoped that Captain Hare will receive a full share of the patronage of the Island settlers."

Apparently the larger *S.S. Isabel*, which also serviced the Gulf Islands route, did not always land her passengers or cargo at the Galiano dock, thereby forcing Island residents to come out and meet her, a sometimes dangerous practice in a small boat.

The hill at Royal Oak was one of the scenic highlights of the V&S Railway, a nemesis to the train crews who had to struggle on the uphill grade, and the subject of many local stories and jokes. Passengers were said to get off and walk up to the Royal Oak Hotel for a drink while they waited for the train to catch up.

At first a pleasant adjunct to the Gulf Islands transport service, the *Mary Hare* was soon a well patronized necessity to many local farmers and fishermen. Unfortunately, her service to the Islanders was to be all too brief.

On an overcast February morning in 1896, the little steamer was putting into Reid Island near Chemainus to obtain a supply of cordwood for fuel. As she approached the shore, the *Mary Hare* struck hard on a rock. After anxious hours spent in trying to get her off, Captain Hare and the crew arranged an attempt to raise her on the next high tide and retired to a nearby farmhouse for supper. They returned to find the *Mary Hare* in flames. She quickly burned to the water line. The steamer was not due back at Sidney until the next day (a Thursday) and so news of her loss did not reach there until Captain Hare arrived in Victoria that day, on the noon train of the Esquimalt and Nanaimo Railway, from Chemainus. The sad news quickly reached the little village of Sidney and there was great disappointment at the loss of a vital link with the Islands of the Gulf.

The *Mary Hare* capsized when she burned, and sank quickly. Her machinery was not badly damaged, so the owner later salvaged this, but the little ship was no more and, in spite of efforts by Captain Michael Hare to replace her, the next schedule of the Victoria and Sidney Railway listed the scheduled operations of the daily trains only, with no connecting steamboat service. It would be four years before there was another scheduled steamer run in connection with the railway. In the interim the trains would run more punctually than they had when forced to wait for the arrival of the connecting steamer service. The Victoria and Sidney Railway operations settled into a routine that would last until 1900 with few interruptions.

One exception was the revival, in April of 1896, of a scheme to make Victoria the terminus of transcontinental railway service as originally envisioned by Amor De Cosmos. The occasion was a meeting of the Council of the British Columbia Board of Trade in Victoria to discuss the possible construction of a bridge over the Fraser River at New Westminster. In an appeal to the Board, Mr. C.H. Wilkinson linked the construction of the bridge with the establishment of a railway and ferry service across the Gulf of Georgia to Victoria, via Sidney. The *Province* of April 11, 1896 liked the idea:

> ...The scheme commends itself to us specially upon the ground that it converts two items of yearly expenditure figuring in the provincial and Victoria balance sheets for $6,000 and $9,000 respectively, as interest on the Sidney Railway's bonds, into assets. As it is none of the taxpayers can be said to be getting any value worth talking about for their money. The Sidney line is of no use to the province at large and such utility as it may offer to Victorians is certainly not commensurate with $9,000 a year. Under Mr. Wilkinson's scheme both city and province would derive large benefits, the latter especially, for what better could be desired than that it should become the terminus of three transcontinental lines. We have not space to reproduce the whole of Mr. Wilkinson's letter but the following condensed extract will show the advantages of the proposed scheme:
>
> "In addition to the direct financial advantages from the proposed readjustment of the provincial aid (i.e., the substitution of a Government guarantee of 3 ½ per cent. on $360,000 bonds for the payment of $18,000 a year for ten years now authorized by the Legislature), the following benefits would accrue: The City of New Westminster proposes to agree with the Government that in consideration of giving the above guarantee it will find the money for the construction of a short line of railway from New Westminster to Garry Point. This line will be connected with the Victoria and Sidney Railway by a ferry boat built on a system now thoroughly understood

Built by the McKenzie family, the Rural House at Saanichton served only briefly as a hotel and was the longtime home of the Ferguson family.

and in successful operation in many places, whereby the freight cars of the railway are shipped bodily onto the ferry-boat and landed on the corresponding rails on the other side of the water. The construction of the bridge and this short line will, therefore, make Victoria the terminus of the Great Northern Railway. (Transcontinental line No.1).

"The Canadian Pacific Railway Co. having already a line running from Westminster Junction to Westminster city, will have access to the new short line, the ferry boat and the Victoria and Sidney Railway, thereby making Victoria the terminus of the CPR (Transcontinental line No.2).

"Powers have been given for the construction of a line of railway from Sumas City and a junction with the Seattle, Lakeshore and Eastern Railway, thereby connecting with the Northern Pacific Railway. This line the promoters state would already have been built had the difficulties in connection with the financing of the Westminster Bridge been settled, and that as soon as the difficulties are settled, the money will be forthcoming to build it. On the construction of this line, the Northern Pacific Railway, the Seattle, Lakeshore and Eastern, and I believe another small railway, the Bellingham Bay Railway, also connecting, will run over the Fraser River Bridge at New Westminster, use the ferryboat, terminating at Victoria. (Transcontinental line No.3)..."

Unfortunately, the construction of the Fraser River Bridge was still some years off and there would be other matters affecting the Victoria and Sidney Railway in the meantime. In the climate of railroad construction mania then so common, this scheme would soon be forgotten, but other ideas would capture the imagination of the public. In the short term, there were few changes in either the pattern and scheduling of operations or in the bottom line profitability of the V&S.

There was a resurgence of tourist and excursion traffic each summer, the line reverting to the twice daily mixed freight and passenger service with extra trains as required only through the winter season. The Victoria and Sidney ran mixed trains exclusively until well after 1900 when freight and passengers were sometimes carried in separate trains. It was not a great money earner, but it had hopes for a more prosperous future and was providing a useful and necessary service to the people.

The downhome style of the V&S established during this period, which was due primarily to the genial railway staff (in spite of frequent delays), lasted until the line's final days. In spite of the established routine along the line, there were developments from time to time which did provide a welcome but brief flurry of activity.

The Elk Lake Project, 1896

The first of these took place in 1896, when the City of Victoria made improvements to its dam, reservoir and waterworks located at Elk and Beaver Lakes. The City let a contract for this work in the spring of 1896, and by July the work was nearing completion when the *Victoria Daily Times*, of July 30th, mentioned the involvement of the Victoria and Sidney Railway with the project:

"In connection with the construction of the waterworks the Victoria and Sidney Railway has proved of great advantage in bringing out supplies and in the accommodation of workmen passing to and fro. It has also proved a great benefit to the whole countryside, more especially since it has been provided with the mail service."

After the usual busy round of excursion traffic through the summer of 1896, the V&S provided a special Labour Day service for the members of Seiger's Council No.85, Y.M.I., running a total of four special trains to and from Sidney. On September 23rd the ladies of the Saanichton Church organized a special evening of

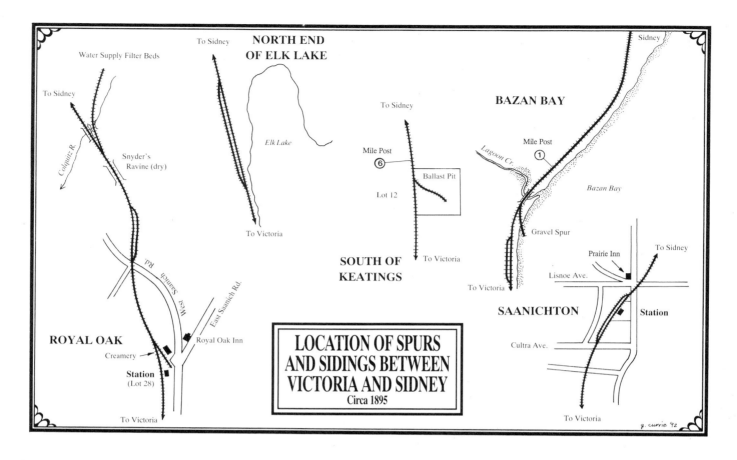

LOCATION OF SPURS AND SIDINGS BETWEEN VICTORIA AND SIDNEY Circa 1895

concert and theatricals in the Agricultural Hall under the patronage of Bishop Perrin. The evening's entertainment included a little production entitled "Betsy Baker." Admission for the concert, supper and theatricals was only 25 cents, on top of the regular Saanichton train fare - a bargain indeed. Upwards of 40 people availed themselves of the opportunity to travel out from Victoria and the performance was deemed a great success with full details of the evening chronicled in the *Times*, including a list of the participants.

The routine scheduling (such as it was) and operation of the Victoria and Sidney Railway, while sometimes lacking in the comfort and punctuality of the Canadian Pacific or the Great Northern, still beat the old hayburning horse or the muddy roads of Saanich when one had to get into Victoria or out to Sidney on an inclement day. There were those who thought that the answer to the railway's operating and scheduling problems would be found in electrification, and the substitution of interurban cars in place of the steam locomotives and coaches of the V&S. While that was touted by some as the solution, local writer Clive Phillipps-Wolley quipped that perhaps "electrocution" would be the more desirable course.[2]

The average Saanich Peninsula resident waiting for a late train probably had no interest in the reasons behind the delay or any detailed knowledge of the growing financial crisis facing the railway management. For Thomas Paterson though, the financial situation was becoming acute. It was clear that before long something would have to be done if the V&S was going to survive into the new century. In spite of these worrisome details, the Railway continued its runs out to Sidney and back each day, doing the best it could. It usually made up for its deficiencies through the force of kindness and consideration shown by the train crews, who could never do enough to placate and appease the long-suffering passengers. The years ran one into another and it sometimes seemed that little or nothing would change for the better - either for the passengers or the financially strapped railway company.

First Fatality

The Growing Financial Crisis

One of the few unforeseen and most lamented incidents during this period was the first fatality on the V&S line, which occurred on January 16, 1898, when Charles Gallagher, a former Member of the Provincial Parliament for the Kootenays, was run down and killed by the evening train near Beaver Lake. Gallagher had gone out to Royal Oak on the afternoon train to visit friends and then walked toward his cabin near Elk Lake. As the train rounded the curve and entered a cut near Beaver Lake, on its way into Victoria that evening, the crew saw Gallagher lying face down on the tracks. He had apparently fallen and struck his head on the rail. On the steep grade there was no time to bring the train to a stop and the unfortunate man was killed. With this accident the Victoria and Sidney Railway entered the ranks of those lines on which sudden and unexpected death were all too common.

The old century was fading fast and with the coming of 1900 there were to be profound changes for the Victoria and Sidney Railway and for its customers at Sidney, along the Peninsula, and in the capital city itself.

On the surface all may have seemed well enough, but for Thomas W. Paterson and his fellow shareholders, the problem was that costs were high, and traffic levels and revenues were just too low. The company could not hope to pay off the bonds that would fall due in 1918 if low traffic volumes and resultant low revenues continued.

The company should have been putting money into a sinking fund, in preparation for the day when the bonds would mature, but it could not raise sufficient funds. To Paterson and his colleagues, and to the City of Victoria and the Province of British Columbia who were paying annual bond interest, it was clear that some action must be taken to pull the V&S Railway out of the red and into a more profitable financial position.

By 1899, the need for action was more urgent than ever and an examination of the Railway's financial and operating records, as reported to the Chief Engineer of Railways and Canals in the Dominion of Canada Sessional Papers for the years 1895 to 1899, tell the tale:

Year	1895	1896	1897	1898	1899
1. Operations					
Train miles:	11,520	24,128	23,808	24,135	24,161
Passengers:	15,052	26,917	18,242	19,294	19,573
Freight (tons):	4,573	28,788	16,646	18,464	19,084
2. Earnings					
Passenger Svc.:	$3,552	$9,848	$7,911	$8,991	$8,353
Freight Svc. :	$2,876	$11,930	$8,360	$9,722	$9,240
Mail & Express:	$20	$234	$415	$409	$409
Gross Earnings:	$6,449	$22,019	$16,686	$18,672	$18,012
Total Expenses:	$10,770	$20,357	$15,194	$14,734	$16,664
Net Earnings:	$-4,322	$1,662	$1,492	$3,938	$1,348
% Earn/Expenses:	60%	108%	110%	127%	108%
Earnings per mile	.5597	.9125	.7008	.7736	.7454

To many observers, it was a financial and operational failure. In 1899, a number of businessmen were selected to deal with the crisis and one of their schemes would be adopted in the search for a solution.

3

THE TRANSPORTATION PROPOSALS OF 1899-1900

A Town
in Need of
a Boom

During 1858, the fledgling community of Victoria experienced its first great economic boom with the discovery of gold on the bars of the Fraser River. Almost overnight, it became a frontier boomtown and was the main point of entry into the country for the prospectors, miners, camp followers and the general human flotsam that followed on the discovery of sudden riches everywhere. Within a few months the local population grew from a mere 3,000 to over 10,000. The Cariboo Gold Rush was on!

As the boom continued, New Westminster and other mainland centres superceded Victoria as the major beneficiaries of the influx. Even before the 1858 Cariboo Gold Rush, Victorians had enviously heard accounts of the rush of '49ers into California, following the discovery of gold at Sutter's Mill on the American River a year earlier. The last half of the 19th century was an era of mineral discoveries, and dreams of sudden wealth and riches were shared by all.

In that regard, little had changed in the 50 years between 1849 and the 1890s when a new tide of miners, following up on rich discoveries of gold, silver and copper in the Kootenay and Boundary areas of British Columbia, flooded into the province. The Government of British Columbia quickly realized the need for railway transportation systems to serve the new mines and smelters. There was to be a flurry of railway construction in the province throughout the 1890s and into the 1900s.

Railways and dreams of economic gain were part of the same expansionist dynamic. To many, a rail link was all that was required to put any town worth its salt on the map. The businessmen of Victoria were no different from others in that regard. They determined to share with other British Columbia cities and towns in the wealth that would come from servicing the new mines - even if they were on an island and physically isolated from the mainland mining areas. The discovery of gold in the Klondike, in the mid 1890s, only served to increase the boom fever and the people of Victoria saw the need to reach out to an even wider trading area. They felt that better transportation would ensure the city's prosperity and economic future.

In the context of this climate, many considered that the Victoria and Sidney Railway was putting in a lacklustre performance. This resulted in a series of proposals to put the Provincial Capital in closer touch with the mining and industrial centres of the province, the Yukon, and even beyond.

Left:
This rare rooftop view of the north side of Victoria's business district shows the Market Building (top centre) and the Masonic Hall (still standing), the latter being illustrated on the cover. The Market Station gave the V&S access to the centre of the city.

Victoria was the nearest Canadian port to the booming Klondike and the growing Oriental trade. It was the first Canadian landfall in the Strait of Juan de Fuca and the fact that it was on Vancouver Island, rather than the mainland, was not seen as an obstacle by the more optimistic members of the local business community. It was considered that trains could be transported regularly and as cheaply over water as they could over the same distances on the transcontinental rail lines.

Victoria as a Terminal Point

With a little luck, and a lot of hard work, it might just be possible for Victorians to share in the wealth of the exotic Oriental trade and to profit as well from supplying the mines and boomtowns of the North. To capture the marine traffic would be easy, once Victoria had a transcontinental railway terminus, as envisioned in the old De Cosmos scheme of the late '80s. But, to get its share of the railway trade, the city would have to be able to convey goods to any part of the province without trans-shipment or change of railway cars.

This could best be achieved through the creation of a railway and rail ferry connection with Vancouver, the western terminus of the CPR. The Canadian Pacific Railway was the largest and most important factor in transportation in British Columbia. The creation of a mainland railway connection to the Island would effectively make Victoria the new western terminus of the CPR.

Some years earlier, the Canadian Pacific had given "terminal rates" to Victoria businesses. That rate structure equalized charges for the two major B.C. cities for the shipment of goods to eastern points; there was no transportation cost differential involved between Victoria and Vancouver, except for a nominal fee on trans-shipments crossing the Gulf of Georgia. It was primarily the inconvenience alone, of trans-shipment, that created a problem for Victoria shippers. All of these factors were known and understood by local businessmen in the B.C. capital and no one was more in touch with the problems and possible solutions than Thomas Wilson Paterson, General Manager and principal shareholder of the Victoria and Sidney Railway.

It had long been clear to Paterson that the solution to low traffic levels along the Saanich Peninsula line and the V&S Company's dismal financial performance would be to reach out for trade from a much wider area. He could see that the old De Cosmos idea for a rail and ferry connection between Sidney and the Lower Mainland was still a good one.

T.W. Paterson's Idea

"What Victoria needs to do," said Paterson, "is to form a company of its own and build a connecting ferry and railway line to some point on the Mainland convenient to the transcontinentals, so that it can offer connections to them all. It's a well known fact that the CPR does the bulk of the transcontinental business and instead of trying to get them to come here, we should go to them there on the Mainland. This would also give us connection with the other transcontinental lines coming into Vancouver. When one road recognizes this point, so will all the other connecting lines."[1]

It was one idea, and a good one at that, but there were others to be considered as well.

Sixteen miles across the Strait of Juan de Fuca from Victoria, was the snug harbour of Port Angeles. It was the first landfall for ships entering United States waters in exactly the same way as was Victoria on the Canadian side. For this reason, and for others given below, it was only natural that at some point consideration should be given to a transportation link between them. Both cities had the potential of becoming transportation terminals. In April 1899, the builders of the Port Angeles and Eastern Railway put forward just such a scheme. That company had already constructed six miles of railway line eastward from Port Angeles. They had the idea of an eventual linkup with the American transcontinental railroads at Olympia, south of the Hood Canal.

A Proposal from Port Angeles

So great was the press of municipal business and the agitation for economic development in Victoria, that City Council had established a "Committee of Fifty" with appropriate sub-committees to investigate matters of economic concern. Sub-Committee No.5 was the Railway Sub-Committee and its chairman was Mr. Noah Shakespeare. The features of the Port Angeles proposal were:

1. To put on a fast twin screw ferry with a capacity of ten freight cars or six passenger cars to make one or more trips daily between Port Angeles and Victoria. This vessel would have a speed of about nine knots.
2. To purchase and operate a second, steel passenger ferry with a speed of 18 knots to carry express and fast freight and capable of running in any weather.
3. To build wharves, docks, slips, sheds, railway tracks and all facilities to give Victoria a transcontinental railway connection through Port Angeles.

The consideration asked from the City of Victoria for this new service would be the provision of a $350,000 subsidy. The promoters also wanted, from Victoria, a guarantee of interest on the Port Angeles and Eastern Railway Company's bonded indebtedness, similar to that granted to the Victoria and Sidney Railway.

On April 11, 1899, Sub-Committee No.5 met to consider the Port Angeles proposal in detail and to prepare its report to the Committee of Fifty. "We are favorably impressed with their proposal and hereby endorse the undertaking of a transcontinental connection via Angeles," said Shakespeare, "and your committee are using active steps to acquire information that will lead to the securing of suitable terminal grounds and hopes to be able to report favorably at the next meeting of the committee."[2] The scheme's importance to the city impressed Shakespeare and his committee, so they were keen to promote it as a possible solution to Victoria's transportation woes.

Thomas Paterson came out loud and clear against the idea. "I oppose the idea as no ferry carrying the freight of just one road would pay. To pay, the ferry needs to have connections that will handle all the rail freight to Victoria."[3] Of course, if the scheme would not cost Victoria anything, that would be another matter and Paterson would not oppose it.[4]

There were clearly both positive and negative aspects to the Port Angeles proposal and on April 29th, Vice-President I.C. Atkinson, of the Port Angeles and Eastern, appeared in Victoria to advance his road's case. In the ensuing debate, Atkinson advanced several good points in favour of the idea but in the end it was clear that there were a number of unacceptable features. The most important of these was that while the Port Angeles and Eastern was asking for generous financial consideration from Victoria, it had no real guarantee of being able to connect with either the Great Northern Railway or the Northern Pacific Railroad in Washington State. Further to this, the establishment of a ferry connection with the British Columbia Mainland, via the Victoria and Sidney Railway, would be much shorter, and more financially feasible. It would guarantee a connection at least with the Canadian Pacific Railway, and would effectively make Victoria the western terminus of that line. The case against the Port Angeles and Eastern was made even more forcibly by Mr. W.J. MacDonald, of Victoria. In a letter to the Editor of the *Daily Colonist* on May 12, 1899, he stated:

> "We must always remember that the building of the railway is not contingent upon a subsidy from us: our refusal would not prevent the road from being built, and if built we will as a matter of course have connection. Yet as a matter of sympathetic friendship with our neighbors, we might fairly contribute the above-named figure ($100,000), but more we cannot and should not do, in justice to our own internal improvement and our many requirements."

The Port Angeles scheme had to be considered in light of the existing Victoria and Sidney Railway bond interest guarantee. It was already costing Victoria taxpayers $9,000 per year and provincial taxpayers a further $6,000. The idea of this guarantee had been to help form a transportation link on Canadian territory. The Port Angeles scheme, if financially supported by the city, would be working directly against the Victoria and Sidney Railway. At this juncture the debate became even more complex. A new proposal that had been under consideration for some time was advanced by the Dunsmuir interests of Vancouver Island.

James Dunsmuir, of the Esquimalt and Nanaimo Railway Company, with extensive coal mining and land interests on Vancouver Island, had only recently returned from a European trip. He had been considering a solution to Victoria's transportation problems for some time. The *Daily Colonist* of May 4, 1899, gave front page coverage to the Dunsmuir proposal:

> "The citizens of Victoria will shortly be called upon to decide the most important question that has ever been submitted to them. They are to be given an opportunity to say whether or not they desire CPR passenger and freight trains to enter the city. What they will be asked to give to secure this long-looked-for railway connection has not yet been made public.
>
> "Since the return from the East of Mr. James Dunsmuir it has been rumoured that before long he would make an offer to give the city railway connection with the CPR system by means of a ferry from some point along the east coast of Vancouver Island, the cars being brought from the Island terminus to the ferry by the E&N Railway. Yesterday Mr. Dunsmuir handed his proposal to Mr. Noah Shakespeare, the chairman of the railway committee of the Committee of Fifty."

Final details of the Dunsmuir plan were not immediately available but were announced in the *Daily Colonist* of May 9th. They included the operation of a rail ferry between Vancouver and Osborne Bay on the east coast of Vancouver Island. A fast ferry would be put in service to carry loaded passenger cars across the Gulf of Georgia to Vancouver Island from whence they would be taken over the Esquimalt and Nanaimo Railway into Victoria.

Dunsmuir later dropped the idea of transporting passengers in cars on the ferry, instead suggesting that a separate fast passenger ferry could be used. If implemented, this scheme would also effectively make Victoria the western terminus of the CPR, but through the agency of the Esquimalt and Nanaimo Railway rather than the already-subsidized Victoria and Sidney line along the Saanich Peninsula.

In return for the provision of this new service, the City of Victoria would be asked to put up a sum of $700,000 and to acquire a 19 acre tract on the Songhees Indian Reserve, in Victoria West, for transfer to the E&N Railway for terminal purposes.

On the surface, the Dunsmuir idea looked promising. It was the only scheme backed by a company with adequate financial resources. The new proposal also added to the complexity of finding a solution to Victoria's transportation problems and the Committee of Fifty met again to consider all facets of the situation.

They examined the Port Angeles and Dunsmuir proposals, as well as the possibility of having the Canadian Pacific Navigation Company, who already operated a ferry into Victoria, improve their service. The debate was complex and at times heated. Alderman A.G. McCandless pointed out that there was another possible solution, one that was better than any of the proposals under discussion. It was to establish a ferry connection running between Point Roberts, on the Canada-U.S. border, and the V&S terminus at Sidney. McCandless pointed out that this would give Victoria a connection with both the Great Northern and the Northern

In 1915, the *Daily Colonist* published an interesting story on the first newsboy on the V&S Railway. This picture was taken in 1894, showing ten year-old Johnnie Burnett by a shed near the Brethour ranch at Sidney, where orders for the paper were received and Sidney subscribers received their morning paper every day. Johnnie would take a bundle of *Colonists* out on the 7 o'clock train, selling some to passengers and delivering others to subscribers along the line (placed in boxes at road crossings or other arranged places) and at the northern terminus. He was able to return by 9 o'clock, just in time to reach school in Victoria West. From this early business experience, John H. Burnett went on to become the proprietor of the Victoria Brass & Iron Works.

Pacific in the Fraser Valley. It could also connect with the Canadian Pacific at New Westminster, once a proposed bridge across the Fraser River was completed at that point.

As always, Thomas Paterson was in the forefront of the discussion. He pointed out to the meeting that Canadian Pacific eventually captured 80 percent of the business coming from Victoria; the two other railways (the V&S and the E&N) did only 20 percent. If the people of Victoria wanted to increase their share of the trade they would have to open up and access a wider area that would provide local merchants with additional business.

Some years earlier, Paterson had obtained a charter for a short line of railway from Point Roberts to New Westminster, but Victoria rejected the idea of subsidizing it. In the final consensus, Paterson had convinced himself of the only way for Victorians to command a greater share of the available trade. That was for local merchants, controlling the business, to build a ferry and run it to a connection with the transcontinental railways on the mainland and who would refuse to deal with anyone who did not use this connection.

The Great Northern Railway, which already had planned for a branch line to Port Guichon, on the Fraser River Delta, was expected to reach Point Roberts before the earliest time a ferry could be built. With such a ferry and rail connection in place, Victoria merchants would be able to tap the considerable business activity of the Fraser Valley. That seemed the best option for any expansion of the Victoria trading area and would be strengthened if Oriental steamers could be induced to make their landfall in Victoria, rather than at Vancouver.

The complexity of the situation, with all numbers of proposals emerging, concerned Victoria Mayor Charles Redfern. He decided that he wanted all of the ideas refined before any one plan was considered for adoption. This refinement process lead to the re-emergence of what was really the original De Cosmos railway and ferry scheme.

Withdrawal of the Dunsmuir proposal simplified the resolution process. Apparently, the Dunsmuirs wanted to establish their own Island railway and rail-ferry terminal facilities at a new coal shipping port on Oyster Harbour, some 60 miles north of Victoria. The existing coal port facility at Departure Bay, near Nanaimo, was too far away from new coalfields being developed. As James Dunsmuir owned both the Esquimalt and Nanaimo Railway and the Wellington Colliery Company of Nanaimo, he wanted to simplify the logistics of operating these companies by combining the ferry connection along with the establishment of a coal port at the new location. This would later become the Town of Ladysmith.

The re-emergence of the old De Cosmos scheme, which had never really died, was favoured by T.W. Paterson. He was anxious to extricate himself from the marginal financial proposition that was the Victoria and Sidney Railway. The old scheme had been granted a federal government charter but was effectively killed by the granting of a provincial charter to the Victoria and Sidney Railway in 1892. Unfortunately, the Victoria and Sidney line, as built, embodied only part of the original De Cosmos plan. Paterson indicated that he would even help things along by selling his interest in the V&S line to any party connected with the new proposed railway and ferry service between the Island and the Lower British Columbia Mainland. Up to this time, the V&S had averaged earnings of only $823.63 per year. This included a net loss of $4,321.56 in the first partial year of operation, ending on June 30, 1895.[5]

At a meeting held in Victoria on May 17, 1899, Mr. C.E. Renouf moved that the Mayor appoint a committee to look into all aspects of a proposal to build a ferry to run from Sidney to Point Roberts and a railway from that point up the Fraser Valley to the agricultural town of Chilliwack. Renouf's motion was passed and Mayor Redfern, T.W. Paterson, E.C. Baker, D.R. Ker, Alex Wilson, James Dunsmuir, N. Shakespeare, M. Baker and Aldermen McGregor and Beckwith were appointed to look into the matter.

The situation became complicated when a new proposal, which was really a variation on the Port Angeles scheme, emerged. This was called the Beecher Bay Scheme. It advocated a rail ferry service from Port Angeles to Beecher Bay and a short line of railway connecting that point with the Esquimalt and Nanaimo Railway at Langford, six miles west of Victoria. This idea was short lived. After one more revision of the old proposal, and several more meetings, the whole Port Angeles rail and ferry route idea was defeated at a public meeting on July 22, 1899, by a vote of 14 to 8.[6] The long suffering citizens of Victoria would see this idea revived once more, even after this defeat, before it was finally shelved in favour of a Canadian route that would be shorter, cheaper and more practical.

The fact that Victoria was discussing a possible rail ferry connection with the Mainland did not escape the notice of Vancouver residents and businessmen. There were those on that side of the water who felt that if such a scheme was to be put into effect, they should be a part of it.

Mackenzie Brothers, a Vancouver shipping firm, showed the first real interest. The Mackenzies were astute businessmen, skilled mariners, and were serious about establishing a new ferry service. The *Daily Colonist*, perhaps believing that the honour of bringing the De Cosmos scheme to fruition should go to a Victoria firm, were skeptical about the Mackenzie proposal.

Early in September 1899, Captain S.F. Mackenzie, of Mackenzie Brothers, visited Victoria to discuss his idea with the citizen's transportation committee. While the Mackenzies had in mind a fast ferry running from the Mainland to a connection with the Victoria and Sidney Railway at Sidney, they had not resolved where the Mainland site would be. Nor was it clear just when this detail would be worked out or when it might be put into contract form for the approval of the taxpayers of Victoria, who would be asked to subsidize it.

In spite of this, the subsidy to be asked was in the neighbourhood of $125,000. With the essential details lacking, the Victoria transportation committee rejected their plan. The Mackenzies, not wanting to lose their chance, immediately set to work on a refinement of their ferry proposal. While these events were taking place, life on the little line of the Victoria and Sidney Railway was continuing pretty much as usual.

The Victoria to Chilliwack Rail & Ferry Scheme

By the fall of 1899, it was more than ever clear to most Victorians that the answer to the city's transportation and business problems lay in the direction of the Fraser Valley. A rail connection, a trans-Gulf rail ferry, and also a railway line east through the Fraser Valley would put Victoria in closer contact with the transcontinental railways. This line would also tap the Valley's booming agricultural trade. The fact that the city of Vancouver already effectively controlled that area's business seemed to matter not a bit. With subtle changes and new backers, the old De Cosmos idea had become the "Victoria-Chilliwack Railway Scheme."

On September 20, 1899, the Citizen's Transportation Committee submitted its report. The main features of the scheme included: the extension of the Victoria and Sidney Railway into the centre of the city of Victoria; the construction of two vessels, one for passengers and the other for loaded freightcars, and; a mainland rail line which would run from Boundary Bay inland along the Nicomekl River for 12 miles to a junction with the Great Northern Railway, at a point six miles north of White Rock, continuing eastward to junctions with the Canadian Pacific Railway and the Northern Pacific Railway farther eastward in the Fraser Valley. This would give Victoria rail connection with all three transcontinental railways in the lower Fraser Valley. The Committee's report gave detailed costs for construction of the railway as well as proposed operating schedules. On closer examination though, the citizens of Victoria were shocked to see the expected cost and the proposed sources of funding. The total cost of the project was estimated at $1,509,000 which would be raised as follows:

Victoria to subscribe stock $500,000

Grants from Dominion and Provincial
    Governments to be not less than $300,000

Stock to be subscribed by municipalities
    of the Fraser Valley $100,000

Citizens of Victoria to be asked to
    subscribe stock in the amount of $100,000

Total $1,000,000

Balance to be floated by debenture,
    or otherwise, to be $509,000

Cost as per engineer's estimate $1,509,000

Debate on the merits and drawbacks of the proposed Victoria-Chilliwack Railway Scheme continued through the fall and winter of 1899. The ratepayers of Victoria finally had a proposed railway acquisition by-law which they could debate. If

THE NEW VICTORIA PUBLIC MARKET.

approved, it would see the City acquire the Victoria and Sidney Railway and build rail extensions into the heart of Victoria's business district. From a harbour north of Sidney, a ferry would connect to the Mainland and another railway line would be built up the Fraser Valley to link with the transcontinental railways.[7]

Victoria people discussed the Victoria-Chilliwack Railway Scheme at a number of public meetings and, while there were many enthusiastic supporters, there were a like number of antagonists. At a meeting in Semple's Hall in Victoria West on the evening of October 12, 1899, the assembled ratepayers heard the details of the emerging scheme.

Mr. C.E. Renouf pointed out that the new transportation link would lead to a four hour saving in travelling time to the Canadian Pacific Railway at Mission in the Fraser Valley. He said that a good central depot for Victoria already existed in the Market Building on Cormorant St, with rear access off Fisgard* Street. It had been erected at a cost of $120,000 and would never be of use until the city of Victoria was placed in communication with the Fraser Valley. The building was costing the City $6,000 a year, whereas, if it were turned into a passenger depot and the adjacent lot into railyards, it might lead to a handsome profit.

If, under this new system, the Victoria and Sidney Railway would double its earnings, it would easily make the $15,000 being paid out in the provincial and municipal guarantee of the V&S $300,000 bond issue. At this meeting the committee indicated that it had no estimate of the cost to buy out Thomas Paterson's interest in the V&S, or the cost to run the line into the city. Paterson was present and indicated that $150,000 would easily buy out his interest in the railway and provide for extension of the line into the city from Hillside Avenue.

Remarkably, it was at this same public meeting that Paterson announced he had a steamer under construction to run through the Gulf Islands in connection with the V&S at Sidney. Paterson had waited long enough in hopes of seeing the promise of the old De Cosmos scheme realized and if the City of Victoria would not help out, he alone would at least try extending business into the Islands of the Gulf to provide more traffic for his railway. The meetings continued through the last months of 1899 and into the new century, with arguments, both pro and con, discussed in detail.

One of the City's key selling points for the Victoria-Chilliwack scheme was the claim that Mr. J.D. Pemberton, a well-known Victoria businessman, would be appointed as the Trustee in charge of the expanded railway and ferry operation. This

This illustration of the Market Building facade, facing south onto Cormorant St.is from the 1891 publication *Victoria Illustrated*.

* Often spelled "Fisguard" on old maps.

feature of the proposal ran into trouble when Pemberton refused to serve in that capacity. A lively debate followed in the local papers with backers and opponents contributing their best arguments. Finally, after months of debate, a proposal was put to the ratepayers of Victoria in the form of a by-law "To aid a Railway Company to be formed for the purpose of acquiring and operating the Victoria and Sidney Railway and extending the same, and operating a ferry system between Sidney or the terminus of such extension on the Saanich Peninsula and some convenient point on the Mainland of British Columbia."[8] At last, a refined proposal was published in the Victoria papers and all concerned citizens were able to see what they were being asked to support.

The by-law also provided for a connection between the extended V&S Railway and the Esquimalt and Nanaimo Railway at Victoria, and if carried out would place the V&S in connection with points as far north as Wellington on Vancouver Island. This would make the V&S the central link in a much larger transportation system. The by-law also required the scheme to be completed and in service within three years; the railway and ferry system had to have a connection with a transcontinental railway on the Mainland, and the new company was to become responsible for the bond interest guarantee, which had been paid since 1895 by the City of Victoria and the Province of British Columbia. The by-law was to raise $500,000 for capitalization of the Victoria-Chilliwack scheme and to purchase the same amount in the shares of the new company. If passed, it would lead to an increase of 2 1/8 mills on the tax bill of every Victoria ratepayer. The by-law was formally titled "The Victoria and Saanich Railway Extension and Loan By-Law, 1900" and the *Colonist* announced that a ratification vote would be held on February 28, 1900.[9]

In the days leading up to the vote, the local papers commented frequently on the matter. The *Colonist*, in an editorial of February 27, 1900, came out against the railway and ferry scheme. The paper was not against a rail and ferry connection with the Mainland, in general - in fact it favoured such a scheme - but, it was against the City asking its ratepayers to back a proposition with inadequate information. Such a statement seems remarkably naive in view of the protracted debate throughout the previous year.

Nevertheless, what the *Colonist* wanted to know about the proposal was: what was the city going to get for its money?; what liabilities, if any, would it incur?; and, how much would the city really have to contribute? "The ratepayers are practically without information on any of these points," said the *Colonist*, "and yet they are asked to put $500,000 into the scheme. We hardly think they will do so. If they decide to invest, and the investment proves a mistake, the *Colonist* will have the satisfaction of knowing that it pointed out the paucity of the information furnished the ratepayers. If it should prove a success, we will have the satisfaction of having done our plain duty in criticizing the project in a thoroughly impartial way."[10]

The vote was finally taken on February 28, 1900, and when over, it resulted in a resounding defeat for the advocates of the joint rail and ferry connection. There were 630 votes against the Victoria-Chilliwack scheme and only 221 in favour. By three to one, the people of Victoria were not in favour of supporting another railway scheme. Apparently, the $9,000 annual bond guarantee then paid by the City was already too much and the people were not about to support another railway without some assurance of financial success.

Thomas Paterson had been working hard all through the previous year to divest himself of the Victoria and Sidney Railway. He had gotten nowhere for all his efforts. The vessel he had been constructing in Port Moody through the fall and winter of 1899-1900 was almost ready to go into service and Paterson was determined to make a success of the joint railway and steamship enterprise. In the meantime, any realization of the old De Cosmos railway and rail ferry scheme would have to wait.

4

THE SIDNEY AND NANAIMO TRANSPORTATION COMPANY

The V&S
Goes to Sea

At the turn of the century, the Victoria and Sidney Railway provided what had become an essential service to the residents of the Saanich Peninsula and Victoria. Unfortunately, commercial success had eluded the railway and it was increasingly obvious that action would have to be taken to reach out for the business of the Gulf Islands and the Mainland if the V&S was ever to become a paying proposition.

The V&S received its first mail contract for the route between Victoria and Sidney in 1895. The contract paid a yearly stipend of $400.64 which was considered a sizeable sum in those days. Gulf Islands residents advocated a mail service on a more frequent basis than the weekly sailings of the Canadian Pacific Navigation Company between Victoria and Nanaimo. In February 1900, the Sidney and Nanaimo Transportation Company, (S&NT), a newly-formed subsidiary of the Victoria and Sidney Railway, was awarded this additional postal contract.

The steamer would make connection with Salt Spring Island every two days and the outer Gulf Islands twice weekly. There was to be an accompanying freight and passenger service to Salt Spring, the outer Gulf Islands, and as far north as Nanaimo.

The
S.S. Iroquois

Thomas Paterson's new steamer was in the final stages of construction and still unnamed when the *Daily Colonist* announced the awarding of the mail contract on March 9, 1900. The new service was to begin April first. The name given the new steamer, the *Iroquois*, was decided upon only at the last moment. Even then, it must have caused some confusion, as there was a steamer of the same name, but of American registry, operating in the Puget Sound area of nearby Washington State.

Paterson's *S.S. Iroquois* was built at Port Moody by Alex Watson and, in late March of 1900, she was towed to Spratt's Wharf, in Victoria, to be equipped with boilers and machinery. The *Iroquois* was registered in Canada as Hull No. 112,073 and was propelled by a 20-horsepower engine and single screw. The Polson Iron Works, of Toronto, supplied her machinery and equipment. The ship was 82 feet in length with a beam of 21 feet, depth of hold of eight feet and net registered tonnage of 94 tons.[1] She was capable of carrying about 100 tons of passengers and freight and her gross registered tonnage was 195 tons. Under favourable conditions, the *Iroquois* could make 12 knots an hour. Her first Master was Captain Cavin, formerly master of the *S.S. Lapwing*.

In the fading light of April 2, 1900, the spectators waiting on Hirst's Wharf in Nanaimo kept an eye eastward on the headland at Jack's Point, near the entrance of

Left:
With her shallow draft, the S.S. Iroquois was able to travel where competing vessels of the E&N Railway and the Canadian Pacific Navigation Company could not. Here she transits the shallow waters between North and South Pender Islands.

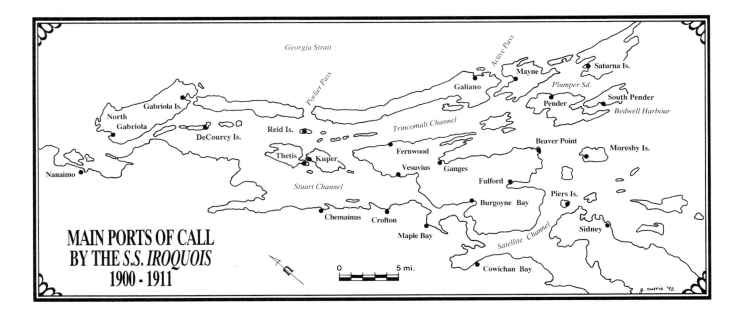

MAIN PORTS OF CALL
BY THE S.S. *IROQUOIS*
1900 - 1911

Nanaimo Harbour. At first, the only hint of her presence was a small wisp of smoke rising over nearby Duke Point. Then at last the little *Iroquois* came round the headland and swung into the harbour, her white hull standing out against the dark, wooded background of Gabriola Island. As she came nearer, the throb of her engines gradually increased. Finally, with a burst of steam and a shrill whistle, the *Iroquois* announced her arrival. She had completed her first run through the Gulf Islands from Sidney to Nanaimo with a cargo of Saanich Peninsula and Gulf Islands produce, along with a complement of passengers picked up along the way.

The *Daily Herald*, of Nanaimo, gave its readers a complete rundown of the arrival the very next day:

> "She is painted white, but is unfinished, the name not being on her, nor the interior even in presentable shape but seems as if she might be a comfortable little boat when finished, having two decks and a cabin.
> "In appearance she is short and stubby and stands an enormous distance out of the water. The general comment on her appearance in Nanaimo being favorable, except that she might be a bit top-heavy in a rough sea."[2]

The *Iroquois* was in service at last and Thomas Paterson had great hopes for her success. The first joint timetable of the Victoria and Sidney Railway and the Sidney and Nanaimo Transportation Company was published later in April 1900, and indicated the steamer made stops at Gulf Island points between Sidney and Nanaimo with calls at Fulford, Plumper Pass, Fernwood, Gabriola, Galiano, Ganges, Pender, Mayne and Saturna.

The *Iroquois*' placement in service signalled the entry of the V&S and S&NT, not only into the mail, maritime freight and passenger trades, but into excursion service on summer evenings and weekends. Many Victoria and Saanich residents were able to make a memorable trip aboard the *Iroquois* on a holiday or day off, and the beauties of the trip through the Islands of the Gulf of Georgia were favourably compared with the Thousand Islands of the St. Lawrence and even more distant destinations. Excursions were also run on summer weekday evenings after the arrival of the *Iroquois* back from her Gulf Islands scheduled route. Connecting train service was provided by the V&S Railway which did a brisk passenger business.

A Season
of Excursions

The *Victoria Times* described an excursion amongst the Gulf Islands on August 2, 1900, and praised the *Iroquois*:

Timetable from 1900.

"It was the privilege of a Times representative on Saturday last to make this journey. The city was left at the reasonable hour of seven in the morning, a quick run on the V&S Railway bringing the traveller to Sidney the terminus, before eight o'clock. The trip by rail forms an interesting prelude to the main portion of the excursion.

"Arriving at Sidney the stout little Iroquois is found puffing impatiently at her moorings. This vessel has been so recently described in these columns that any further details are unnecessary here. Eighty feet in length, with 21 feet of beam and an eight-foot hold, she has ample accommodation for the limited freight and passenger travel of the Island route. With a draft of seven feet she is able to navigate passes which would be impossible for a craft of deeper draft, and thus to abbreviate in a number of instances the route over which she plies. Her hull was constructed at Fort Moody (sic), while the Polson Iron Works of Toronto installed her engines.

"Her cabin and saloon accommodation too, is ample for all requirements. The demand on the vessel since her commissioning has been so constant that no time has been available in which to embellish the interior, but this will be remedied shortly. There is a delightful afterdeck, where passengers may view the scenery at their ease, parlors for the ladies, as well as a general sitting room, while immediately below it, the steward serves the most appetizing of meals in a cosy dining room.

"The vessel scarcely leaves the wharf before she commences to thread the maze of islets, for directly across lies Big Shell, with its parklike clothing of pines and the white beach from which its name is derived. Holding to the left, the Iroquois pushes through Canoe Pass, with Coal Island, where Ah Foo holds undisputed sway on the right, while on the neighboring ones a few Kanakas eke out an existence by an intermittent pursuit of agriculture and fishing.

"An hour's run brings the company to Moresby Island, owned by Captain Robertson, where that gentleman and his sons were found deep in a study of the intricacies of a new self-binder, and an attempt to circumvent the depredations of the cutworm pest. Here again the steamer circumvents the wider channel and steams recklessly out into Windy Strait, where a salty sou'easter indicates the capabilities of the locality when a strong tide lifts. Far ahead the American Archipelago is partially obscured in a bank of fog, while looking backward, the white hooded Olympics push their heads above the wooded hills of Vancouver Island...

"From Ganges the little vessel starts on the last leg of the journey, with the exception of the home run. The coastline is faithfully followed, until, rounding a point, Fulford Harbor is reached, lying like a Norwegian fjord between the giant hills...At the entrance of the harbor is Isabella Point, where the warlike Cowichans built their signal fires and off which their patrol canoes kept constant watch, in the old days, for their dreaded enemies, the Haidas.

"Sidney is again reached and in ample time for the excursionist to be in the city at his own dining table. Interesting as the route is from a tourist point of view, it has a commercial value which is highly prized by the Islanders. Prior to the Iroquois being placed on the run, mail was delivered only once a week...Under the new order instituted by Manager Paterson mail is delivered daily, the exclusive trip being made on Wednesdays and Saturdays, while the Nanaimo run is followed twice a week. Sunday the packet ties up for necessary alterations and repairs.

"Eighty miles of continuous steaming is covered in the trip described above, and already the route is so well timed that the Islanders set their clocks by the whistle of the boat. Needless to say, Captain Cavin, Mate Fraser and Purser Harrison are most popular on the run.

"In conclusion, the Island trip of the Iroquois offers an unique opportunity to the man of affairs who finds it impossible to take a protracted vacation, to snatch a day from the desk and counter and to undertake a cheap, yet ideal outing with his family. The Iroquois has accommodation for nearly 40 passengers in addition to her carrying capacity of 50 tons. When the beauties of this trip become well known, it is a safe prediction that a much larger vessel will be necessary in the summer season to carry the throng of tourists who will find this outing, so easily undertaken, a respite from work and worry."[3]

The S.S. Iroquois made numerous stops at small settlements throughout the Gulf Islands on her way north to Nanaimo, pictured above in 1905. At left, she is tied up at the Sidney dock.

A picnic excursion by students of Sidney School about 1902. Teacher, Miss Currie, stands two places to the right of the smokestack. The bunting and decoration suggests a very special occasion.

The summer of 1900 was a busy time for Thomas Paterson and the two companies he controlled. It appeared that the new Gulf Islands and Nanaimo connection with Sidney and the V&S line into Victoria would at last put some badly needed revenue into the companies' coffers. The combined railway and steamship service was an operational success, but the original dream of Amor De Cosmos to have a rail and ferry connection with the lower British Columbia mainland seemed as remote as ever.

By summer's end the S&NT was taking Victoria and Nanaimo freight business that had previously been monopolized by the rival Esquimalt and Nanaimo Railway. This competition would become so great that a year later the E&N would actually take steps to put the S&NT out of business.

The *Daily Herald*, of Nanaimo, watched the battle unfolding and commented in an editorial, citing the old story of the two rival steamboat companies that cut freight rates until they were reduced to the vanishing point. The *Herald* went on to describe how the victorious competitor, after having eliminated its competition, went back to the old practice of charging as much as the traffic would bear. If the Esquimalt and Nanaimo Railway and its steamship service had been successful in its competition with the S&NT, it would probably have done just as the paper predicted. Fortunately, the tactic was not successful and, while the E&N would try again, the Sidney-Gulf Islands-Nanaimo ferry run completed its first two seasons with pronounced success and looked forward to even better business in following years.

In the meantime, other events of a more pressing nature were to challenge Paterson and his V&S colleagues. The old rail and ferry connection with the mainland had again become the subject of public debate. The idea of a mainland rail and ferry connection with Victoria, in spite of the defeat of the scheme in February of 1900, was revived again before the year was out.

5

THE VICTORIA TERMINAL RAILWAY AND FERRY COMPANY

From Defeat

Left:
In February 1912, a few of the employees of the V&S posed with locomotive No.1. Crew members from top left include Engineer Bill Walker, (left); Conductor Albert Lacoursiere, (right); Cliff Ferguson of Saanichton; Conductor Herman Shade; Fireman R. Peterkin; Freight-Handler Paul Singh; Shopman R. Mellado, Master Mechanic Jenkins, (lower right); and Brakeman D. Laird, standing lower left.

The defeat of the Victoria and Saanich Railway Extension Loan By-Law, in February of 1900, had been a blow to local businessmen who were still anxious to secure connection with at least one of the transcontinental railways on the B.C. mainland. It seemed a good idea to the entrepreneurial segment of Victoria's population, but to the ordinary ratepayers of the city the price was just too high.

Notwithstanding these reservations, in the autumn of 1900, the idea was still firmly entrenched in the minds of Victoria City Council and the Vancouver Island Development League. Fortunately, for advocates of the railway and ferry scheme, events elsewhere in the railroad world in the Canadian and American West were working towards a solution that would give Victoria the rail and ferry connection it so badly needed.

On October 1, 1900, Alderman Williams, of Victoria, requested that council have the city clerk write to the management of the Canadian Pacific Railway, the Great Northern Railway, or any other railway company that would be prepared to build a railway and rail ferry connection into the city. Williams was frustrated. Most of the year had passed since the defeat of the earlier by-law and nothing had been done.

President Shaughnessy, of the Canadian Pacific Railway, happened to be in Victoria only a few days later and was questioned about the CPR's possible role in a revived transportation scheme. "My visit to the Coast," said Shaughnessy, "at this time has no significance whatsoever. We are simply making a tour of inspection over the lines, and, I am pleased to say, that we have found everything in good shape...I am informed that the steamboat service between Victoria and the mainland is not satisfactory to the Board of Trade, and this afternoon I expect to confer with a committee appointed by the Board of Trade on this subject. Of course, we do not have anything to do with the boat service, controlling only the end of it, as it were. But we have always found the CPN (Canadian Pacific Navigation) Company, which owns the boats, ready to meet us to make any arrangement that will be satisfactory all around...I have really nothing further to say."[1]

When the Victoria and Sidney Railway Company held its annual meeting in Victoria a week later, there was no expectation that there would be an early solution forthcoming for the company's flagging railway business. The steamer *Iroquois*, on the other hand, was doing quite well in the inter-island freight, passenger and mail service.

A possible solution to the transportation dilemma came forward only a few days later, on October 16th. Victoria Council and the Board of Trade met to consider a proposal that had apparently come from the Great Northern Railway, who were said to be considering an extension of their road into the capital city.

Great Northern Railway officials had been in the city looking over the local transportation situation for some time. James J. Hill was apparently anxious to extend the western terminus of his railway from Liverpool, on the Fraser River opposite New Westminster, across the Gulf of Georgia to Vancouver Island and to reach Victoria by the shortest possible route.

The GNR officials liked what they saw in Victoria and forwarded a favourable report to Hill. The Great Northern plan would be to put on fast rail ferries that would at first run down the Fraser River from Liverpool. This portion of the route would later be replaced by a railway line to some point near Point Roberts or closer to the mouth of the Fraser.

The Great Northern would cross the Gulf and run along the Victoria and Sidney Railway line into Victoria, thus making it the western terminus of the Great Northern system. This new link would also give Hill's railway a Canadian port for the British portion of its Oriental shipping trade and the first landfall for the Great Northern's two trans-oceanic steamers, the *Minnesota* and *Dakota*. The plan had some complications, at least one of which is worthy of comment.

After years of competition between the Great Northern and the Canadian Pacific in the west, the two companies had only recently agreed to respect each other's territory. An open move by the Great Northern to enter Victoria might be seen as a breach of this compact. If the GNR wanted to get into Victoria in the short term, it would have to do so by subterfuge or in some way that would not openly break its agreement to respect CPR territory. In hindsight, this is an interesting comment, because although Victoria was served by the V&S and the E&N Railways, it did not have an actual CPR direct railway connection.

It is notable that the CPR had already been resorting to this same kind of subterfuge for a number of years, extending its railway lines into the Kootenay and Boundary regions of British Columbia by setting up and then taking over companies that were incorporated specifically to avoid a restriction against the CPR building south of its transcontinental mainline for 25 years after completion of its line into Vancouver, in 1885. The Nakusp and Slocan Railway, the Kootenay and Columbia Railway, and the Shuswap and Okanagan Railway were all examples of this methodology.

In spite of this minor stumbling point, it appeared that further details of the Great Northern's entry into Victoria had already been worked out. The Great Northern wanted to secure depot space in Victoria's Market Building. Access would be gained to this site off Fisgard Street by routing the V&S line along city streets from Hillside Station to the new site.

Mr. E.V. Bodwell, of the firm of Bodwell and Duff, Barristers and Solicitors, represented the Great Northern Railway and its subsidiaries in Victoria. Bodwell made a formal presentation to Victoria City Council and a group of interested citizens on October 19, 1900, and introduced a letter, purportedly from the Great Northern, confirming its plans and outlining details of financial assistance that would be asked from the city in return for the extension of this new service. There were three main features to the plan:

1. The Great Northern Railway was to construct a line of railway from a point near the mouth of the Fraser River through the Delta on the south side and connecting with the New Westminster and Southern Railway (a GNR subsidiary) at a point near Cloverdale.

2. To build a line of railway through Victoria to connect the terminus of the Victoria and Sidney Railway with the Esquimalt and Nanaimo Railway.
3. To operate and maintain a railway ferry between Sidney and the Lower B.C. Mainland.

Construction was to begin just as soon as a new company could be incorporated to carry out the work. This would be after the Great Northern had undertaken to provide a temporary service so that carload freight could be transported from the Mainland to Vancouver Island without breaking bulk, unloading, or transferring freight from one car to another.

If the plan was implemented there would be a connection between Victoria and the transcontinental line of the Great Northern, making the British Columbia capital its *de facto* western terminus. Local trade unions wanted the new rail ferry to be built in Victoria, if possible, to give the maximum benefit to local workers. They even went so far as to say the assistance by-law would not pass unless there was an undertaking to do so by the new Railway Company.

In return for its undertaking, the newly incorporated company would require several concessions from the City of Victoria:
1. A permanent right-of-way over certain streets in the city;
2. A cash bonus of $15,000 a year for twenty years; and
3. A lease of the Market Building in Victoria for a term of fifty years at a nominal rent and exemption from taxation for that period.

Concessions
from Victoria

The pilot beam flags indicate this is a festive occasion, possibly a May Day in the early 1900s and two belles decorate the No.1 as she waits at the Sidney dock for the arrival of the *S.S. Iroquois*.

So far so good, but then another problem intervened. It would not be possible to incorporate a company to undertake the project until the next sitting of the British Columbia Legislature. It was suggested that in the interim a trustee could be appointed to enter into an agreement with the city that would be transferred to the new company after the Legislature had given assent to its incorporation. Bodwell expected that if such an arrangement was made, it would be possible to commence work on the project almost at once and to complete the new connection with the Mainland within twelve months.

Bodwell's argument was smooth and well organized. He compared the new scheme with the original, unfulfilled De Cosmos proposal, but pointed out that the Great Northern would deliver something that none of the other plans had been capable of doing - to give a connection with a transcontinental railway. He concluded his speech with the assurance that the plan had already been submitted to James J. Hill of the Great Northern, through the company's senior officers, and had been approved.

The Great Northern was then at the height of its power and prestige in British Columbia and was, in spite of an apparent agreement to the contrary, in a struggle with the Canadian Pacific Railway for domination of the railway trade in Western Canada. In 1900, the GNR owned or controlled the New Westminster Southern, the Bedlington and Nelson, the Nelson and Fort Sheppard, the Red Mountain and the Kaslo and Slocan Railways in British Columbia and was actively planning even more route extensions in the province. The GNR also controlled the International Steamship and Trading Company, which operated routes on Kootenay Lake, and had connections with a number of other U.S. transcontinental railroads.

The Great Northern was a transportation empire that had been built by the energy and business acumen of James Hill, an expatriate Canadian who had made his fortune in the United States. If the new scheme for extending GNR routes to Victoria was realized, it would put Victoria in direct connection with points as far away as the U.S. Atlantic Seaboard. It appeared that the idea was the best one yet submitted and might be sold to the Victoria ratepayers who would be asked to subsidize it.[2]

Jim Hill's Master Plan for Victoria

The plan would make Victoria the terminus of an extensive transportation network and would greatly benefit local businesses on Vancouver Island. It was estimated that with a railway and ferry connection between the Great Northern and the Esquimalt and Nanaimo Railway in Victoria, there would be at least 600 carloads of freight per year coming into the city. There would be other advantages: the railway ferry would be efficient and capable of handling all business in sight; the rail line from the mouth of the Fraser River to Cloverdale and beyond would open a rich agricultural district that would become tributary to Victoria; if the line connected with the E&N and that line was extended to the northern end of Vancouver Island, and a new port built there, as advocated in some circles, they would even be able to tap the Klondike trade and become the closest Canadian port to Skagway, Alaska. Finally, the Great Northern would have direct access to the Vancouver Island coalfields and would become a major factor in coal shipments to both the rest of Canada and the U.S.

The plan was well received in Victoria, being far and away the best scheme that had been proposed since the old De Cosmos days. Many Victorians also thought that once there was a Great Northern Railway connection, the Canadian Pacific Railway would be eager to follow.

Along with his presentation, Bodwell introduced a petition from Victoria businesses, representing over $5,000,000 in real estate values, urging the city to enter into an agreement with the Great Northern.[3] It was at this point that another difficulty intervened.

A Victoria resident, who was not convinced that all available information was being given to local ratepayers, wrote to James. J. Hill of the Great Northern and asked him to confirm that he was backing the construction of the railway and ferry scheme. Hill's reply indicated that he had agreed to nothing more than a traffic agreement for his railway to move cars as far as its Liverpool terminal. Hill stated that he was not otherwise involved. This caused some consternation among Victorians, but they were finally reassured by E.V. Bodwell, who affirmed that he had never said that the Great Northern were financing the project, but that they were agreeing to provide the new service with a transcontinental railway connection. It turned out that Bodwell, himself, was the head of a syndicate wishing to build the ferry and the required railway connections on the Island and lower mainland. His answer was all the explanation deemed necessary by local Victoria backers of the plan. The final determination was left to Victoria ratepayers at large, who would decide whether or not to back the joint rail and ferry system.

As always, and in spite of great enthusiasm, there were some who still advocated a even closer look at the whole plan before the city entered into an agreement with the Great Northern or any other railway company. In spite of these cautions, City Council quickly prepared a by-law for submission to the local ratepayers. This by-law passed both first and second readings, between Bodwell's presentation of the 19th of October and the end of that month.

The vote for ratification of the "Victoria Terminal Railway By-Law, 1900" was held on November 29, 1900, following a month of debate at public meetings throughout the city. It resulted in a major victory for the backers of the new railroad scheme, a total of 1,728 voters had approved of the agreement and only 319 were opposed. It was a stunning victory after the defeat of the railway assistance scheme earlier in the year.

With passage of the by-law, the backers of the plan continued with preparations for incorporation of a new company, and construction of the Victoria and Mainland railway sections, as well as the building of a new rail ferry. In the interim, the Sidney and Nanaimo Transportation Company and the steamer *Iroquois*, which was still being managed by Thomas Paterson, was ending a successful first year and looking forward to a continuation of service to the Gulf Islands and Nanaimo in 1901. The link between the Victoria and Sidney Railway and the Sidney and Nanaimo Transportation Company continued, with the two companies still taking advantage of the mutually beneficial link between Nanaimo, the Gulf Islands and Victoria. This part of our story will be taken up again in the next chapter.

The first year of the new century was coming to an end, but fate had one more accident in store for the V&S - just the latest in a long series of minor mishaps along the rusty streak of rails between Sidney and the capital city. At 9:30, on the morning of December 22, 1900, the inbound mixed train was approaching Mark's Crossing, near the head of Elk Lake, when the passenger coach derailed. There were several passengers on board at the time, but no one was hurt. The engine and boxcar in front remained on the rails. Another passenger car was brought out from Victoria and the passengers were taken into the city, shaken but otherwise unharmed.

Pages 68 and 69:
One of the most popular and frequent travellers on the V&S trains was Rev. Father A.J. Vullinghs, who was the resident priest around Saanichton from 1893 to 1908. He built up a strong following and established the Indian Missionary school, along with churches at East and West Saanich.

As a testimony to his popularity, after returning from Holland in April 1901, where he had been for six month upon the death of his parents, the local populace at Saanichton turned out in full to greet his return. "The Indian Band played lively airs...the procession formed a line nearly half a mile long..." Father Vullinghs received annual free passes on the V&S railway (and ferry to Vancouver). One memorable occasion was the day, in 1907, when he was a passenger in the cab as the No. 1 hit a fallen tree on the tracks near Elk Lake.

A few of his photographs are shown here.

Top:
The V&S passenger train at the Sidney dock.

Above:
Father Vullinghs poses with a local Native Indian dressed in traditional wear.

Right:
V&S locomotive No. 1.

North-Saanich Hopfield abou[...]

2 snapshots of accident (with insuf-ficient light) by a passenger at my own request.

hilly-side

my place at the time of the acci... dent.

on the other side : edge of Elk-Lake.— engine dragged tree 28 yards.—

Above:
Hops were a popular crop on the Saanich Peninsula at the turn of the century.
Below and Left:
Scenes from the 1907 accident at Elk Lake when the train hit a fallen tree.

With passage of the Victoria Terminal Railway By-Law on November 29, 1900, the backers of the new organization moved ahead with plans to build the new rail lines, construct the ferry and put the new system into service. A January 1901 announcement indicated that a company had been formally organized and was working in concert with the Great Northern Railway. Active operations would begin by April and the works would take about a year to complete. Few other details were available.

Within a month or so, Captain S.F. Mackenzie, one of the group of investors in the new project, purchased the car barge *Georgian* for temporary use on the interim run between Liverpool and Sidney. The *Georgian* had been in service between Vancouver Island and Skagway in the coal trade with the White Pass and Yukon Railway. She had a capacity of 800 tons but needed some structural changes to make her ready for her new role as a rail barge. On April 13, 1901, the *Daily Colonist* covered the preparations being made to place the *Georgian* in service:

THE VICTORIA FERRY

Preparations for Temporary
Service via Great Northern

"The cars of the Great Northern will be landed in Victoria, at least as far as the present accommodation of the line of the Victoria and Sidney Railway will allow, in a very short time. The big barge on which the tracks are to be placed for the cars to ferry them over from the present terminus of the Great Northern at Liverpool, will be taken up next week, for the purpose of preparing and fitting her for the work. The detail of a tug has been arranged for, and as soon as the barge is fitted up there will be another great transcontinental line sending its freight in its own cars direct to this city without breaking bulk.

"Yesterday Captain Mackenzie of the Victoria Ferry Company and Mr. Paterson, of the Victoria and Sidney Railway, made a special trip over the road to Sidney and there made arrangements for the barge to be pulled up for the work of preparation. The gentlemen were accompanied by Mr. J.D. Lynch, a gentleman from New York, who is said to be here representing the interests of Mr. Hill, of the Great Northern, and Mr. J. Pierpoint Morgan, the syndicate which is said to have a hand in the scheme for control of all the great continental railways. Mr. Lynch evinced great interest in the details of the proposed ferry service and looked carefully over the ground which is proposed to be the terminus. He left last night for Vancouver, accompanying Captain Mackenzie. The latter gentleman said he was not yet able to say when the ferry for freight service would be inaugurated, but it was only a question of a short time, as the preparing of the barge for the tracks to carry the cars was not a task of great magnitude."

Top Right:
Locomotive No.3 (captioned as "The Flying Dutchman") crosses Douglas at Fisgard Street on her morning run from Victoria to Sidney, circa 1905. The adjacent Masonic Hall is still a prominent feature in downtown Victoria.

Bottom Right:
The northbound passenger stirs up dust on her run up Rose (First) Street approaching Hillside Avenue, Victoria.

The company also planned for a passenger steamer that would operate over the same route. In spite of Captain Mackenzie's optimistic assessment, the completion of these arrangements would take some time. For most of 1901, traffic on the Victoria and Sidney Railway between Victoria and the Saanich Peninsula would continue much as in previous years.

By June, it was estimated that the little engines of the Victoria and Sidney Railway had consumed about 7,800 cords of wood fuel. This was a significant financial windfall for Thomas Paterson who still held the contract. Besides keeping Paterson's personal finances in the black, to the tune of about $13,000, the arrangement to buy

cordwood from local farmers also enabled many of them to make it through an otherwise bleak winter.[4]

While Paterson may personally have done well with the wood contract, the V&S Railway itself was still not even making enough money to pay off its bond interest and each year the City of Victoria and the Province of British Columbia had to ante up their respective subsidies of $9,000 and $6,000.

In an effort to stem the flow of red ink on the company ledgers the Victoria and Sidney Railway, in August of 1901, announced new, reduced freight and passenger rates on the steamer and railway service between Nanaimo and Victoria.

A passenger could travel from the "Coal City" to Sidney and Victoria for $1.50 one way, and $2.50 return. Freight charges were pegged at the reasonable rate of 7 1/2 cents per hundred on shipments up to 600 pounds, and 5 cents per hundred on heavier freights. The *Daily Herald*, of Nanaimo, announced on July 13, 1901, that traffic on the route was on the increase, many customers taking advantage of the cheap, convenient and enjoyable route through the Gulf Islands to Sidney and Victoria.

The existence of the combined V&S and S&NT service led to some pretty interesting freight routings. One such shipment was described in the *Victoria Times* of May 3, 1901:

A NEW SERVICE

V.&S. Railway and Steamer
Iroquois Now Carrying Passengers
and Freight to the Coast

"Certainly the transportation problem assumes some very peculiar phases these days. As an instance of this it may be mentioned that a Times reporter hearing of a carload of flour and feed being hauled from the E.&N. Railway station, on Store Street, to the Victoria and Sidney Railway station, asked for particulars, and much to his surprise was informed that this large shipment was not intended for the Saanich district but was destined for Cowichan, forty miles up the E.&N. Railway. With several other shipments, it was now being carried to that point by the Victoria and Sidney Railway and the steamer Iroquois.

"One very remarkable feature about the movements of this particular carload of freight is the fact that it had already been hauled past within almost a stone's throw of its destination. It would appear, however, that owing to the very complex nature of modern railway business methods it must first be hauled to Victoria, and then hauled back again before delivery could be made, the car having been shipped from Enderby via the new Ladysmith ferry.

"The Victoria and Sidney Railway and the owners of the steamer Iroquois have recently inaugurated a freight and passenger service between Victoria and the various districts on the east coast of Vancouver Island between Victoria and Nanaimo. This service is said to be a great advantage and convenience to the shippers along that route, and it would seem they are showing their appreciation by patronizing the new arrangement very liberally."

From this congratulatory description of the new railway and steamer service it was clear that the V&S and the steamer *Iroquois* were doing much better than before the inauguration of their joint service. Unfortunately, very little news seemed to be available on the new company behind the mainland rail and ferry scheme that had been so loudly hailed at the passage of the Victoria Terminal Railway By-Law in November of 1900, six months earlier.

The summer and fall of 1901 were marked with the usual excursion trains to picnics at Sidney or points along the line. Specials were run for Victorians wanting to attend the Saanich Agricultural Association's Fall Fair. For October 1901, in order to tap more revenue traffic, the V&S announced that it would run special hunting trains from Victoria out to the Peninsula with a morning departure at seven o'clock, two hours earlier than the usual passenger train.

The longer than usual "consist" indicates a special occasion as the vintage No.1 pulls up to the Sidney Station on a day of admirable commerce.

Under Way at Last

Finally, after nearly a year of preparation, the Victoria Terminal Railway and Ferry Company began to move into high gear on the railway and ferry project. On October 15th, the *Daily Times* announced that Captain Mackenzie had ordered steel rails from England for the new rail line from Liverpool to the mouth of the Fraser River. Further details were available the next day when the *Colonist* announced that the "Ladner-Sidney Ferry scheme, which is to give the Great Northern Railway a terminus in Victoria, is progressing favorably. Rails for 13 miles of railway from Westminster south to a point just below Ladners, have been ordered in England and will come by sailing ship. It is reported that during the summer the line will be completed to the water's edge from the Great Northern Railway station at South Westminster (Liverpool). This winter the attention of the promoters will be directed to putting on fast steamers for the ferry service."[5]

The first general meeting of the Victoria Terminal Railway and Ferry Company was held during October 1901, and E.V. Bodwell, the principal shareholder, was elected as president. The other shareholders included Captain S.F. Mackenzie, Mr. A.E. Henry and Mr. James Anderson, the General Manager designate who would be taking over from Thomas Paterson as head of the Victoria and Sidney Railway and S&NT operations after a period of familiarization.

The Saanich Land Company, which was still the holding company for the V&S and VTR&F, also had a new list of officials. Captain Mackenzie was president, his brother Duncan was vice-president and Victorian Samuel Rounding was the company secretary in addition to his duties as the Victoria station agent. Construction on the proposed rail ferry had yet to begin, but plans were made to proceed with it as soon as possible.

The Victoria Railway Extension

On October 22, 1901, after many months of apparent inactivity, the VTR&F finally announced that work would begin on the railway extensions immediately. The promoters indicated that they had experienced difficulty in obtaining funding because the Great Northern Railway was at first unwilling to enter into a traffic agreement for the delivery of cars to the company for a period of more than ten years. Prospective investors wanted an agreement of at least 25 years duration and it took some time for the VTR&F people to negotiate with the Great Northern. Finally, the promoters were able to persuade them to enter into a long-duration traffic agreement which broke the impasse. Soon ample investment funds were available. Since non-compliance of the terms of agreement with Victoria were stringent, it was imperative that work begin as soon as possible.

To speed things along, the company decided to delay construction of its new rail ferry. This would not take long, and in the interim a rail barge service would be run between Liverpool and Sidney. Plans for the Victoria portion of the VTR&F got under way.

The preliminary survey for the Victoria extension of the Terminal Railway was commenced on October 23, 1901, by Mr. H.P. Bell, C.E. The route chosen proceeded from the existing V&S terminal, near Hillside, along A Street, thence along Bay, First, Blanshard and Fisgard Streets to the Market Building.

Thomas C. Sorby, a Victoria resident and civil engineer, submitted a proposal through the *Times* newspaper suggesting that connection be made with the Esquimalt and Nanaimo Railway in Victoria by routing trains over the tracks of the British Columbia Electric Railway Company (BCER):

VICTORIA TERMINAL RAILWAY

"To The Editor:- When the Railway and Ferry By-Law was before the public in October last year, I called Mr. Bodwell's attention to the desirability of connecting the V.&S. Railway (as part of a transcontinental road) with the Victoria Tramway System, so that freight coming in from the Eastern factories could be delivered direct to the Western salesrooms in unbroken bulk.

"Their present position is to extend the line from Hillside Avenue along First and Blanchard, and then down Fisguard (sic)Street, to the Market Hall, a distance of about 1,400 yards, through a residential section to which it offers no traffic advantages. It would be a source of danger to wheeled vehicles throughout its whole length. My suggestion was that instead of cutting up and damaging 1,400 yards of public streets, they should run their junction diagonally across a vacant piece of land of small value, from a point south of Topaz Avenue to a point on the car line north of Market Street, a distance of about 200 yards, which would place them at once in connection with the whole of the existing tramway system and its future extensions. This would inflict no further nuisance on the public and open up a splendid prospect of business for the company and provide corresponding public advantages.

"I mentioned this matter to you, sir, at the time, and discussed it with many of our leading importers, with the local manager of the British Columbia Electric Railway Company and others. But Mr. Bodwell particularly requested me to keep it out of the papers for fear it might be regarded as a rival proposition and, by confusing the voters, imperil the passing of the by-law. It is a matter which should have careful consideration before it is too late, for it must be remembered that these acts of folly of the passing generation leave a fearful legacy of debt and embarrassment on those that follow us. A memorial to your council is under consideration.
Victoria, Oct. 28th,1901.   THOS. C. SORBY"[6]

Sorby's idea was sensible and would have eliminated eleven street crossings along the new VTR&F line, but the B.C. Electric Railway Company would have nothing to do with it. The engineering staff began to consider several possible routes for the railway extension in Victoria. The sod breaking ceremony, which was originally scheduled for November 4, 1901, was delayed because they had not yet

Victoria Extension Begins

completed their cost evaluations. On November 6th, the *Colonist* announced that the engineers were still at work and that a despatch had been sent to a U.S. steel company for a cargo of 65-pound steel rails to be delivered as soon as possible. This steel was in addition to the outstanding order then in transit by sailing ship from England to the lower mainland. Finally, after another day's delay, the ground breaking ceremony was held on November 7th:

GROUND HAS BEEN BROKEN

Route For First Section
of Extension of V.&S. Railway
Approved

Rails, Ties and Other Materials
Will Be Brought in By Rail

"Ground was broken on A Street yesterday morning for the extension of the V.&S. Railway to the market building which is to be the depot for the Victoria Terminal Railway and Ferry. This is the first practical step towards giving Victoria direct connection with the American system of railways through the Great Northern, which road the line will eventually join at Liverpool, its present British Columbia terminus. The company intend to push to completion the piece of road to bring the Victoria and Sidney line into the heart of the city. The work will be done from the Hillside Avenue station, the V.&S. being used as a feeder during construction. The rails, which are to come from Seattle, will be landed at Sidney and the ties will be brought from points along the line of railway, so that all the transportation for construction purposes will be by rail. Announcements in regard to the construction of the ferry steamer and the line from Liverpool to the mouth of the Fraser River will be made shortly.

"Under the by-law it is necessary for the company to supply the city engineer with plans before commencing any work. The plan for the extension of the V.&S. through the city was not quite complete, but yesterday morning the city council met and approved the plan for the first section from the V.&S. to the corner of Blanchard and Fisgard streets. This first section parallels the V.&S. along A Street, and then crosses private property to First Street; along First Street to Bay Street; through Finlayson's fields to Blanchard Street, and then along the latter street to the corner of Fisgard. The second section will have to show the route to the Market and the connection with the E.&N. Railway."[7]

Taking Over the V&S

The Victoria Terminal Railway and Ferry Company formally took over the assets and obligations of the Victoria and Sidney Railway on October 31, 1901. The commencement of a thrice daily ferry service to the mainland was announced on the same day. In spite of the takeover, the Victoria and Sidney Railway was to remain a separate corporation and the railway line from Victoria to Sidney was, in effect, operated by two separate legal entities. All subsequent reports submitted to federal and provincial authorities listed the Victoria and Sidney Railway and the Victoria Terminal Railway and Ferry Company separately. This led to the company practice, in its publication of local timetables, of informally calling itself the "Victoria Terminal and Sidney Railway Company."

After being delayed for most of the previous year, the first actual work on the Victoria Terminal Railway and Ferry Company was at last under way. Work on the new section of the line from Topaz Avenue towards the Market Building began on

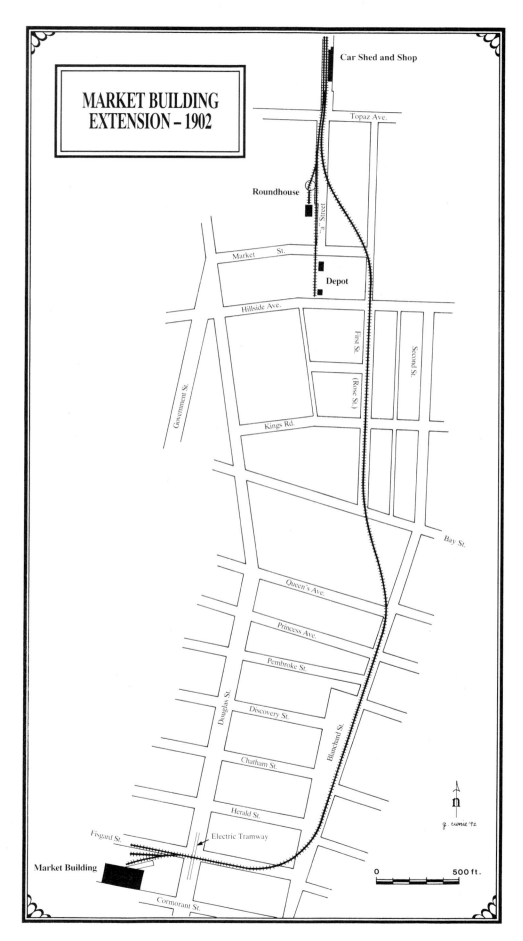

MARKET BUILDING EXTENSION – 1902

Car Shed and Shop

Topaz Ave.

Roundhouse

"a" Street

Market St.

Depot

Hillside Ave.

Government St.

First St.

(Rose St.)

Second St.

Kings Rd.

Bay St.

Queen's Ave.

Princess Ave.

Pembroke St.

Douglas St.

Discovery St.

Blanchard St.

Chatham St.

Herald St.

Fisgard St.

Electric Tramway

Market Building

Cormorant St.

g. currie '92

0   500 ft.

November 8, 1900, under the able superintendence of Thomas Paterson who was retained by the new owners to provide that service. Also, it was finally stated that an announcement on the construction of the ferry and the mainland section of the VTR&F was imminent.

Six hundred tons of 65-pound (per yard) rails for the Victoria extension arrived in the city from Seattle on the steamer *Clansman* on November 15, 1901, and were landed at Raymond's wharf in James Bay. A gang of men was already hard at work on grading along Alpha Street and the rails would soon be put to use.

It was during this same period that the Victoria and Sidney Railway experienced yet another accident on its Saanich Pensinsula line. The daily mixed train was returning to Victoria when, along the west side of Elk Lake, the rails spread and the passenger coach and two wood cars skidded to a halt along the ties. Mercifully, there were no injuries. After necessary repairs to the track, the cars were re-railed and taken into Victoria. Regular scheduled service was restored the next day.

Notwithstanding the occasional minor accident, or the dearth of hard cash in the company coffers, the Victoria and Sidney Railway and the new Victoria Terminal Railway and Ferry Company ended 1901 on a more optimistic note than had been the case a year earlier. This time the plans were not just on paper, but were being carried out by an apparently energetic management. That brought hope to the residents of Victoria and Saanich who looked forward to the impending developments of the coming year, 1902, with enthusiasm.

By the first week of December 1901, the new Market extension had been graded to a point on First Street near King's Road and a work train was moving dirt and ballast as the workmen ditched and graded their way into the main part of the city. By December 15th, the new line was half completed and work was continuing apace through Finlayson's field in the direction of the Market Building. After a few finishing touches on the completed section of line, work would proceed along Blanshard Street. Rails were on hand to complete the extension in Victoria and Captain Simon F. Mackenzie, on an inspection visit to the city, indicated that rails for the mainland section of the line would soon be arriving from England.

In the first week of January 1902, survey work was also well under way for the (never built) mainland section of the line from Liverpool towards Canoe Pass. It was announced that a temporary railbarge service would be in operation from Liverpool to Sidney by the beginning of February.

Work on the ferry dock and barge slip at Sidney was begun in mid-January and was expected to be completed within a month or so. While prosecuting work on the Victoria and mainland extensions of the VTR&F, the new management did not neglect the operations of the steamer service by the *S.S. Iroquois* which was doing well in the trade through the Gulf Islands to Nanaimo. Several exciting developments on Vancouver Island would make 1902 a very important and busy year for the Gulf Islands and Nanaimo steamer service. We now turn to the operations of the *Iroquois* and its role in the development of the Island in the first years of the new century.

V. T. & S. Ry. Sunday Excursion Train leaves Market Building at 9 a.m. instead of 8 a. m., as heretofore. Excursion rates: Beaver Lake and return, 25 c: Saanich or Sidney and return 50c Crofton and return, $1.50. The V. T.& S. Ry. has the finest points for holiday; trips around Victoria. Return train arrives 6 30 p m.

6

IN THE GULF FERRY TRADE, 1901-1902

As in the previous year, 1901 was a successful year in the Gulf Islands trade and the *S.S. Iroquois* entered 1902 with promise of even greater success. A copper mining boom which had begun in 1897 on Mount Sicker, just north of Duncan, led to the development of the new smelter town of Crofton, on Osborne Bay, along the east coast route of the *Iroquois*. It was named after Henry Croft, the brother-in-law of B.C. Premier James Dunsmuir, and one of the unsuccessful V&S bidders in 1892.

Booming Crofton

Crofton was the site of a smelter operation initiated by the Northwestern Smelting and Refining Company. The smelter operators were Herman Bellinger and James Breen, who had constructed the famous smelter at Trail, in the Kootenay Region of British Columbia, in 1896. It was built to treat the low grade ore from nearby Mount Sicker. It was also intended to attract ore shipments from points as far away as Alaska and South America. The location was a good one, as it was close to supplies of coal, coke and limestone that were a necessary part of the smelting process. It was also easily accessible to shipping. Many vessels often ran empty from the U.S. West Coast to load coal from the Nanaimo or Cumberland coalfields of Vancouver Island. They could carry cargos of ore coming north instead of running in ballast and would thereby augment the maritime trade from the U.S. West Coast to Vancouver Island. Since the new smelter town was on tidewater, but did not have railway connections, the *Iroquois* was in an advantageous position to become the main method of transport for smelter workers, equipment and supplies going into the new town.

The smelter operation had been induced to come to the new townsite of Crofton by Henry Croft, the major landholder in the area. While Croft was married to the sister of James Dunsmuir, the two were not friends and Dunsmuir viewed Croft's new enterprise as a threat to his own E&N transportation monopoly on Vancouver Island.

Dunsmuir was the owner, not only of the Esquimalt and Nanaimo Railway, but also of the E&N Steamship service along the east coast of Vancouver Island. It was only natural that Croft and the new smelter owners would look to the Sidney and Nanaimo Transportation Company to break the E&N freight monopoly. The result was an added incentive to the S&NT and prospects for 1902 looked even brighter than they had a year earlier when the service had been slated for takeover by the Mackenzies and the VTR&F.

Left:
On a warm spring day in 1902 the *S.S. Strathcona*, newly placed in service, meets the southbound passenger train at Sidney dock. The passengers are being transferred and the No.3 will soon head her train south towards Victoria.

In those days, the *Daily Colonist* was acknowledged to be a "Dunsmuir paper" and the *Daily Times* was noted for a more independent stance with regard to local Vancouver Island issues. It followed then, that the *Times* should comment in detail on the unfolding drama along the Island trade routes at the beginning of 1902:

"The Victoria and Sidney Railway has been referred to in bantering tones in many quarters; in one quarter it and its tin-pot ferry connection have been sneered at and alluded to in terms of withering contempt. We hope this feeling may long continue, for the Victoria and Sidney Railway is the one transportation concern that stands between the people of Victoria and a monopoly which seemingly would be pleased if it could transfer the business of this port to other places on the Island and mainland. The farmers and country people generally, as well as the businessmen of this and other cities

who have been brought together through the medium of the Victoria and Sidney Railway, realize what a cheaper means of communication has accomplished for them. In a comparatively small way monopoly has been broken and modern methods have been substituted for the mossback methods of a few years ago. There is not so much complaint as formerly about exorbitant charges. It has been asserted in interested quarters that there is no virtue in any railway competition. At any rate, few of the residents of the Islands want to go back to the old system. Competition is of the utmost importance to Victoria - of vastly more importance at the present time than many of us imagine. The development of the Island's metalliferous mines has commenced.

"It is a matter for congratulation that the first producing mine of importance is in control of a man who is friendly to this city, who is not one of them that takes delight in injuring rather than benefitting to the utmost of his power the place which should be the centre of all his interests. In the vicinity of Mount Sicker there will soon be thousands of people working in the mines and smelters connected therewith. We understand that the Victoria and Sidney Railway intend to run a steamer from the terminus of the road to this rapidly growing place. We hope that the report is true and that our Board of Trade is doing all in its power to bring about such a consummation. Our natural advantages should make the business relations between Victoria and the Mount Sicker communities most intimate. But we shall have competition and in view of recent developments it is not unreasonable to assume that we might be compelled to compete at a disadvantage, but for an institution which we admit has cost us much, but which promises to return value in full unless the monopolies should unfortunately be driven to the conclusion that there is virtue in competition and gobble it up."[1]

It was true - the Victoria and Sidney Railway had cost Victorians much, but so had it given them their only relief from the monopolistic Dunsmuir railway and steamboat empire which had hitherto had a stranglehold on transportation routes in the Southern Vancouver Island area.

The businessmen of Nanaimo were even more supportive of the Sidney and Nanaimo Transportation Company than their colleagues in Victoria. The presence of the *S.S. Iroquois*, now styled the *R.M.S.* (for Royal Mail Steamer) *Iroquois*, even on her 1900-1901 schedule of two trips per week to Nanaimo, had given the businessmen there and along the east coast route hope for cheaper rates and a more competitive service than the E&N.

All Aboard for Crofton

The genesis of the new town of Crofton was a fortuitous windfall for the S&NT and soon excursion trips on the *Iroquois* to the new smelter town were a popular weekend pastime for Victorians. The new smelter town had its own newspaper, *The Crofton Gazette*, a paper "devoted to The Mining and Agricultural Interests of Vancouver Island, Texada Island, and Coast Mainland Districts." In its first issue on February 27, 1902, the *Gazette* featured a fine description of an excursion to Crofton from Victoria and Sidney on the railway and *S.S. Iroquois*:

ALL ABOARD FOR CROFTON

"At 7:45 a.m., punctually, the Sidney train started from Fisguard Street. By twos and threes the various parties of sportsmen dropped off at wayside stations, and after the final dispersion at Sidney the little band that wended their way to the steamer 'Iroquois' might all be counted Crofton pilgrims, as indeed they were.

"There was the real estate agent, spruce and tidy and looking full of business. There were several contractors who had been down before and were wisely provided with big gum boots. There was the doctor. There were also various business and professional men who would be speculators in town lots. There was the general manager of the railway, there was the smelter chief and colleagues and friends - all aboard for

Crofton! The talk ran of stone and lumber, estimates, dollars in tens of thousands, and of course smelting, with an occasional reference to refreshments. And presently, with its eager human freight, the little steamer was plying through the picturesque waters between Salt Spring Island and Vancouver Island.

"About two and a half hours brought us past Cowichan Arm and on to Maple Bay. We could now perceive ahead of us, to our right, the Vesuvius Bay settlement lying in a cosy nook of Salt Spring Island. To the left a wooded promontory cut off our view, but rounding this we caught our first fair glimpse of Osborne Bay.

"At the foot of a gentle slope of wooded hills lies the clearing upon which are dotted the earliest habitations of Crofton. To the left Mount Richards stretches, green and forest covered, whilst in the distance to the right Mount Brenton arises, a misty blue mass with scattered fields of snow. But the little patch of land with the yellowish wooden buildings is the mark of all eyes.

"The large double building on the high ground to the left is pointed out to be the smelter offices, and to the left of them again is the smelter site. To the right, stretching back, are a couple of ranches. Their weather-stained buildings denote that they are not part of the new townsite...The wharf confronts us. It is at present a small structure erected merely for Mr. Ward's convenience, but five or six weeks hence there will be extended in its place an imposing structure 750 feet long and 60 feet wide, and having a depth of water for the largest ships at its extremity...The prospect looking down on the bay is admirable. The avenue has been so laid out that there is an uninterrupted view across the waters of the bay to a deep dip in the rugged hills of Salt Spring Island, through which may be caught a glistening vista of glorious Mount Baker on the far off American shore...

"And now returning down Joan Avenue and bearing across Robert Street, we cross into the smelter domain by a light bridge over a small stream. Here we come to two large buildings connected by a covered way. These are the smelter offices and living quarters of the staff. Their luxuriousness bears witness to the handsome way in which the smelter syndicate are known to treat their employees...Beyond the high ground the foundations for the various smelter buildings are being prepared. Behind are the ore and sampling houses, and below them again the boiler house and furnaces...Below, again, excavations are being made for the works...Here the Victoria Transfer Company are employing 50 or 60 Chinamen and the scene is a busy one.

"A couple of hours have now passed in what has seemed but a few minutes in this interesting place, and the steamer is whistling for our return. A few weeks hence these impressions will be obliterated as ancient history, but they will serve as a contrast to the hustling future, and to suggest the rapid development that is now taking place."

Above:
The new smelter town of Crofton was an important destination for the S&NT Company during the construction boom of 1902-03 and most inbound freight was trans-shipped across the smelter dock from the *S.S. Iroquois* and the *S.S. Mystery*.

Left:
The smelter dock at Crofton featured a three-track barge slip and moveable overhead ore bunkers.

Right:
Cars of limestone, coke and
ore were all part of the
smelting process and were
stored in this small yard
before treatment in the
blast furnace complex
nearby.

Development of the new smelter town at Crofton meant a substantial increase in the business of the S&NT. The company announced that it was looking for another steamer so that it could serve the Gulf Islands, as before, while upgrading its Nanaimo and Crofton service to a daily schedule.

As of March 1902, the *Iroquois* was making only a weekly stop at Crofton, on Tuesdays, as it proceeded north to Nanaimo. Clearly, this would be inadequate to meet the transportation requirements of the new smelter town, so the search for an additional boat was under way. In the interim, the company announced an increase from semi-weekly to daily sailings between Sidney and Nanaimo. To accomplish this, the VTR&F, in June of 1902, leased the newly completed steamer *Unican*, of the United Canneries Company, to serve on a daily Sidney to Crofton service. A new wharf had been erected on Osborne Bay and heavy equipment for the construction of the plant of the Northwestern Smelting and Refining Company was moving over the shore in increasing amounts.

In addition to its use on the Nanaimo run, the *Unican* also made stops at Ladysmith, thereby increasing competitive pressures on the Esquimalt and Nanaimo Railway Company which regarded that place as its private domain. The *Unican*, sailing in conjunction with the *Iroquois*, was able to bring a great deal of additional

traffic to both the S&NT and the VTR&F. Intended as a temporary vessel, the company still desired a larger, and preferably faster, steamer to serve the east coast route.

Arrival of the S.S. *Strathcona*

The search for such a new vessel stretched from the U.S. West Coast to northwestern British Columbia. Finally, the company purchased the sternwheel steamer *Strathcona*, which had been constructed for the Hudson's Bay Company's Stikine River run but was considered to draw too much water for the river's extensive gravel bars and shallows.

The *Nanaimo Herald* of June 7, 1902, announced the sighting of a sternwheel steamer being moved down the Gulf of Georgia in tow of a tug and speculated that it must have been the *S.S. Strathcona* - and it was. The *Strathcona* was a much larger ship than either the *Iroquois* or the *Unican*, with a gross registered (loaded) tonnage of 596 tons and a net (empty) registered tonnage of 376 tons. She was 142 feet in length with a beam of 30 feet 4 inches, and drew five feet of water. She had two high pressure horizontal engines with a 24 inch bore and 72 inch stroke. The *Strathcona* was fast and her ability to run in water little more than five feet deep made her a natural for the shallow harbours of Vancouver Island's east coast.

Sale of the Railway and Ferry Companies

As arrangements for the purchase of the *Strathcona* were being concluded, the Victoria Terminal Railway and Ferry Company and the Sidney and Nanaimo Transportation Company were changing hands as well. In May, it was announced that the railway and ferry interests had been sold to a Victoria syndicate, represented by E.V. Bodwell. Under the new ownership Captain Mackenzie was transferred to Vancouver, to look after the interests of Mackenzie Brothers and the VTR&F mainland rail ferry service. (See Chapter 7.) James Anderson, Traffic Manager of the VTR&F, became the new General Manager.

To inaugurate its new daily service between Sidney and Nanaimo, the owners of the *Strathcona* announced a free excursion from Nanaimo, to Sidney and return, on June 24, 1902. Accordingly, the sternwheeler arrived in Nanaimo on the evening of the 23rd and was met by an enthusiastic crowd of well-wishers. The next day the *Nanaimo Herald* gave a complete description of the vessel:

"The Strathcona is a three-decker, standing a way out of the water in imposing proportions. To those who are not used to sternwheel riverboats it seemed impossible that they should draw only three feet of water but such is the case. Her first deck is devoted to the storage of freight and it is certainly a commodious store room and well able to carry the immense amount of merchandise that gravitates between here and Victoria.

"The second deck has two cabins fore and aft, the former being more of a smoking cabin and the latter for ladies, being handsomely fitted up with wicker chairs and upholstered seats. Part of the furniture of this saloon is a piano.

"Between these two saloons is the Strathcona dining hall which is furnished with small tables and chairs, it being the intention of the management to serve meals on the European plan. You are supplied with a menu card and pay for what you get. The deck is exceptionally roomy and pleasant, the top deck is not supposed to be for the use of passengers.

"Outside there is the stern of the boat, quite a large platform for those who prefer sitting outside and a promenade entirely around the outside of the boat. Altogether she is a very handsome and comfortable boat, both for freight and passenger traffic...She is to leave this morning on her initial trip to Sidney with a large number of Nanaimo's representative citizens onboard as invited guests of the V.&S. Railway Company in connection with which the boat is being run. She is expected to return to Nanaimo at seven o'clock this evening."

Photo Above:
The S.S. Strathcona waits for passengers from the arriving northbound passenger train No.1. The *Strathcona* served the route for only a few months in 1902 before blowing a cylinder head and being withdrawn from service. Some say she was just too much ship for the job.

Above:
This picture was taken on the same day as the previous photograph. The merchandise in the car on right was waybilled to Bella Coola, probably by ship from Vancouver.

The Master of the *Strathcona* was Captain Riley and her purser, Mr. L.C. Newlands. The day of the initial, free excursion dawned brightly and the *Strathcona* pulled away from the dock just before 7:00 a.m. Unfortunately, affairs did not go as planned. As the sternwheeler was opposite Gabriola Island, the packing blew off one of the cylinder heads and there was a delay of one hour for repairs. Then a strong wind came up which left the high-standing *Strathcona* struggling for headway. Finally, the excursion party reached Sidney - three hours late.

The VTR&F train whisked the passengers into Victoria and the party returned to Sidney later in the day, well pleased with the outing. The *Strathcona* sped away from the Sidney dock at 6:15 p.m. and all went well until she was forced to pull into the harbour at Chemainus to replenish her water supply. None was immediately available and it took another three hours to make arrangements, the boat finally returning to Hirst's wharf at Nanaimo at 2:30 a.m., the next morning.

In spite of the snags of the previous day, the *Nanaimo Herald* was complimentary in its description of the way the *Strathcona* handled herself in the rough water and strong headwinds. Other crewmembers included First Officer Fred Anderson, Chief Engineer C. McGuire, Steward William Luke and various deckhands totalling, in all, fifteen. The hospitality of General Manager James Anderson and Captain Riley received special mention and the passengers even handed Mr. Anderson a letter of appreciation after the boat arrived at Nanaimo. It thanked the crew for their kind treatment, and wished the sternwheeler and her crew all success in the new service.

The summer of 1902 was noteworthy for the large number of rail and ferry excursions and the *Crofton Gazette* gave coverage to each one:

VICTORIA TERMINAL RAILWAY AND FERRY COMPANY

Left:
The timetables for 1902 were numerous, and show the various vessels used for the east coast Vancouver Island and Gulf Islands service that year.

"Several delightful excursions have recently been made available on this beautiful line of country by the railway to Sidney and thence by the steamer 'Strathcona' or the steamer 'Iroquois' to Crofton or Nanaimo, or around the Islands. No more charming trip than any of these can be imagined, and we congratulate the new management on their energy and enterprise."[2]

87

The *Strathcona* had made a good start in the new service but was plagued by boiler problems that should have been fixed before she was placed in service. This had not been done because of company's haste. The result was that the vessel had to be taken off the east coast run at the beginning of July to undergo repairs. After a week or so she was back on her Sidney-Gulf Islands-Nanaimo duties and the Nanaimo *Daily Herald*, citing an earlier article in the Victoria *Daily Colonist*, commented again:

"The sternwheel steamer Strathcona of the Victoria Terminal Railway and Ferry Company has been thoroughly overhauled and refitted and sailed this morning at four o'clock for Sidney to connect for Crofton with the regular morning train. Her boilers and machinery have been thoroughly gone over, 105 new tubes have been put in, and her motive power is now in excellent shape for fast time.

"The Strathcona has been newly painted, her cabins and staterooms newly upholstered, and she is now provided throughout with electric lights, including a searchlight and boom lights installed by the Hinton Company. With her new dress and her interior fittings the Strathcona is practically a new boat and one of the most elegant and comfortable passenger steamers sailing from this port.

"On Saturday she will carry the Orange excursion to Nanaimo and on Monday she will resume her regular trip, leaving Nanaimo at 7:00 a.m. and arriving in Sidney in time to allow her passengers to arrive in Victoria with the train which arrives at 12:15 p.m. Returning, she will leave the city at 2:00 p.m. and arrive in Nanaimo at 7:00 p.m."[3]

"T.W. Paterson, Esq.,　　　　　　　　　　Victoria, B.C.

The *Strathcona* at the Pender Island wharf.

Until the *Strathcona's* refit, the S&NT seemed to have encountered a streak of bad luck, but most of the causes were beyond the foresight of her owners and crew. When she returned to her regular scheduled route after repairs it was expected that her luck would change and it did so, however briefly.

On July 13th, the *Strathcona* was scheduled for another excursion from Nanaimo but this plan came under direct attack from the forces of James Dunsmuir and the Esquimalt and Nanaimo Railway and its affiliated steamship line. The day trip to Crofton was jointly sponsored by the Nanaimo Silver Cornet Band and the Nanaimo Athletic Association and had been well advertised. The fare for the round trip was at the moderate rate of only one dollar (children 50 cents).

After the excursion was announced, it took only a day or so for George M. Courtney, the Esquimalt and Nanaimo Railway's Chief Passenger Agent, to visit Nanaimo and announce that the E&N's steamship, *Joan*, would run a similar excursion to Crofton on the same day, but with one major difference. The E&N was going to charge only half the rate advertised for the *Strathcona*.

While some might have considered this a windfall, it came close to causing a riot among the members of the Silver Cornet Band and Athletic Association who had pre-paid their charter fees on the *Strathcona*. If they could not sell the tickets they had been issued, they would stand to lose a substantial amount.

The Nanaimo papers got hold of the breaking contest and loudly condemned the actions of the E&N in trying to undercut the S&NT. Another factor in the case seemed to be that the Athletic Club had just previously refused to pay an exorbitant sum to charter an E&N steamer for a trip to Seattle. It appeared that the Esquimalt and Nanaimo Company was trying to scuttle the activities of both the Athletic Association and the S&NT.

It might have seemed, to George Courtney, poetic justice and an opportunity to punish both the Athletic Association and the VTR&F. Unfortunately for the E&N,

Versus
the E&N

it didn't work. On the morning of the excursion, the crew of the *Strathcona* were forced to pull up the gangplank with 250 passengers on board and even more left standing on the dock. When the Esquimalt and Nanaimo steamship *Joan* pulled away from her berth, she had only 22 passengers.

The *Joan* made a stop at Ladysmith on her way south to pick up more passengers. Those unfortunate few who decided to take the trip were astonished as, with the *Joan* sailing out of Ladysmith Harbour, the E&N purser came around to collect fares - not of 50 cents as had been advertised by the company in the Nanaimo papers, but at the regular rate of one dollar. The 140 unfortunate passengers had no choice but to pay up, and did so, under protest. The *Joan* was well on her way and it would be a long swim back to shore if they didn't.

The day's excursion to Crofton was a great success and the ordinary residents of Nanaimo who had taken the trip derived considerable satisfaction from the apparent humiliation of the E&N and the *S.S. Joan*. Bloodied, but unbowed, the E&N retired from the field of action to return another day.

Just when all seemed to be going well for the VTR&F, disaster struck. The *Strathcona* was proceeding south from Nanaimo on the evening of August 19, 1902, and was only nine miles from Sidney. Chief Engineer McGuire, handed control of the steam engines over to Second Engineer McKay, a new man on board.

After McGuire went topside, the steam engines began to prime, drawing water as well as steam from the boilers. The usual solution to this problem would have been to slow the engines and drain the cylinder cocks (a valve on the bottom of the cylinders). Unfortunately, this precaution was neglected. The cylinder head blew off, tearing out bolts and blowing away part of the cylinder. The ship made it to Sidney, and then Victoria, on one engine. In dock for expensive repairs, her career, in the service of the S&NT at least, came to an end.

The End of a
Short, Sweet
Season

Co-incident with the *Strathcona's* misfortunes, the Crofton Smelter had been forced to close by the shutdown of the Mount Sicker mines, its main source of ore. It would be several years before operations at the smelter resumed. Traffic on the east coast ferry routes declined, the *Iroquois* resumed her old schedule on the run to Nanaimo, and the *Strathcona* was sold.

Up to this time, the summer of 1902, along the Saanich Peninsula, through the Islands of the Gulf, and at Crofton and Nanaimo had been redolent with excitement and optimism. The freight and passenger business was doing so well that the Sidney and Nanaimo Transportation Company introduced yet another vessel, the tug *Mystery*, to its growing fleet.

As Christmas approached, the company announced special excursion rates for the holiday season in an attempt to keep up sagging passenger revenues and while it enjoyed some success, the tenor of operations returned to their previous levels.

The year 1903 was not a good one for the S&NT and, with VTR&F operations between Sidney and the mainland gaining in volume and importance, the company decided to sell off its Gulf Islands ferry routes. In October 1903, the company announced the pending sale of the S&NT and the steamer *Iroquois*. The two associated companies became independent of each other but would work together as formerly for a number of years. The story of the *Iroquois* and her new owners will be taken up later. For now, we return to the year 1902 and the increasingly complex affairs of the Victoria Terminal Railway and Ferry Company.

Pt Guichon 1903 AD

7

COMPLETING THE MAINLAND CONNECTION

For the Victoria Terminal Railway and Ferry Company, in January of 1902, work was well under way on the Market Building extension in Victoria. The construction of a railferry barge slip at Sidney had been ongoing for more than a month, the barge *Georgian* was being refitted to carry railway cars, and survey work for the construction of a section of railway from Liverpool to Canoe Pass was about complete. A great deal had been accomplished since the first general meeting of the VTR&F only three months earlier, but the next few months would prove to be an even busier time for the combined railway and ferry companies.

These developments were proceeding in a spirit of optimism and the only regrettable event in connection with the new works was the disappointing news that Thomas Paterson, the guiding spirit behind the V&S from construction days, was to leave the company. On February 1st, Paterson formally severed his connection with the Victoria and Sidney Railway and the new Victoria Terminal Railway and Ferry Company.

The employees of the companies made a farewell presentation to Paterson and wished him well in the future. The able Andy Forbes, conductor and friend to all along the line, warmly saluted Paterson and the memorial he presented still gives a clear indication of the high regard in which Paterson was held:

> "Sir:- We the employees of the Victoria and Sidney Railway and the steamer Iroquois, having learned of your retirement from the management of the above companies, respectfully request you to be good enough to accept at our hands the accompanying token as a token of the high regard and esteem in which you are held by each and every one of us.
>
> "We also earnestly desire to assure you of our sincere appreciation of the singularly cordial and friendly relations which have ever existed between yourself and us during our service with the company.
>
> "We greatly regret the severance of your connection with the company, but we advert with pleasure to the fact that, owing almost solely to your persistent efforts and tireless industry, the Victoria and Sidney Railway has been successfully operated and has amply justified its existence from the date of its inception.
>
> "We are not forgetful of the fact that to your able guidance and careful management must be credited the consummation of the important ferry project which is now rapidly approach-

Left:
The *S.S. Victorian* at the Port Guichon dock of the VTR&F Company in 1903.

ing completion. This, we are sure, must be a matter of especial satisfaction to you, as undoubtedly the work must prove of great and lasting benefit, not only to the city of Victoria, but also to the province generally.

"Wherever your future ventures may lead you, it is our earnest hope that all of your enterprises may prove abundantly successful."[1]

Paterson was succeeded by Captain Simon F. Mackenzie. The new General Manager became engaged in directing renovations on the Victoria Market Building to fit it up as a station. The carpenters were converting one end of the building into a large waiting room, a ticket office and two private offices for company staff. Work on the railway extension had been suspended for a week by a heavy snowfall but would soon recommence.

Mackenzie was also busy on the maritime front and announced that the steamer *Iroquois* would be withdrawn from the Gulf Islands route temporarily, to be put on a daily run to the new smelter town of Crofton. The *Iroquois'* replacement on the Islands run was to be the *Mystery*, a steam tug originally purchased by the VTR&F for service with the railbarge *Georgian*. She was temporarily reassigned to the Gulf Islands pending completion of the barge slips at Sidney and Liverpool. After the company found another, larger vessel for the Crofton and Nanaimo run, they would then put the *Iroquois* back on the Islands route and the *Mystery* into service with the *Georgian*.

While work on the Market Building renovations and the Victoria extension was well under way, conditions of the agreement between the City of Victoria and the VTR&F required that the rail barge service be in operation before the company commenced to operate out of the Market Building. In mid-February the local newspapers reported that work was to be immediately commenced on the barge slip at Liverpool. The company was anxious to comply with its agreement but also announced that it would not, at first at least, compete with the Canadian Pacific Navigation Company in the Gulf of Georgia passenger trade. Other changes were also under way.

Simon Mackenzie was succeeded by James Anderson as General Manager, of the V&S and VTR&F. He soon became a popular figure in Victoria and on the Saanich Peninsula. He even took to working with the crew on the Gulf Islands run on an occasional basis. Mackenzie had proven to be a capable manager during his short time in charge and was being succeeded by a man who was considered to be equally capable.

By mid-February, the rails on the Victoria extension had reached the corner of Fisgard and Douglas Streets but was temporarily held up by a dispute with the British Columbia Electric Railway Company, whose tracks the VTR&F had to cross to reach the new station building. By the 20th of the month, the locomotives were bringing passengers as far into town as this same intersection and the final completion of the railway trackage in Victoria was eagerly awaited. The temporary dispute with the BCER was soon relieved - just in time, for another impediment to completion of the new service took place at Sidney.

In early March 1902, the Victoria area was struck by a severe storm. The dock at Sidney was dangerously exposed to southeast winds and the piledriver had been tied to the unfinished barge slip wharf. When the storm began to drive heavy seas against the uncompleted wharf, the piledriver tied alongside crashed into it and inflicted heavy damage. Not only did the piledriver largely destroy the wharf, it completely destroyed itself. Sheer legs were broken off, the large iron hammerhead was dropped into the harbour and a shelter housing the machinery was completely demolished.

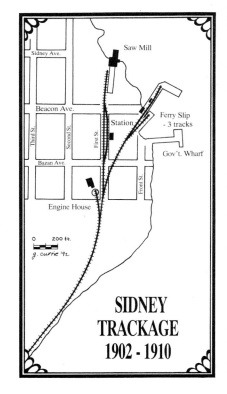

SIDNEY
TRACKAGE
1902 - 1910

The *Iroquois* at the Sidney dock, 1902. The counter-balances on right are for the ferry-barge slip.

A new piledriver was brought in and work quickly resumed on the new ferry slip. Operations on the railway and barge service were scheduled to begin by April 1st. Notwithstanding the occasional difficulty, all appeared to be well. It therefore came as a surprise when a major change in company ownership was announced in Victoria, on May 13, 1902.

The Victoria and Sidney Railway was acquired by a new group of investors, headed by none other than E.V. Bodwell, who had been at the head of the VTR&F. He had participated in most of the debate prior to the approval of the scheme in 1901. The only major change brought about by this acquisition was the resignation of Captain S.F. Makenzie from the directorate and, while it has not been confirmed, it seems likely that Bodwell had simply bought out his interest in the companies. Bodwell had close ties with Jim Hill of the Great Northern Railway and many assumed that the GNR must have been the hidden buyer behind the sale of the properties. Only time would tell.

The new directorate hurried the railway and the barge slips at Sidney to completion, while the Great Northern finished the barge slip at Liverpool. The Great Northern assisted developments by announcing another new rail barge service from their Liverpool terminus to Vancouver. (Another link was being forged in Hill's invasion of Canadian territory.) The old Victoria and Sidney Railway and its new successor company were closely tied to the Great Northern through a traffic agreement. It seemed likely that the Great Northern even had designs on the nascent VTR&F and its associated companies. These complicated developments were applauded in a special edition of the *Victoria Daily Times* on August 23rd:

VICTORIA TERMINAL RAILWAY

"...In 1901 an agitation began for the extension of the Victoria and Sidney Railway system on the lines originally contemplated in the De Cosmos scheme...

"In December of the same year, a by-law was passed by the City of Victoria of which the principal provision was the granting of $15,000 yearly to this company for a period of twenty-five years. In consideration of this bonus the line was to be extended into the city, making its depot in the market building, for which a lease was granted for the sum of $100 yearly. On the completion of its undertaking the city was to remove the fire department from the market building and to receive $7,500 therefor...

"Contracts were to be made with the Great Northern for the carriage of unbroken Great Northern freight into the city. The passenger rate was limited to $2 each way. In the city, connection was to be made with the E.&N. Railway system.

"This arrangement is now in process of being carried out, and already the service by the road has been greatly improved. The steamer Iroquois was purchased by Mackenzie Brothers from T.W. Paterson, and with the little steamer Mystery, also purchased by this firm, was placed under the house flag of the Sidney and Nanaimo Transportation Company. The big barge Georgian was bought and fitted up at a cost of $7,000, and strengthened so as to carry twelve ordinary freight cars. Towed by the Mystery this barge forms the forerunner of the regular steam ferry system which it is proposed to install, and for which the contract is shortly to be let. Ferry slips were constructed at Sidney, while the Great Northern built a slip at its terminus at Liverpool, on the Fraser River opposite New Westminster. From this slip Great Northern cars are transferred to the Georgian, and carried, not only to Victoria, but to Vancouver where a slip has been built at False Creek...

"At Sidney a new wharf has been built 270 feet in length, while $4,000 has been expended in improving the roadbed of the line from Sidney to Victoria. Contractor T. Bryden is just completing a fine double-tracked car shed at Hillside Avenue, 200 feet long and 28 feet wide, with a capacity of twelve coaches.

"The railway has been extended to the city market, a distance of one mile and an eighth...

"A new engine has been bought from the Victoria Lumber Company, while the company is now completing an order for two new coaches.

"The Great Northern has so far recognized the advantages of the system that they now quote Victoria as one of their terminals and insure all cars crossing the Gulf to this city."[2]

Throughout all these changes, with new facilities and equipment, the old Victoria and Sidney and the new Victoria Terminal Railway and Ferry Company struggled on as in previous years, but with the anticipation of better things to come. What did not change was the continuation of small accidents.

On August 28th, the Sidney bound mixed train jumped the track. No damage was done, other than to the patience of the beleagured passengers, especially those boarding the *Iroquois* for the trip to Nanaimo. The steamer did not get in there until eleven o'clock in the evening. This relatively minor incident was soon overlooked by local Victoria and Saanich residents. They were looking forward to a much improved railway and ferry service in the months ahead.

The Sidney-Liverpool Ferry

By the end of August, the VTR&F was finally ready to call tenders for the construction of its proposed new rail ferry to be operated between Sidney and Liverpool, and construction of the railway line from Liverpool to Canoe Pass. The new ferry tenders were to be submitted by September 10th, with a completion date for the ferry of April 10, 1903.

Under its agreement with Victoria, the company was required to construct a ferry in that city. It had to be capable of a speed of fourteen knots an hour, carry up to eight railway cars of standard gauge of not less than 10,000 pounds capacity, and also have accommodation for 400 passengers. A capacity to run in the shallow waters of the Fraser River estuary was also a necessary requirement.

As the date for submission of tenders grew near, the *Times* again gave details of the ongoing work on the joint railway and ferry system, and more details of the ferry itself were made public. The specifications called for a regular car ferry with 'tween decks laid with two lines of standard gauge rails. The freight deck was to have clear headroom of 15 feet and the stern was to be specially constructed for lining up against a floating landing stage. Freight cars were to be moved on board with minimal delay at each end of the trip. Space for a passageway would be made along the midline of the ship with suitable stairways giving access to the passenger deck. As mentioned above, the ferry required seating capacity for 400 passengers and four cargo gangways were required along each side of this deck to enable the vessel to take on ordinary freight when required.

The roof of the passenger deck would be extended to the full width of the vessel and about ten feet beyond the house at the forward end to serve as an awning deck and to carry the regulation number of lifeboats and rafts.

Passengers were to be excluded from the forward end of the passenger deck and a bridgehouse was to be constructed there with accommodation for the ship's officers and crew. A pilothouse and flying bridge would occupy the top deck with wings extending the full width of the vessel. Other specifications required the vessel to be built of Douglas-fir and all equipment to pass the Canadian Marine Board standards. The new ferry was to be 200 feet long, with a beam of 40 feet, and depth of 13 feet. The *Times* also published a plan and profile view of the proposed ferry. The VTR&F were working hard to comply with the conditions of their agreement with Victoria. Just when it seemed the revised directorate was nearing the completion of its various projects, there was another organizational change in the joint companies.

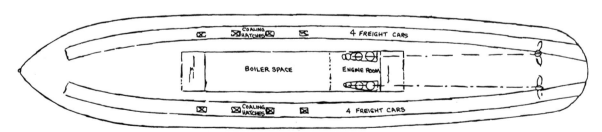

PLAN OF FERRY STEAMER.

THE DECK PLAN.

The GNR Takeover

During August 1902, the Great Northern Railway, through its local agents in Vancouver, B.C., began to bargain with the Terminal Railway Company with a view to a Great Northern takeover of the Victoria Terminal Railway and Ferry Company. The purchasers were John Hendry and J. Jaffray, both of Vancouver, and A.H. Guthrie, of St. Paul, Minnesota - an old Jim Hill ally. It had long been clear that if Guthrie was involved in a takeover, he would likely be acting for President Hill of the Great Northern Railway. Hendry and Guthrie had represented them in their 1890s acquisition of the Kaslo and Slocan Railway, in the Kootenays.

Negotiations did not go smoothly at first. The buyers had tried to make a secret and informal agreement with the City of Victoria to obtain an extension of time for completion of the railway extensions and ferry system. When the VTR&F people heard about this, they broke off negotiations with the Great Northern Railway. However, by the end of August it was obvious that this problem would be overcome. An agreement for the Great Northern purchase of the Railway and Ferry Company was possible, and on October 4, 1902, it was completed.

By arrangement, E.V. Bodwell's controlling interest in the company was sold to the firm of Archibald Guthrie and Company, of St. Paul, Minnesota. As will be seen later in this book, the Hill method of takeover by proxy, as it were, gave the Great Northern control while keeping the parent company at arm's length from any legal repercussions that might arise. The Great Northern would use this to their advantage in the years ahead.

With their acquisition of the Victoria Terminal Railway and Ferry Company and the Victoria and Sidney Railway, Guthrie and Company assumed responsibility both for building the fast ferry, to run between Sidney and the Mainland, and to complete the remainder of the railway line between the mouth of the Fraser River and a connection with the New Westminster Southern at Cloverdale. The old Liverpool and Canoe Pass survey route along the lower Fraser River had finally been abandoned. The transfer of the VTR&F properties did not include the Sidney and Nanaimo Transportation Company, ownership of which was retained by E.V. Bodwell.

The acquisition was a clear sign that Jim Hill was still in competition with the Canadian Pacific Railway and was moving into an area that had previously been dominated by the latter. The entry of the Great Northern into Victoria would also provide the city with a connection, at Sumas, B.C., with the Northern Pacific Railway, another American transcontinental, via the Great Northern's Vancouver, Victoria and Eastern Railway that was to be built eastward through the Fraser Valley.

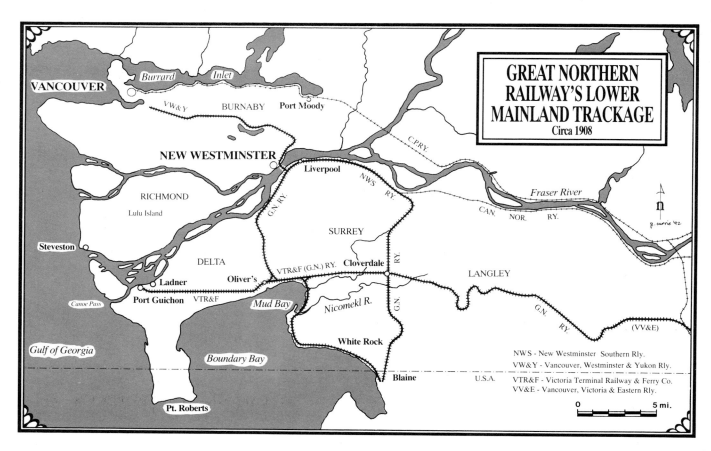

Negotiations for the sale had been conducted by General Manager James Anderson, acting for E.V. Bodwell, and Captain S.F. Mackenzie, acting for Guthrie, Hendry and Jaffray. It was therefore no surprise when Captain Mackenzie took over from Anderson as the new General Manager (for the second time) on October 9, 1902. The exact details of the takeover, which involved the City of Victoria through the VTR&F By-Law, were not at first known but these leaked out over the following few weeks.

The VTR&F, through its new owners, asked for an extension of time in which to carry out the terms of the original agreement of 1900. Specifically, they wanted a six month extension in which to put a suitable rail and passenger ferry on the run between Sidney and the Mainland.

They also wished to substitute, in place of a combined rail and passenger ferry, a separate, fast passenger ferry capable of a speed of 18 knots, and a slower rail ferry capable of a speed of ten knots. The VTR&F was also prepared, if the city agreed, to extend the Victoria and Sidney Railway line as far as Swartz Bay at the northern end of the Saanich Peninsula. From there, the fast ferry would carry passengers to the Mainland through Canoe Pass, putting them on the Mainland in only four hours from time of departure from Victoria. As evidence of its sincerity in the matter, the VTR&F was prepared to put up a guarantee of $150,000. They would carry out, to the letter, the agreement entered into by the original promoters of the Victoria Terminal Railway and Ferry Company with the City of Victoria - provided that the six months extension was granted.

The proposal was acceptable to some Victorians but others were disgruntled with the actions of the VTR&F which had still not paid the claims of city residents along the streets passed through by the Victoria Extension. Other Victorians were convinced that, while it was known that GN's Jim Hill was in some way involved in the deal, his role was still not clear. Both of these matters had to be addressed before any revised agreement could be struck with the city council. Some gesture of good faith was required and, at the end of November 1902, the VTR&F deposited a cheque for $9,110 in damages with the manager of the Canadian Bank of Commerce in Victoria, to be paid out when a revised agreement with the city had been reached.

To clarify the Great Northern's official involvement in the matter, a letter from Hill to A.H. Guthrie, of the VTR&F, dated November 6, 1902, was published in the Victoria *Daily Colonist*:

> "Dear Sir,- In answer to your question as to this company's business to and from the city of Victoria, I beg to say that as soon as your line (The Victoria Terminal Company) is in a position to connect with ours, we are ready to handle all our business over your line.
> "In order to do this it should be understood that the business will be handled with promptness and dispatch in every way, and that your facilities will be such as to ensure this.
> J.J. Hill"[3]

The nominal President of the VTR&F, on Guthrie's behalf, was Mr. A.E. Wood, who said that he did not think that any other "construction" could be placed upon the letter above, than that Hill was prepared to make Victoria a terminal point on his Great Northern system so far as was possible. Probably no one in Victoria was really sure what all this double-talk meant, but they were diverted from a clear answer by another complication which arose on December 23rd. After a short time as General Manager, Captain Mackenzie again retired, being replaced by Mr. Frank Van Sant. He was to hold the managerial position for many years. This change caused a slight delay while both sides regrouped. During this time, yet another complication arose.

A deputation from the Victoria Trades and Labour Council asked the Mayor and Council to amend the VTR&F By-Law to make it necessary for the railway company to build its rail and passenger ferry in Victoria. They insisted that if the by-law was not revised to include this, it would have no hope of passing. The Trades and Labour Council was in a powerful position and could likely cause this speculation to be fulfilled.

For his part, A.E. Wood was non-committal and asked for more time to consider the matter. He did say that he would have no objection to the ferry being constructed in Victoria, so long as it could be done at the same cost and with the same quality of work as elsewhere. This seemed to satisfy the Trades and Labour Council for the time being. It was only a stalling tactic on the part of the VTR&F though, as the company had already taken steps to acquire a vessel which could be used as a rail and passenger ferry on the Sidney-Port Guichon run.

Purchase
of the
S.S. Victorian

The first indication that the VTR&F were looking for a vessel to purchase, as a cheaper alternative to building a new one in Victoria, was an announcement in the *Victoria Daily Times* on January 8, 1903. The paper stated that the *S.S. Victorian* was to be purchased from Dodwell and Company for service between Vancouver Island and the lower Mainland.

The *Victorian* was a large vessel with a gross (loaded) tonnage of 1,504 tons, and net (empty) tonnage of 809. The vessel was 256 feet in length with a beam of 34 feet, depth of hold of 16.6 feet - a fine ship, constructed of yellow fir with galvanized fittings and equipped with triple expansion steam engines.[4]

The *Victorian* was also well-known to residents of Victoria. She was originally built in 1891 for the Oregon and Washington Navigation Company in the Steffen Yards at Portland, Oregon, under the supervision of Captain J. Troup, of the Canadian Pacific Navigation Company. She made only one trip for the former company on the Columbia River and then was shipped to Victoria to enter service on the Puget Sound run. Later, she did return to the Columbia, but was soon after brought back to replace the *City of Kingston*, a CPN vessel sunk in a Puget Sound collision. When Dodwell and Company acquired her, she was placed on the passenger and freight service to the Klondike via Seattle and Skagway, Alaska. The *Victorian* had been lying idle at a berth in Tacoma, Washington, for sale by Dodwell since August of 1902.

President John Hendry, Vice-President A.E. Wood and solicitor Thornton Fell, of the VTR&F, made the purchase after the ship was inspected in Tacoma by the Provincial Boiler Inspector, J.A. Thomason; Inspector of Hulls, Captain Collister; and engineer H. McGuire, formerly of the S&NT's *Strathcona*.

The VTR&F's initial plan was to use the engines from the *Victorian* in a large barge, the *Washington*, which was available for purchase at a cost of $30,000. However, the *Victorian* proved to be perfectly sound, and suitable for conversion as a rail and passenger ferry, so the plan to use the *Washington* was abandoned. The company hoped, or even assumed, that a refit of the *S.S. Victorian* at Victoria would be sufficient to satisfy the terms of the subsidy agreement with the city. In spite of the obvious advantages to the Victoria Terminal Railway and Ferry Company of buying her, rather than building a new vessel, the Victoria City Council was not satisfied.

Council passed a resolution on January 12th condemning the purchase of the *Victorian*, after Mayor Hayward pointed out that failure to do so might lead the company to think that the city was condoning their action in breaking the earlier ferry construction agreement. The situation was complicated by the VTR&F's negligence in failing to repair streets after the extension of their line into the Market Building, and by their not having compensated local landowners for damage to their property

during construction. The company was no longer popular with many Victorians.

Speaking to the Mayor's motion, Alderman Yates felt that the company should have more time in which to comply with the agreement. The Mayor, on the other hand, contended that according to the terms of the contract with the city, the company was required to submit its ferry plans to competitive bids. An extension of time for compliance had already been granted once, when A. Guthrie and John Hendry acquired the VTR&F. Alderman Grahame felt that it was impossible to convert the *Victorian* to a combined rail and passenger ferry.[5] All in all, the City Council was running short of patience in the matter. Besides, the granting of a lease to the company for occupancy of the Market Building was in the balance and would soon have to be addressed by both parties. In spite of the city's mood, the VTR&F proceeded with the conversion of the *S.S. Victorian*. This issue would remain a sore point between the city and the railway and ferry company for some time to come.

While the controversy over the railway and passenger ferry raged on, the company announced that it would immediately undertake construction of the mainland section of the VTR&F between Port Guichon and Cloverdale.

The distance between those two points was about 18 miles, and the railway would run through a rich agricultural area where crops of every description were grown - much of the trade from this area could be made tributary to Victoria. The actions of the VTR&F in moving ahead with its rail and ferry connections was noted by the Canadian Pacific Navigation Company who announced that they would place a competing steamer on a run between Victoria and Steveston, on the Fraser River north of Port Guichon.

On January 31st, Manager Van Sant of the VTR&F announced that the railway and ferry connections would be in service by the first of May. The plan was to run the *Victorian* on a daily schedule so that passengers travelling from Victoria to New Westminster would reach the Royal City within four hours of their departure from Victoria. To fit her up for the new service the *Victorian* was extensively refurbished.

The bow was sponsored but the changes did not affect the shape of her hull at or below the waterline. The stem of the ship was cut away about a foot below the level of the main deck as far aft as the engineroom. The first passenger deck above was removed to make way for the railcar deck. Staterooms in the way were done away with, leaving a total of only 14 to remain. The ladies salon and dining salon were left unaltered. The most important alterations were to the large steerage quarters with which the ship had originally been constructed. These areas had been important when the ship was on the Alaskan run but were no longer necessary in the ship's new role.

While the lines of the ship's hull remained unchanged, she was considerably strengthened and Mr. MacDonald, the superintendent in charge of the work, stated she would be as strong as required for her new role as a combined rail and passenger ferry. The vessel arrived at Victoria in tow of the tug *Sea Lion* on January 12, 1903, and was met by the tugs *Albion* and *Sadie* who towed her to her berth at the Victoria Machinery Depot in the upper harbour. Work on the refit was begun the next day. Meanwhile, work was also under way at Port Guichon on the Mainland.

The *Victoria Times* of February 3, 1903, gave a detailed description of the work under way on the extension between Port Guichon and Cloverdale:

BUILDING LINE
TO POINT GUICHON

Rushing Work
on Cloverdale Branch

Municipality of Delta
Arrange Terms Upon Which
Right-of-Way is Granted

"The Victoria Terminal Company are vigorously pushing their line to connect this city with transcontinental lines on the Mainland. While the ferry steamer Victorian is being hurried to completion so that she may be ready to enter service by the 1st of May, the company are also looking after the other branches of the service, which is to be established so as to have everything in working order by the beginning of May.

"The grading of the railway line from Cloverdale, where connection is made with the continental railway system, to Port Guichon is being done as rapidly as possible. The contract for this work is in the hands of A. Guthrie and Company, of St. Paul, one of the largest contracting firms which has dealings with the systems controlled by J.J. Hill. Mr. Guthrie, the head of the firm, holds a controlling interest in the Victoria Terminal Company, and is thus interested in seeing that the work is carried out with all expedition.

"The commencement was made at the Cloverdale end. For some weeks past that work has been going forward. Now the Delta end has been begun by C. Foliott.

"The question of a right-of-way through the Delta Municipality has been settled in a conference held a few days ago between the members of that municipality and representatives of the railway company. The Terminal Company's interests were in the hands of John Hendry, president of the company; Thornton Fell, solicitor; J. McMillan, engineer; and C. Foliott, contractor.

"The matter was amicably settled and the railway company will be given a right-of-way over the road allowance lying north of the dredge ditch, and the municipality's interests will be protected by provisions regarding railway crossings, ditch and cattle guards.

"The company agree to put in three sidings for the convenience of the residents of Delta. These will be Slough, Goudy and Mather's Road, and probably at one of the following: Benson, Tasker, or Smith Road. It is necessary for a by-law to be passed giving the railway company these privileges and this will be submitted in a week or so which will be voted on by property owners. It only requires a majority of votes to carry the by-law.

"Large gangs are now working along various points of the right-of-way through Delta. Sub-contracts have been let and the work will be rushed to completion..."[6]

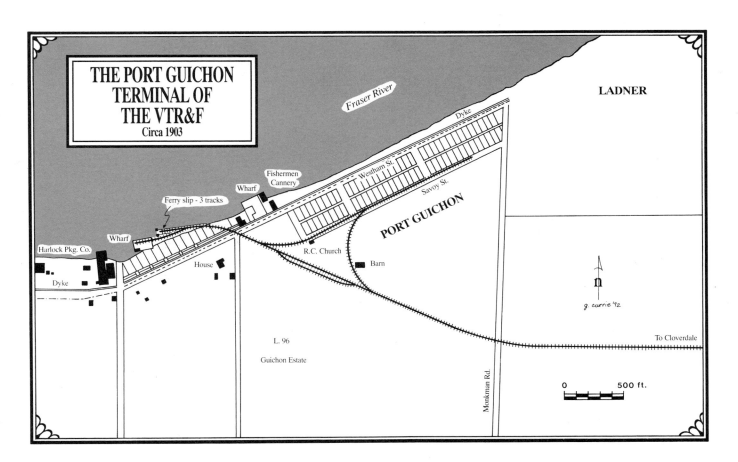

THE PORT GUICHON
TERMINAL OF
THE VTR&F
Circa 1903

LADNER

Fraser River

Dyke

Westham St.

Savoy St.

Fishermen Cannery

Wharf

Ferry slip - 3 tracks

PORT GUICHON

Wharf

Harlock Pkg. Co.

R.C. Church

House

Barn

Dyke

g. currie '92

To Cloverdale

L. 96
Guichon Estate

Monkman Rd.

0   500 ft.

Things were going well on the Delta extension and on the refit of the *Victorian*, but were not so good between the VTR&F and the City of Victoria. Hendry and Wood of the company assured the council that their arrangements for the service would comply fully with the original agreement for ferry service and passenger accommodation and that connection would be made with the Esquimalt and Nanaimo Railway in Victoria as well.

By March, the work was continuing apace on the Delta extension and the New Westminster Southern, another Great Northern Railway property on the Mainland, announced a start on its line from New Westminster to Vancouver. This would give the VTR&F direct connections with Vancouver via the New Westminster Southern. Tracklaying was commenced on the Delta extension at Cloverdale on March 4, 1903.

Work on the *Victorian* and the railway extensions was changing the face of the old Victoria and Sidney Railway dramatically and some of the old reliable members of the staff decided it was time for them to change as well. At the beginning of April, J.J. White, who had been the stationmaster at Sidney since the inception of the V&S, finally decided to leave the company's employ. White had been a highly regarded official of the company and his move to the world of private business was regretted by some. He would remain an important figure in the Sidney community and on the Saanich Peninsula for many years.

The combined works of the Victoria and Sidney Railway and the VTR&F was moving towards as close a realization of the old De Cosmos dream of the 1880s as they would get, when the new Gulf ferry service with the *S.S. Victorian* was inaugurated on May 7, 1903. On the inaugural day, the *Victorian* left Sidney at 8:00 a.m., with President Wood and General Manager Van Sant of the VTR&F and Robert Irving, Manager of the Kaslo and Slocan Railway, another Great Northern property, on board. The *Victorian* made her landfall at Port Guichon at 11:05 a.m. A train running on this schedule would reach Cloverdale at 11:50 a.m., New Westminster at 12:50 p.m., and Vancouver at 2:00 p.m. Returning trains would leave Vancouver at noon, New Westminster at 1:00 p.m., and would reach Victoria at 6:45 p.m. It wasn't the touted four-hour trip that had been predicted earlier but it was a direct rail and ferry connection between Victoria and Vancouver - and more importantly - a connection with the transcontinental system of the Great Northern Railway on the lower B.C. Mainland. The only cargo on the return trip was a partial carload of paper that came in over the Great Northern through Cloverdale. The company officials having checked out the new system, an invitation was extended to the Mayor and Aldermen to Victoria to take a grand excursion over the line.

The first car to arrive in Victoria over the new ferry system from the Mainland was boxcar No.7028 of the Grand Trunk Railway. The car was loaded with fruit jars destined for J.H.Todd and Son of Victoria. The shipment originated in Chicago and came directly over the Burlington and Great Northern Railways to Liverpool, and by barge to the V&S system at Sidney.

An unidentified Great Northern or Vancouver, Westminster and Yukon Railway locomotive on the Mainland Extension between Port Guichon and Cloverdale. Flatcars are from the VW&Y and caboose is from the parent Great Northern Railway. This may have been the small 4-4-0 that briefly served the V&S on Vancouver Island.

Mayor McCandless and City Engineer Topp, of Victoria, were anxious to inspect the whole system with a view to ascertaining its compliance with the original Victoria Terminal and Ferry Company agreement. The City's concerns were legitimate. The combination of the old bond interest guarantee and the new subsidy of $15,000 per annum agreed to by the City of Victoria meant that the combined subsidies received by the VTR&F from the municipal and provincial governments aggregated $30,000. That was a considerable sum in 1903 dollars. The $15,000 annual subsidy from the City to the VTR&F was to be paid for a period of 20 years with the first payment due on June 30, 1904. The *S.S. Victorian* and the new Delta extension of the VTR&F had an excursion of government, company and public dignitaries over the combined system on May 16, 1903. This trip was described in the Victoria *Daily Colonist* the next day with great detail:

TERMINAL FERRY
TO MAINLAND

Enjoyable Trip to the Fraser River
by Way of Sidney

Steamer Victorian Now in Service
and Makes Good Time.

"Through the courtesy of the Victoria Terminal and Sidney Railway Company the representative of the Colonist made the round trip between Victoria, to the Delta and return, yesterday.

"A very quick connection is made at Sidney, where the palatial steamer Victorian is awaiting the arrival of the train from Victoria. Friday she left at once, and, after a quick run across the Gulf, tied up at Port Guichon at 11 a.m. At Port Guichon the train was waiting, and in a very few minutes afterwards was off with the passengers among whom, by the way, was the wife of the Member for the constituency, Mr. John Oliver.

"On the way over Chief Engineer Fraser very courteously showed our representative through the engine room, which has been remodelled, under his direction. The engines have

been re-bolted to the frame of the steamer and so fixed that the very objectionable vibration which was, as is so well known, such a drawback to comfortable travelling when she was on the Sound Service, has been practically stopped. The engine room and stoke hole are both cool and well aired. Chief Engineer Fraser designed and the Marine Iron Works made an automatic draught apparatus which goes quicker as the pressure goes down, and slows as the pressure increases, by this means a regular pressure of 130 pounds is maintained. The engines are driven by three boilers, with three furnaces apiece. Each boiler is nine feet three inches diameter, and 26 feet long. The ashes are ejected by means of water power, a pump for which purpose is placed on the port side of the engineroom. The engines are triple expansion with cylinders 26, 44 and 68 inches diameter, and 34 inches stroke, with 105 revolutions per minute when going full speed.

"The railway, from Port Guichon on, is not quite completed yet, though sufficiently graded to permit passenger traffic. Awaiting the steamer were two full cars of freight for Victoria, which, on account of the rapidly falling tide, were at once run aboard. The ship works admirably, the whole transaction not taking over fifteen minutes.

"The inhabitants were nearly all away at Boundary Bay (only five miles away) holding their annual May Day Picnic. Unfortunately, the weather was very showery, and consequently the participants had not all unalloyed pleasure. On account of this exodus everything seemed quiet, although the railway company have a large gang of men, ballasting the road, and the saw mill was running full blast. The lumber business on the Fraser is in a very prosperous condition this spring, every mill having orders booked six months ahead, and this despite the almost prohibitive price of the same.

"The Victoria Terminal Railway and Ferry Company's good sense in placing such a ferry as the Victorian on this route cannot fail but produce good results for traders at both ends of the system. It opens the Delta to the Victoria merchants giving them an incomparable daily service and freight rates which

Great Northern's 2-6-0 No.477 was one of a number of engines that served the Mainland Extension of the VTR&F between 1904 and 1907, when the line was transferred to the Vancouver, Victoria and Eastern Railway and Navigation Company.

compare most favorably with the opposition routes. Furthermore, for passenger traffic to the Delta or even New Westminster, it is a great boon, saving as it does over eight hours travelling. The railway company intends running quite a few excursions this summer to the Delta, which most undoubtedly will be largely patronized.

"Our representative has nothing but kind words to say for Purser Harry Howard, Captain Rogers, Chief Mate Mansell, Steward Brown and Chief Engineer Fraser, who one and all did everything in their power to give him a thorough insight into the working, both of the steamer and the whole system. It is the intention of the company to institute a lunch counter, at which sandwiches, etc., and a pot of coffee or tea can be obtained for the nominal figure of 25 cents. This should prove very popular to the travelling public, so many of whom most strongly and justifiably object to paying 75 cents for a meal when they require nothing more than a cup of tea.

"Up to date, owing to the unfinished state of the road at the Delta end, the trains have been very late in arriving, and so far the time schedule has not been very well adhered to, but the officials assured our representative that once the line is completed that a quick and fast connection would be made and passengers landed here no later than 6:30 p.m.

"Friday the train reached Port Guichon at 3:10 p.m. The Victorian left at 3:15, arrived at Sidney at 6:15 and the train reached here at 7:30.

"Quite a large complement of passengers came down, who expressed very freely their appreciation of the accommodation and the speed of the ferry."[7]

So, after many years of trial and difficulty, the Victoria and Sidney Railway and the Victoria Terminal Railway and Ferry Company, now unofficially listed on company timetables as the "Victoria Terminal and Sidney Railway," achieved the realization of the dream of Amor De Cosmos for a combined rail and ferry system between Victoria and the lower Mainland, with transcontinental railway connections. But the scheme would soon flounder on a new sea of difficulties, both political and economic, that would confound the VTR&F, the V&S and their owners until the last days of the railway and ferry company. The years of tribulation were not at an end, but only lapsed into a temporary respite between quarrels with city and provincial officials, the long suffering public, and the Canadian federal government. So far, the history of the Victoria and Sidney had been colourful and it was to see even more of the same through its final years.

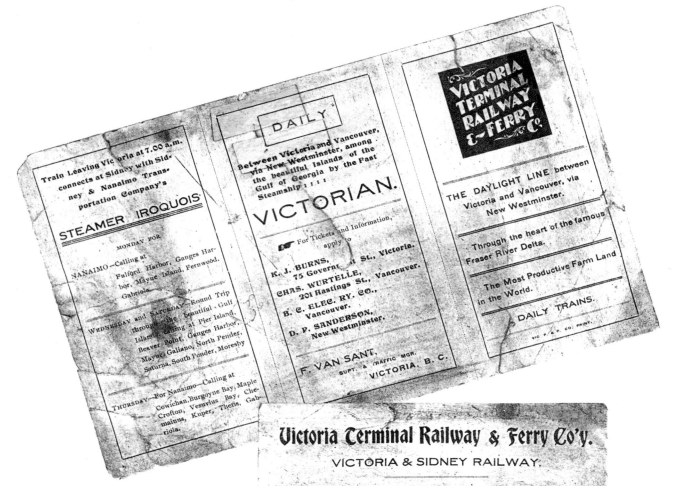

Victoria Terminal Railway & Ferry Co'y.

VICTORIA & SIDNEY RAILWAY.

TIME TABLE No. 2.   In Effect June 25th, 1903.

No. 5 Saturday and Sun.	No. 3 Except Satur'y & Sunday.	No. 1 Daily.	Miles from Victoria	STATIONS.	No. 2 Daily.	No. 4 Daily.
LEAVE	LEAVE	LEAVE			ARRIVE	ARRIVE
2 00 P.M	4 30 P.M	7 00 A.M	0	....Victoria	7 20 P.M	10 00 A.M
2 05 "	4 35 "	7 05 "	1	...Hillside Ave..	7 10 "	9 50 "
2 18 "	4 50 "	7 18 "	6	...Royal Oak...	7 00 "	9 35 "
2 25 "	5 00 "	7 25 "	9	....Elk Lake...	7 50 "	7 25 "
2 30 "	5 10 "	7 30 "	11	.....Keating...	6 45 "	9 10 "
2 38 "	5 30 "	7 38 "	13	..Saanichton..	6 48 "	8 45 "
2 50 "	6 00 "	AR 7 50 "	17	...Sidney...	6 30 "	LV 8 30 "
		11 30 "	65	...Pt. Guichon..	3 00 "	
		11 35 "	66	...Challuckthan.	2 45 "	
		11 45 "	68	...Inverholme..	2 38 "	
		11 53 "	73	.....Bayside..	2 28 "	
		12 00 "	77	...Alluvium	2 20 "	
		12 07 P.M	81	...Surrey....	2 15 "	
		12 10 "	82	...Cloverdale...	2 12 "	
		12 25 "	87	...Pt. Kells...	1 50 "	
		12 40 "	94	G. N. RAILWAY. ...Bon Accord...	1 32 "	
		12 50 "	97	G. N. RAILWAY. ...Liverpool...	1 25 "	
		1 00 "	99	G. N. RAILWAY. ...Brownsville...	1 20 "	
		1 30 "		G. N. RAILWAY. New West'r Ferry.	1 00 "	
	ARRIVE	2 45		Vancouver B. C. ELEC. CO.	12 00 M.	LEAVE

CHEAP EXCURSIONS

SATURDAY and SUNDAY between Victoria and Guichon and Intermediate Stations.

THE ONLY LINE by which a DAYLIGHT TRIP in Both Directions is possible between Victoria and Vancouver.

8

A NEW SYSTEM
WITH AN OLD PROBLEM

With the inauguration of the "Victoria Terminal and Sidney Railway" connection from Sidney to Port Guichon on the Mainland, the old De Cosmos scheme seemed almost a reality. The majority of residents in Saanich and Victoria, on the Island, and in Delta and elsewhere on the Mainland, had high hopes for the new rail and ferry connection utilizing the *S.S. Victorian*. The abundance of farm products from all over the Fraser Valley, and manufactured goods, could be readily shipped to Victoria by this alternative route. Freight from Victoria could easily be shipped to New Westminster and Vancouver, or points east, over the new Great Northern Railway connections. Passengers could do likewise, or use the route to connect for transcontinental trips. The elation was short lived.

On June 2, 1903, the *Colonist* was describing this new Mainland ferry connection as a boon to the travelling public.[1] However, less than a month after the May 16th opening of the VTR&F combined rail and ferry system, complaints were, once again, being aired by those who depended on the railway for either passage or for shipping. A June 9th accident on the VTR&F gained press coverage typical of previous years:

ACCIDENT ON THE TERMINAL RAILWAY

Caused Some Stir on Sunday

"(Special to the Colonist) Sidney, June 9 - The Victoria and Sidney Terminal Railway Ferry Company train, which left the Market Building on Sunday at two o'clock, had an accident on its way out to Sidney. It ran off the track and did not reach its destination until 9:30 p.m. The steamer Victorian was getting up steam in order to make the trip to Victoria. The huge bugle blast of the whistle was heard all over the district, many of the residents wondered what had happened, as it was an unusual occurrence to have so much stir on the weekly day of rest..."[2]

Left:

The VTR&F timetable from 1903.

The derailment was only one incident in a long list of complaints forthcoming on the new railway and ferry service. The matter was well aired in the *Colonist* on June 17, 1903:

SERIOUS FLAW IN SERVICE

Victoria Terminal Ferry Company's Contract Before City Council

Alleged that Great Northern Freight Service is Short of That Promised

"The city council at an adjourned meeting yesterday and later sitting as a Streets, Sewers and Bridges Committee, wrestled with a problem of particular interest to the ratepayers - shall the Corporation accept the service provided by the Victoria Terminal and Ferry Company as fulfilling the terms of the contract made with the city when the big yearly bonus and concessions were voted by the ratepayers? It appears from the short discussion which took place in open council, that there are grave omissions in the service as now provided - it being, for instance, pointed out by Alderman Vincent that the contract with the company alleged to have been made with the Great Northern Railway in respect to the delivery of freight to Victoria, is far short in its provisions, of what it was represented to be.

"The matter came up on the reading of a report of a special committee, consisting of His Worship the Mayor, the city solicitor, and city engineer, in which a recommendation was made that the lease of the Market Building be granted, and the contract be recognized as being fulfilled - all without prejudice to the city's right to dispute at a later date the fulfillment of the contract. The report omitted any opinion as to the suitability of the Victorian as a ferry steamer such as was called for by the contract.

"On the report being read, Alderman Vincent said the main point was: had the company fulfilled its contract in respect to the ferry boat?

"The city barrister explained that many documents accompanied the report which would help the council to form an opinion as to the points in question. He could mention one important particular in which it was shown that the service given by the company was short of that called for in the terms of the contract. He had a copy of the contract made between the Victoria Terminal Company and the Great Northern Railway and it was shown by an examination of the latter that the document had no seal, was signed by the fourth vice-president, and only agreed to deliver freight in Victoria which was consigned to Cloverdale. The agreement was a direct contravention of the sort of freight service, via the Great Northern promised by the Victoria Terminal Co. when the city made a contract with the latter.

"Alderman Vincent remarked that it was clear that the Victoria Terminal Railway Company could not carry out the provisions of its contract with the city. The whole matter had better be referred to the city barrister for an opinion as to whether the contract had been fulfilled.

"Alderman Grahame was of the opinion that the Victoria Terminal Company would never accept the lease of the

Market Building on the understanding that it might be annulled at some future date.

"Alderman Barnard wanted more information. If it were established that the railway carried out the terms of its contract, why the council would not hesitate to perform its part in the matter. But the company should fulfill its contract to the letter - there should be no loopholes in it. He thought it was a proper thing to refer it to the city barrister, and fight the matter out with the full legal knowledge of what they were doing.

"Ald. Vincent, 'Oh, that's bosh!'

"The Mayor thought the matter had better be discussed privately in committee.

"A motion to do this was put and carried and the reporters withdrew." [3]

The problem of the City's agreement with the VTR&F and the company's possible non-compliance was to drag on. In the meantime, there were continuing complaints. In a forceful letter in the *Colonist* on June 17th, a local ratepayer, identifying himself only as "Weary Traveller" put the matter quite clearly:

"I do not believe that on one single occasion since the Victorian has been on the route between Sidney and Port Guichon has the train arrived at Victoria on time, excepting two or three times when the train left Sidney with local passengers and subsequently returned for those from the Mainland...I take this opportunity of voicing the unanimous sentiment of those who travel from this district and adjacent Islands that it is an unbearable outrage that such a service should be tolerated.

"This evening the steamer Iroquois arrived from Nanaimo and way ports at 4:00 p.m., and those passengers, together with those from Sidney and way points had to wait until 9:00 p.m., at which hour the mail train - advertised to leave at 5:30 - left for Victoria.

"...I think, as do all the residents who are dependent on this service for their supplies and travelling facilities that the time has arrived when it, the company, should give us a train service that can in some measure be depended upon."[4]

Finally, after another month of debating the pros and cons, Council agreed to grant a lease on the Market Building, but conditionally. As had been suggested by the City Solicitor, it was offered without prejudice to the City's right to contest fulfillment of the contract at a later date.[5]

Sidney Sawmill Reopened

The one bright spot on the horizon occurred when the Sidney sawmill was reopened after a lengthy shutdown. From its beginning in 1892, the Sidney sawmill turned out to be a disappointment to the local people. They had looked on it as a source of jobs, but the mill had operated only sporadically.

The Toronto and British Columbia Lumber Company opened the 50,000 board-foot per day "temporary" mill and obtained the large contract to supply lumber and timber necessary for construction of the V&S Railway. It had extensive timber holdings on Vancouver Island comprising 4,261 acres in the Port Renfrew district, 24,525 acres in the Clayoquot district, and 11,126 acres in the Barclay district. These leases had a duration of 30 years and as a condition to obtaining the timber rights, the company was required to construct a sawmill of a certain capacity in relation to the acreage of timberlands held.

In 1893, the Toronto and B.C. Lumber Company informed the B.C. Government that depressed lumber conditions did not warrant an additional outlay of funds for a larger mill with a capacity of 250,000 feet per day, as originally proposed. The government made concessions by granting further time for completion of the second mill, but raised the annual lease payment to 5 cents per acre. This meant the company had to pay out $2,000 yearly, even if the mill was not in operation.

With the onerous lease payments and the lack of expertise in marketing its product, the mill was in trouble almost as soon as its contract to supply material for the V&S construction was completed. The property changed hands in 1894, being sold to Mr. Ewen Morrison of Victoria's Rock Bay lumber yard.

Morrison's tenure was also brief. The mill passed to a Mr. Patterson, of Vancouver, who also obtained the timber leases. This company was called the Vancouver Island Lumber Company and, it too, was soon in financial trouble. By 1903, the mill had been closed far more often than it had been open and Sidneyites were relieved to learn, in July 1903, that the operation had been purchased by a group of American investors who would place it in running order almost immediately.

Sure enough, the plant was ready by the end of August and the first big boom of logs, from the Port Renfrew timber limits, arrived on November 1st. The mill's operation was a welcome relief to local workers in an otherwise dismal time.

The complaints about irregular service on the Victoria and Sidney Railway did not cease during the latter part of 1903. On October 7th, the Victoria *Daily Colonist* published a short news item under the heading "Want Waiting Shed:"

The Complaints Just Keep On Coming

> "A large number of patrons of the Victoria and Sidney Railway Co. are of the opinion that if a lean-to shed was erected at the Beaver Lake and Prospect Lake Road railway station it would be a great convenience to the large number of shooters and corporation men who are employed on the filter beds, and who have often to wait for a long time in the exposure from cold and rain on account of the boat being late. The train was two hours late last Saturday night, and there were ladies and children waiting, as well as about a dozen others. On the evening following there were 18 people (five ladies) again waiting out in the open, and the cold and rain, for the delayed train. Anything would be appreciated to escape the misery that is now endured by the large number of passengers who have to wait."[6]

Only a week later, more V&S patrons revealed themselves to lay more complaints, through the newspaper, about the absence of passenger shelters. At the end of the month a petition with 150 signatures was submitted to City Council demanding action in the matter. The railway, at the time, was in the process of being inspected by the Provincial Government engineer and it was hoped that such pressure would speedily lead to better facilities. The year ended, without any action taken, and the disgruntled V&S ridership could only hope for a better year ahead. In the meantime, there were other developments taking place in connection with the Sidney and Nanaimo Transportation Company and the steamer *Iroquois*.

Rumours of a pending sale of the *S.S. Iroquois* by E.V. Bodwell first surfaced in the *Vancouver News-Advertiser* of October 1, 1903. It came as a surprise to many, as it was regarded that the S&NT was still doing well financially. The sale was confirmed in November when it was announced that the Company had been purchased by Captain Albert A. Sears, a Master Mariner formerly in the service of the Pacific Coast Steamship Company, and Mr. A.D. Munro of Victoria, a former purser with the same company. The price of the vessel was said to be $20,000 and the new owners issued their first timetable to go into effect on November 19, 1903.[7]

The *S.S. Iroquois* Changes Hands

While the *Iroquois* was changing hands, developments were progressing, in connection with the Great Northern Railway, that would have an effect on the operations of the Victoria Terminal Railway and Ferry Company.

Mixed train No.4 northbound on Rose Street shortly after the opening of the Market Building extension in 1903. Two of the line's three boxcars were in the consist that day.

On December 31, 1903, the Great Northern ran its first passenger train over a new line from New Westminster to Vancouver. As the GNR had an interchange with the VTR&F at Cloverdale, the new route between New Westminster and Vancouver created a direct rail and ferry connection between Victoria and Vancouver.

The Great Northern Railway ran trains more or less directly north and south between White Rock and the ferry connection at Liverpool. Part of the line, from White Rock as far as Cloverdale, had a steep downgrade for northbound trains and, conversely, a steep adverse grade against southbound traffic. To deal with this operating problem, Great Northern decided to realign its railway lines in the lower Fraser Valley. It was announced that a line would be extended south from Liverpool to Oliver's, on the line of the Victoria Terminal Railway and Ferry Company. Later, the new line would be extended southward from Oliver's, past Mud Bay and White Rock to the U.S. border by a waterlevel route.

These changes promised great improvement on the Fraser Valley end of the rail and ferry connection from Victoria. Nevertheless, the dispute between the City of Victoria and the Victoria Terminal Railway and Ferry Company over the construction of a vessel locally was still unresolved in the early months of 1904 and the time was fast approaching when the company would be asking the City for the first installment of its $15,000 annual subsidy.

The confused state of operations and lack of passenger shelters along the Victoria and Sidney line was still receiving a great deal of adverse publicity. An accident on the line, in March 1904, reinforced the V&S's bad reputation.

Accident to Brakeman Hasker

On a cool Sunday evening, No.1 locomotive, panting quietly with occasional bursts of steam from leaks in her boiler, was kicking cars around in the Sidney railyards in preparation for the evening mixed train to Victoria. As the engine backed the train slowly towards Beacon Avenue, the brakeman, E.A. Hasker, moved forward to open a coupling. Suddenly, Hasker fell forward under the car. Caught by the wooden brake beam and dragged for several yards, miraculously, the train wheels did not pass over his body. He did suffer, however, a severe compound fracture of the forearm and other injuries and was rushed to Victoria's St. Joseph's Hospital in critical condition. It was a painful experience for him, but he recovered to work for many more years on the V&S. The notoriety from this accident led to yet another "black eye" for the VTR&F.

In response to the continuing criticism, the company decided to begin upgrading the right-of-way along the Victoria to Sidney line. New ballast was to be spread, old cattleguards that had been in service since 1894 were to be replaced, and the line side-fenced. The arrival of springtime saw this work well advanced. Soon, the summer weather would return and the usual round of weekend excursions and outings from Victoria would begin, leading to an increase in ridership to and from all points on the line.

All, however, was not well. Being at odds with the City and short of operating capital, the upgrading of service by the VTR&F was a desperate move in anticipation of its application for payment of the first year's $15,000 subsidy. In contrast, the new owners of the Sidney and Nanaimo Transportation Company and the *S.S. Iroquois* were faring better.

The *S.S. Iroquois*, 1904

The spring schedule for the *S.S. Iroquois* was announced on May 2, 1904 - twice weekly service between Sidney and Nanaimo with runs on alternate days to the Gulf Islands and weekend excursions from Sidney. The stops on the Nanaimo to Sidney southbound run, Tuesdays and Fridays, included Gabriola, DeCourcy, Thetis, Kuper, Vesuvius Bay, Burgoyne and Sidney. Northbound landings were made at Gabriola, DeCourcy, Read Island, North Galiano, Fernwood, Ganges Harbour, Mayne, North Pender, Fulford Harbour and Sidney on the Monday and Thursday of each week. It was a far cry from the daily service of two years earlier but the *Iroquois* was still a welcome sight as she plied the calm waters of the inside passage.

The route was scenic, the crew was described as genial, and the Islands along the way were beautiful. Captain Sears' command was much less pretentious than that of the larger ships of the Pacific Coast Navigation Company, but this little boat was at least partly his own.

The summer of 1904 was definitely a good one for the *Iroquois*, and those fortunate enough to make a voyage with her.

On the Peninsula, it was a long, hot summer for the VTR&F and the V&S - both literally and figuratively. There seemed never to be an average summer, weatherwise - some were hot and dry while others were cool and wet, as they are today. The summer of 1904 was of the hot and dry variety. By early July there had been a number of fires along the line. On or about July 10th, a fire ignited near the V&S line in the vicinity of Keatings. It quickly got out of control. Fires, in those days, if they did no damage to buildings or livestock, were considered to have occurred without loss. At first, such was the case with this fire, until July 12th when it began to threaten the line of the Victoria and Sidney Railway. Manager Frank Van Sant realized that there was little the train crews and section gangs could do, so he decided to call on the government for assistance.

Fires and Money Problems

The response was quick and Superintendent Bullock Webster, of the B.C. Provincial Police, sent out Constable Campbell and a squad of 12 men to fight the conflagration. They were at first easily successful in their efforts, but when high winds fanned the flames to new heights, several local farmsteads had close calls. Fires continued along the line for some days and other outbreaks were reported along the line of the Esquimalt and Nanaimo Railway and elsewhere on the lower Island. Continued drought and high winds made the situation very hazardous. Just when the VTR&F and V&S joint management thought things were hot enough, they got even hotter.

At a special chamber session of Victoria City Council, held on July 14th, a motion was passed to refer the matter of the first annual $15,000 bonus for the Victoria Terminal Railway and Ferry Company to the City's solicitor. Legal advice would be sought before any decision was made on payment. This was seen by many as a preliminary to the City testing its case against the VTR&F, for non-compliance with the assistance agreement, within the court system.

For its part, the railway company was trying to do its best. Earlier, on May 1st, they had announced an improved daily service between Victoria and Sidney with two passenger-only trains, instead of the mixed freight and passenger service that had been in vogue since the opening of the line. On the new schedule, the passenger trains would leave Victoria at 7:00 a.m. and 4:30 p.m. daily and return from Sidney at 8:30 a.m. and 6:20 p.m. Merchandise would be carried in a separate train consisting of freight cars only.

By this time the improvements to roadbed and ties were well underway and loads of ballast from the gravel spur at Bazan Bay were being put down all along the line. While this upgrading was taking place on the Island service, the VTR&F and associated companies on the Mainland were also making changes.

VICTORIA TERMINAL RAILWAY & FERRY CO'Y

VICTORIA & SIDNEY RAILWAY

TIME TABLE No. 6.   In Effect May 1st, 1904

NO. 5 Sat. Sun. only	NO. 3 Ex. Sat. Sun.	NO. 1 Daily	Miles frm Victoria	STATIONS	NO. 2 Daily	NO. 4 Daily
LEAVE p.m.	LEAVE p.m.	LEAVE a.m.			ARRIVE p.m.	ARRIVE a.m.
2 00	3 45	7 00	0	.... Victoria	7 20	10 15
2 10	3 55	7 08	1	...... Hillside Ave.......	7 12	10 05
2 25	4 10	7 23	6	.........Royal Oak.......	6 58	9 45
2 35	4 20	7 32	9	.... Elk Lake........	6 46	9 30
2 45	4 30	7 38	11	.... Keating..........	6 40	9 15
3 00	4 45	7 44	13	........Saanichton.......	6 34	9 00
3 15 ar.	5 00 ar.	8 00	17	.... Sidney	6 20 lv.	8 45 lv.
		11 30	65	........Pt. Guichon......	3 00 lv.	
		12 15	82	.........Cloverdale........ G. N. RAILWAY.	2 12	
		1 05	99	........Brownsville....... G. N. RAILWAY.	1 15	
		2 00		...New West'r Ferry...	1 00	
		2 45		.......Vancouver......... B. C. ELEC. CO.	12 00	

Train Leaving Victoria at 7.00 a.m. connects at Sidney with
Sidney & Nanaimo Transportation Company's

STEAMER IROQUOIS

MONDAY for NANAIMO

Calling at Fulford Harbor, Ganges Harbor, Mayne Island, Fernwood, Gabriola. Returning, leaves Nanaimo Tuesday morning for Victoria and way ports.

Wednesday and Saturday—Round trip through the beautiful Gulf Islands, calling at Pier Island, Beaver Point, Ganges Harbor, Mayne, Galiano, North Pender, Saturna, South Pender, Moresby.

Thursday—For Nanaimo—Calling at Cowichan, Burgoyne Bay, Maple, Crofton, Vesuvius Bay, Chemainus, Kuper, Thetis, Gabriola. Returning, leaves Nanaimo Thursday Morning for Victoria and way ports.

1904 Timetable

The port of New Westminster, at the head of navigation for seagoing ships on the Fraser River, was well endowed with railway links as both the Canadian Pacific and Great Northern Railways had local connections. The new Vancouver, Westminster and Yukon Railway, a Great Northern affiliate, was next to enter into service. The completion of the VW&Y line between New Westminster and Vancouver, on August 22, 1904, created an effective rail and ferry connection between Victoria and Vancouver proper. It was hailed as a transportational landmark. With the opening of this link, it was possible to make a VTR&F, Great Northern and VW&Y connection between the capital city and Vancouver.

On opening day, at the invitation of President John Hendry, the city councils of Vancouver and New Westminster made an inaugural trip over the line between the two cities. The roadbed was described as "a good one," and the cars rode easily and smoothly over the iron metal. At New Westminster, the guests were entertained at the Westminster Club, and in Vancouver, the honours were done at the "Maison de Ville."[8]

These events were marred slightly, afterwards, by a collision on the VW&Y line between Vancouver and New Westminster on October 5th, but fortunately there were no injuries.

As 1904 drew to a close, the newly completed mainland connection of the VTR&F and its link with associated railways seemed to portend a prosperous future. Great Northern was endeavouring to increase the freight business to Vancouver Island and, in January 1905, the company's Eastern Canadian agents made special efforts to capture shipments from Ontario to the Lower Mainland and Victoria. Papers in Ontario and elsewhere were kept well supplied with details of the new connections on the West Coast.

The failure of the City of Victoria to yet meet its expected subsidy payment to the VTR&F had, in the meantime, led to cancellation of the scheduled Sidney to Port Guichon runs of the *S.S. Victorian*. While this was a blow to the expected passenger trade, the Great Northern issued special circulars to prospective freight customers. They indicated that those who had favoured the Great Northern with their freight business in the past could continue to rely on a Great Northern connection between the Lower Mainland and Victoria by means of a new freight car barge service between Liverpool and Sidney. While they were still in the market for railcar freight shipments, their joint passenger trade was over almost as soon as it had gotten under way. This was, in part, because of the failure of the VTR&F to gets its subsidy. It was also because of very effective competition - the passenger service provided between Victoria, New Westminster and Vancouver by the Canadian Pacific Navigation Company.

The new year of 1905 brought a number of changes to the VTR&F and its associated companies. These changes in Victoria, at Sidney and elsewhere led to new challenges.

The Sidney sawmill changed hands again at the end of 1904, but Sidney traffic was shortly to be supplemented by a new industry. In February, the Saanich Canning Company opened a clam cannery to process shellfish that had previously been put up at canneries on the B.C. Mainland or in the American Gulf Islands.

This new business was capitalized at $50,000 and had sufficient capacity to put up 100 cases of clams per day. A ready market was available for the product all across Canada and local wholesalers in Victoria had already made commitments with the new firm. Managed by Mr. J.J. Call, the cannery was owned by J.J. White, formerly of the Sidney Sawmill and the Victoria and Sidney Railway, along with Mr. J. Wilson, a prominent Sidney resident. Favourably situated in close proximity to an abundant supply of crustaceans, the cannery anticipated a prosperous future.

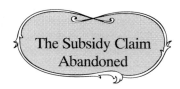
The VTR&F Company had worked hard to get the City of Victoria to pay the anticipated subsidy, but the year wore on and there was no sign that it would be paid out. Consequently, in March, it was announced that the Company had abandoned all negotiation towards resolution of the ongoing subsidy conflict. When the Victoria Labor Council had demanded specific performance on the agreement, to construct a rail and passenger ferry in Victoria, they had meant it, and their power base in the local municipal council was strong.

The decision was made to continue the *status quo*, with the VTR&F operating its railbarges between Sidney and Liverpool. The *Victorian* would serve no more, languishing through her final years at quayside in Victoria. The company and its parent, the Great Northern, had conceded the passenger trade to the Canadian Pacific Navigation Company but was not conceding the Vancouver Island freight trade to its arch rival, the Canadian Pacific.

The first train over the Market Extension was able to back down Fisgard only as far as Douglas Street. A dispute with the B.C. Electric Company prevented completion of the diamond crossing of the two railways for several months.

In June 1905, the GNR-owned Vancouver, Victoria and Eastern (VV&E) announced that it would petition the provincial legislature for a charter to construct the previously planned rail line from Oliver's, on the VTR&F between Port Guichon and Cloverdale, to existing Great Northern/New Westminster Southern rail connections at Liverpool.

The lower Fraser Delta between Port Guichon and Cloverdale was a verdant wonderland of farms, forest and marshes. The line of the VTR&F ran inland, in a straight line eastward, towards the new junction at Oliver's. Port Guichon was really a suburb of Ladner, a prosperous cannery, fishing and farming community of substantial homes. The little town was well supplied with its own newspaper, general stores, two hotels and several churches. Before the arrival of the tracks of the Victoria Terminal Railway and Ferry Company, Ladner was connected with the outside world only by river steamers running down into the Delta from New Westminster.

The new railway connection would shorten the run between Victoria and Vancouver. The VV&E charter had been purchased from the Canadian railway magnates, Mackenzie and Mann, some years earlier, and was the key chip in James J. Hill's bid to compete with the Canadian Pacific Railway in British Columbia. Within a short time, the Mainland portion of the VTR&F, between Port Guichon and Cloverdale, would be absorbed into the new VV&E system. While there were many developments on the railway scene, the summer of 1905 was also a very busy season for the maritime operations.

Sears and Munro anticipated that 1905 would be a prosperous year, but, could hardly have expected the dramatic events about to unfold in the Gulf Islands. In anticipation of a busy season, the owners had the *Iroquois* in dock for her annual inspection during April, and the trim little vessel was pronounced fit after some routine attention to boilers and paintwork.

The British naval base at Esquimalt was still, at this time, an important facility and ships of foreign nations frequently visited there. That summer was made notable by the arrival of the Italian Navy's cruiser *Umbria*, a heavily-armed ambassador of national goodwill, far from its home waters in the Mediterranean.

After the exchange of pleasantries between senior officers of the British and Italian navies, and a round of diplomatic garden parties and receptions, the *Umbria* set out for some training manoeuvres in local waters. Target practice was the order of the day, and a Royal Navy hydrographic survey party working in the Gulf Islands was more than pleased to help the Italian gunners set up a target on a rocky headland, clearly marking the bullseye with whitewash.

However capable gunners that the Italians were in scoring several direct hits, several shells managed to overshoot their target and bombarded the peaceful community on Pender Island with dramatic results. There were no fatalities as the shells did not contain any explosives, but local citizens were sent running for cover and a sharp protest lodged with Naval authorities in Victoria. The matter was quickly settled, but Sears and Munro gained a new attraction for their Gulf Islands charter service.

WHERE SHELLS FELL

"Steamer Iroquois, Captain A.A. Sears, carried a good complement of passengers on an excursion among the Gulf Islands on Sunday. Leaving Sidney on arrival of the morning passenger train, the steamer proceeded past Pier Island, the home of Captain Phillipps-Wolley, writer and poet, to Beaver Cove on Salt Spring Island. Here the excursionists were given a run ashore. Continuing her cruise, through the narrow verdure lined waterways, and over calm, sun-lit reaches, the Iroquois voyaged to Mayne Island, where luncheon was served at the Mayne Island hotel...A call was made at Pender Island where the (H.M.S.) Egeria's bluejackets are in camp, making a record of the tides. It was in the bay and on shore near there that the cruiser Umbria's shells fell during her now famous bombardment of Pender Island. Leaving the harbor, the Iroquois steamed around the point into Pender Reach, where the target at which the Umbria's gunners fired, a whitewashed patch on the rocks about twelve feet wide, was viewed by the excursionists. The cruiser had stood off about three miles while her gunners practiced with plugged shells and non-explosives. The bombardment of the Egeria's camp and farmers nearby had resulted from the over-elevation of the guns causing the shells to carry over the point to the bay beyond. The general practice of the gunners was, however, better than would have been expected considering the vagrant flights of the shells which overcarried. The rocks about the target show a large amount of shell-marks scattered near the white-washed patch which the gunners aimed at. The excursion was a very enjoyable one."[9]

While the bombardment provided momentary excitement in the tranquil lives of the Gulf Islanders, the summer of 1905 was otherwise usual - steamer runs through the Islands to Nanaimo, the weekend excursion traffic, visits to the fish traps at Bedwell Harbour in the American San Juan Islands, and the excitement of an occasional misadventure along the Victoria to Sidney railway line.

Train No.1 prepares to depart Market Street Station in 1905 with four coaches. One of the passenger cars was on loan from one of Great Northern's Mainland subsidiaries.

On the July 1st Dominion Day weekend, city residents deserted the town in larger numbers than ever before. The V&S trains were full of passengers for picnics on the beach at Sidney or fetes at locations along the Peninsula railway line. The Catholics convened at Saanichton and the Reformed Episcopals at Bazan Bay. The *S.S. Iroquois*, with Sears and Munro in charge, made its usual rounds of the Gulf Islands and the *Colonist* even commented on the humanity of Captain Sears in saving the life of a "passenger". A naive white feline had been taken onboard at Sidney, bound for Ganges, and when it fell overboard part way across the channel, Sears quickly put his vessel about to rescue the poor creature. That act endowed him with the universal admiration of his passengers.

September brought the Labour Day celebration, and October, the usual Saanichton Fall Fair.

While it was business as usual on the maritime front, there were developments in connection with the railway trade. In July, a party of Great Northern officials, in company with Mr. Glen Andrus, Railway Editor of the *Chicago Times*, and company photographers, made a quick visit to Victoria. They arrived in a special Great Northern car, wheeled into Victoria over the V&S and VTR&F for the occasion, to gather material for a series of articles to be published under the auspices of the Great Northern Publicity Department. The target audience was travellers and shippers in the East. While in Victoria, they looked into all aspects of local business and tourism. This writer has not been able to locate any of their published articles on the visit but it seems likely that at least some photos of the spectacular scenery along their countrywide route must survive.

A month after the publicity visit, GN's Vice-President Louis Hill and a party of officials arrived in Victoria over the Great Northern and VTR&F systems. They made what was billed as a purely pleasure visit to the B.C. capital. Back at Great Northern headquarters, in the American Midwest, James J. Hill was growing old in harness, but had, for all intents and purposes, handed control of the Great Northern over to his son Louis more than a year earlier. Unwilling to fully retire, the old railroader was determined to fight his battle with the Canadian Pacific to the last.

If there was some cause for optimism, in the efforts of the Great Northern to improve its railway connections and freight service into Victoria, there was still the nagging problem of public dissatisfaction with the Victoria and Sidney Railway line and its VTR&F connection in Victoria.

At a mid-November 1905 meeting of City Council, the subject of the V&S was again raised. Complaints had been received from residents of Fisgard Street about the fire danger created by cinders from the locomotives. Nevertheless, Mayor Hayward was able to say that manager Van Sant of the VTR&F had assured him that the company had taken precautions to prevent any such outbreak. Their incentive was a penalty of $5,000 for any conflagration caused by their negligence. While the V&S was able to end its year by negating this complaint, the *S.S. Iroquois* was to end its 1905 season on an unfortunate note. The little steamer blew a cylinder head on Christmas Day, resulting in a long delay for holiday passengers. It could only be hoped that the following year would begin on a more auspicious note.

With the winter of 1905-06 well advanced, the Great Northern's Vancouver, Victoria and Eastern Railway construction was underway in the British Columbia interior and was scheduled to begin in the Fraser Valley. The Hill incursion into Canadian territory was again raising the ire of the Canadian Pacific and there was much talk in the press about the threat of an American industrial invasion, no doubt aided and abetted by the Canadian Pacific. The railway wars were a familiar part of the provincial scene and were looked forward to eagerly in almost every issue of the Vancouver and Victoria papers.

The Year 1906

For the Great Northern, the building of the VV&E was a positive step, but on January 15, 1906, a fatal accident occurred on the Vancouver, Westminster and Yukon line between New Westminster and Vancouver. Engineer C.W. Jones, of Seattle, was crushed "between the backhead and boiler of his engine"(sic). Pinned by the legs, he begged rescuers not to cut off his legs, which would have effected his release. He was consequently scalded to death. It was a sad beginning for the VW&Y Railway.

The summer brought with it another examination of the financial viability and public utility provided by the Great Northern's Vancouver Island subsidiary. The story of company successes and failures in the years from 1900 to 1905 is clearly shown in reports submitted to the Chief Engineer of Railways and Canals at Ottawa. Freight shipments over the Great Northern connection increased by about 50% between 1900 and 1906. Tonnage was up - from about a low of about 17,000 tons in 1900, to about 23,000 tons by 1906. The number of passengers more than doubled in these early years of the century, and, although passenger fares were not high, revenues for passenger traffic were up, from $18,000 to about $27,000 - a 50% increase. At least something was looking up. If the company could keep improving its equipment and roadbed, it just might have a chance to be a financial success after all. Unfortunately, operating expenses ate up all of the extra passenger revenues. In 1903 and 1905, they topped the $34,000 mark, a dramatic increase from the annual operating costs experienced in the first five years of the Victoria and Sidney Railway. The year 1906 was much like the five years preceding it, with only a minimal profit to show for the company's efforts. If the 1907 financial picture was to see any improvement, the V&S and its parent, the VTR&F, would have to improve the facilities of the railway and make a better showing in the areas of scheduling and public service.

VICTORIA AND SIDNEY RAILWAY STATISTICS
JUNE 30, 1900 TO JUNE 30, 1906

Year end June 30th:	Passengers Carried	Freight (tons)	Gross Income	Total Expense	Net Income
1900	21,783	17,051	$17,920.97	$18,062.84	$-4,321.56
1901	22,761	18,726	20,386.27	20,232.53	1,667.71
1902	26,703	23,255	24,062.51	22,595.66	1,492.00
1903	34,379	21,783	27,046.73	34,647.00	3,937.78
1904	41,694	23,633	26,729.23	29,206.23	1,348.22
1905	46,456	23,037	26,987.05	34,407.89	-141.87
1906	48,980	23,200	26,795.69	23,833.92	153.74

The incorporation of the Victoria Terminal Railway and Ferry Company and the construction of the Victoria and Mainland extensions, together with the inauguration of the railbarge and ferry services had all been tried between 1900 and 1906, but when all was said and done, the problem of the Victoria and Sidney Railway and its associated companies was still the same as it had been at the inception of service in 1894 - there simply wasn't enough traffic to justify the cost of maintaining a railway and ferry system. In spite of this, the Great Northern was not finished with its efforts to make the companies pay. The V&S was a public necessity for many Saanich Peninsula residents and this alone guaranteed that further efforts would be made to see the railway and shipping operations succeed.

9

BRICKBATS, BARGES AND BREAKDOWNS

The year 1907 was anticipated to be one of progress and change for the VTR&F. The financial profitability of the Victoria and Sidney Railway and the Victoria Terminal Railway and Ferry Companies was still very marginal, but there was hope for the eventual success of the combined rail and barge system as a link in the expanding Great Northern/Vancouver, Victoria and Eastern Railway empire.

The year began with talk of electrifying the Victoria and Sidney Railway but nothing definite was decided. Another impending change was announced at the beginning of February. Tenders had been invited for the construction of two new railbarges and a tug for use by the VTR&F on a new run between Sidney and Mud Bay, near Blaine, Washington. This would be a much shorter route than the one in use via the Great Northern and the barge slip at Liverpool.

At this time, the tug and barge service between Liverpool and Sidney was maintained by the tug *Fearless* and the barge *Sidney*. On the proposed Blaine route, with a shorter run of 40 miles, the tug could make the trip to Blaine with her tow in only six hours. That would put the company in a good competitive position with its arch rival, the Canadian Pacific Navigation Company, which was operating the barge *Georgian* between Vancouver Island and the city of Vancouver.

The Great Northern and the VTR&F still had an image problem in Victoria. There was the outstanding matter of unsettled damages, arising out of construction of the Market Building extension some years earlier, and pending legal action between the City and the VTR&F, over non-compliance with the original subsidy agreement. The company announced that it would finally pay for damage it had caused to the landowners along its Victoria extension during construction and, at the same time, make a number of improvements to the V&S, the VTR&F and their physical plant.

During the first week of May, work began on rebuilding all wooden culverts and bridges along the Peninsula line. The wharf at Sidney which had been in poor condition, was under repair. All of the company's rolling stock was shopped, for the application of airbrakes and automatic couplers, a long-felt want. The cars were all given a new coat of paint, and new ballast was to be laid down along the entire length of the line. One of the engines was sent east, to Delta, Michigan, for a complete overhaul at the Great Northern shops.

The work was going well until a May 10th mishap on the ballast spur, just outside of Sidney. The spur had originally been laid at low water and the tracks ran right out

Upgrading the VTR&F System

Left:
V&S No.3 crosses Colquitz Creek in this 1910 photo. The structure in the foreground is the water aqueduct running from Beaver Lake to Victoria.

into Bazan Bay. Two loaded gondola cars were spotted on the spur at the watermark, loaded to capacity with gravel. On arrival, the afternoon mixed train paused at Bazan Bay, to retrieve the two loaded cars. The engine was cut off from the train, and panting quietly, it ran through the connecting switch and backed down the spur. We now pick up the story as reported in the Victoria *Daily Colonist* of May 11, 1907:

> "...The passengers were left on the mainline as the antiquated little 'snorter' which is made to answer the purpose of a locomotive went to take the freight out of the water. Owing to the grade, the task of pulling the two cars at once was too much for the engine, and after a coupling was made the conductor went to the one which was deepest in the bay to detach it.
>
> "When the separation was effected something went wrong with the brakes, the wheels went over a slab that had helped to hold them, and the car, with the conductor, proceeded out into the briny deep, becoming more and more submerged as it went.
>
> "The passengers who witnessed the disappearing scene became slightly excited. For a few seconds it looked as if it were good-bye forever to the rolling stock, and a case of sink or swim with the man who struggled heroically at the brake handle. There were neither life preservers nor ropes in sight, and as the car rolled on rescue seemed out of the question...
>
> "A reporter from the Colonist who was one of the excited spectators, launched a raft, and with the aid of a pole set out to the rescue. The craft was a trifle light for its navigator, and caused him to perform several remarkable balancing feats in order to keep afloat...
>
> "The conductor was sent to shore alone, and the raft returned, unmanned, to the relief of the reporter...
>
> "This morning an attempt will be made to recover the runaway car."[1]

It turned out to be a longer stop than anticipated and while the passengers were vexed at the resulting delay, they at least had some entertainment while they waited for the train crew to do their chores. So ended the first, but not the last, accident of 1907.

V&S Locomotive No.1 and three passenger cars at Sidney Dock, circa 1905.

The Victoria and Sidney Railway and the VTR&F were favourite topics for local people and seldom did a month go by without one complaint or another being aired in the press. On May 4th, Captain Clive Phillipps-Wolley, the well known local businessman and journalist, gave *Colonist* readers his feelings on the struggling Victoria and Sidney Railway:

THE V.&S. RAILWAY

"Sir:- Those who read your valuable paper will remember excellent articles in it to demonstrate the importance to Victoria of a thriving suburban district on the Saanich Peninsula whilst all know how rapidly this district is filling up, and at what satisfactory prices the land in it is selling. Any menace to the prosperity of the peninsula and the district is therefore a menace to the merchants and general public of Victoria...

"The system of communication between Victoria and the above mentioned district has become absolutely intolerable. It would cause a rebellion in Timbuctoo. Here are some recent facts: The V.&S. Railway which, we understand, exists upon a subsidy from your city (the original Victoria and Sidney Railway bond interest guarantee), has two trains a day. The evening train is advertised to leave Victoria at 3:00 p.m., and to leave Sidney on the return journey at 5:35 p.m. and a patient public is content if it covers the short distance in about an hour.

"On Wednesday the evening train started from Sidney at about 6:30 p.m., on Thursday it left Sidney at or about 6:45, whilst on Friday it arrived at Sidney at about 5:40. When it left I can only conjecture.

"One of the chief reasons for this abominable state of affairs is that the old engine which drags the train is stopped at a gravel pit a short distance on the Victoria side of Sidney, and is there employed to haul gravel, the passengers meanwhile being retained on board in sight of their homes, but unable to get there because the engine can't pull the gravel.

"It is unnecessary to detail the losses and inconveniences arising from this state of things and it is only the immense popularity of Mr. Forbes which prevents a daily outbreak. I may say that I am writing at the insistence of those who feel as I do.

"Frequent complaints have probably reached you about the state of the Sidney wharf. If you want to prevent a ghastly catastrophe, you will insist upon an investigation of it by a trustworthy man, unconnected with the railway.

"On the 13th the first of the boxcars was landed upon it, and went through, although the slip had been examined and presumably passed the day before. You understand the car was lying half over and halfway through the slip, whilst its corn was being unloaded. So much for the railway.

"As this is such a long letter I will deal with the question of the steamer on another occasion. I have to go in, in my own boat, five or six miles to post this because the steamer omitted to call on her bi-weekly trip with the mail. And I maintain a wharf at an annual cost of about $120 for her convenience. On my own authority I beg the government to inspect at once the wharf onto which the train runs. If an accident occurs the person responsible should be hanged.

May 4, 1907   CLIVE PHILLIPPS-WOLLEY"

On July 8th, the locomotive sent to the east earlier in the year for repairs, returned to service. Summer traffic increased as in previous years. The VTR&F was really trying to improve its service to the public but nothing seemed to go right and finally, on July 14th, the railway hit a new lowpoint in its history when there were two separate accidents in a single day. The harder they tried the more difficult it became.

The City of Victoria's legal action against the VTR&F was again in the public eye and the City decided to proceed in the courts.

At the end of July, the question of electrifying the Victoria to Sidney line again received public attention. Vice-President Louis Hill was known to be more favourable to the idea of electric railways than his father had been. A newspaper article indicated that a proposition had been made whereby the British Columbia Electric would take over the V&S line and operate it themselves. Jim Hill had previously resisted such a scheme, but this time the plan was only to rent the V&S line to the BCER, for a period of years, as had been done with the Lulu Island Railway on the B.C. Mainland.

Final arrangements were still a matter of speculation and depended on the acquisition of an adequate supply of electricity, then not yet available to the Peninsula. While the scheme did not immediately materialize, the idea foreshadowed the eventual construction of a Saanich Peninsula line by the B.C. Electric a few years later.

The rumour of electrification ended for the time being, but soon another possible scheme was put forward. It was indicated that the Grand Trunk Pacific was negotiating with the Great Northern for purchase of the V&S and VTR&F system, with a view to making it the first section of its planned Vancouver Island lines. Neither was this to happen, but again it foreshadowed the construction some years later of a Canadian Northern Pacific Railway line along the Saanich Peninsula. It was not long before the Saanich Peninsula, which did not really generate enough traffic to support one railway, would be blessed with two more.

It was another long, hot summer. On August 14th, the northbound passenger train was derailed on a curve at Elk Lake after it ran into a fallen tree. The spare locomotive was sent out from Victoria to assist, and the train proceeded, landing the long-suffering passengers at Sidney three hours late. A few days later, the No.3 engine fell through the badly rotted ferry slip at Sidney wharf and had to be retrieved from a very precarious situation. Even with the VTR&F's stated goal of upgrading the line, affairs were not going well. In Sidney, on the other hand, things were better than they had been for a long time.

No.3 attempts to rescue loaned Vancouver, Westminster and Yukon combine from Bazan Bay after she had run off Sidney wharf. The summer of 1907 was a bad time for accidents on the V&S line. The combine was soon back in service.

Locomotive No.3 stranded on the Sidney wharf with her tender in the saltchuck on July 14, 1907, the worst day for accidents in the history of the Victoria and Sidney Railway.

Sidney In 1907

The Sidney Brick and Tile Works

Sidney essentially owed its survival as a town to the construction and operation of the Victoria and Sidney Railway. Its early years as a commercial centre had otherwise been marked with frequent closures of the local sawmill and a marginal existence. By the early 1900s, the local economic situation was improving and in 1907, Sidney was poised to assume a much more important role in the commercial life of Vancouver Island.

The sawmill was operating again, as the Gulf Lumber Company, and it appeared that it would finally be a financial success. Sidney was becoming a residential centre and new housing was going up at a steady pace. A new butcher shop, a new fruit cannery and the clam cannery contributed to local employment and the cash economy as well. The rumour of an electric railway line from Sidney to Victoria was still alive and whether it was to be undertaken by the Victoria and Sidney or another company seemed problematical.

Of importance, in new local industries, was the cannery of Brodeur Brothers, which processed the apples, pears and prunes of the Saanich Peninsula, providing much needed revenue for local farmers and a tidy profit for the owners. The new Sidney Creamery in its fine cement building was rising fast and was to commence operations by October.

Another new industry at the Peninsula town was a brick and tile works, established at Bazan Bay in the autumn of 1907. The owners were said to be wealthy Chinese businessmen from Victoria, who were anxious to manufacture brick, tiles, drain tiles and earthenware of all kinds for the Victoria market. They had 1,500 acres under option and plans were under way to ship the products of the new plant by scow or rail, not only to Victoria, but to points as far north as the new town of Prince Rupert on British Columbia's North Coast. The rails of the V&S passed right through the property of the new plant and the railway was well situated to provide service.

For many years previous, coal had been known to underlie the northern end of the Saanich Peninsula - a southerly extension of the famous coalfields farther up the Island at Nanaimo and Cumberland. It had actually been mined, in a small way, in the vicinity of Sidney before the turn of the century and some shipments were made to Victoria at the time.

A Captain Bissett, acting for a firm of U.S. investors, had bonded or leased 2,000 acres of coal lands in the Sidney area and $50,000 was to be spent in an exploratory diamond drilling program. The properties included those of Percy Winch, Christopher Moses, Rufus Hall, H. Birch, W. Scalthorpe, Towner Macdonald and W.J.Taylor. An option was given for a period of six months, during which time the drilling program would be completed.

In the end, the coal proposition did not succeed. Had it done so, the presence of the mines, within four miles of Sidney, would almost certainly have lead to extensions of the V&S Railway to the mines and increased traffic for the VTR&F. As it was, the Victoria Terminal Railway and Ferry Company was about to be shortened - not lengthened.

In September 1907, the Great Northern Railway's Vancouver, Victoria and Eastern Railway made an offer to the VTR&F for the purchase of its Mainland trackage between Port Guichon and Cloverdale in the Delta and Surrey Districts. The deal was approved, in reality being little more than a change in the corporate structure of the Great Northern and its subsidiary operations on the Lower Mainland. A similar move had taken place a month earlier when the Vancouver, Westminster and Yukon Railway was transferred from independent ownership to the Great Northern. These changes to the VTR&F shortened its route. Now, only the extension trackage

Coal Again

Sale of the Mainland Section of the VTR&F

between Hillside Avenue and the Market Building in Victoria - 1.14 miles - remained. There would be a short term financial gain for the VTR&F from the sale, but a long-term loss of the revenue from the Mainland section of the line. Nevertheless, it was logical and feasible for the Great Northern to consolidate its Mainland holdings under one single ownership.

The formal transfer, including the tug and barge service, was concluded on November 1, 1907. While the Island lines were not taken over directly by the VV&E, the Victoria and Sidney Railway and the Vancouver Island section of the VTR&F were still an important connecting link in the Great Northern Railway system.

The last months of 1907 were busy ones. There was another successful agricultural fair at Saanichton during October. It was the 40th season for the event and the V&S did yeoman service in transporting residents from all points along the line to the fairgrounds. During November, a special train was run from Victoria to Elk Lake to allow local ratepayers to inspect the city's water supply system.

In December, a party of Great Northern engineers visited the Island lines and although very little information was available on the reasons for their visit, locals hoped its purpose was to formulate plans for improvements to the local railway during 1908.

Later that same month, one unusual item of freight was shipped over the rail barge service - a motor lifeboat destined for service at Bamfield on the West Coast of Vancouver Island. The lifeboat was intended to be launched on the Sidney ferry slip by the simple method of lowering the apron until the boat floated away from the flatcar on which it had arrived. Despite this simple plan, the launching was fraught with difficulties. The work was directed by Captain Jones of the Dominion Marine Department. Because of the boat's heavy weight, it was necessary to construct a slip

V&S No.3 and scheduled train passing through the Rogers Farm, just north of present day Mackenzie Avenue. View is facing east towards the Rogers' house on the far hillside. Picture of the "Big Snow" of 1916 on page 180 was taken from this house.

of heavy timbers with large rollers to carry the cradle on which the lifeboat arrived. It took time to put the temporary slip in place but when it was ready, two full days later, the vessel was finally rolled into the water without even a scratch to its paintwork.

The year was ending, but before it could, there was one final mishap to be contended with by the railway company. While making a run up from the Bazan Bay gravel spur, engine No.3 blew a piston rod, driving it right through the wall of the locomotive cylinder. After considerable work on the part of the crew and local railway mechanical staff, the broken one was removed and the engine ran light into Victoria on a single cylinder.

It seemed an inauspicious ending for a busy year.

Meanwhile, the subject of improved railway and ferry connections was still receiving coverage in the local papers and the *Colonist*, in an editorial on May 4th, offered comment as part of a general discourse regarding the situation on the Saanich Peninsula:

The Improvements of 1908

> "Its present great need is transportation. The Victoria and Sidney runs out sixteen miles. On the principle that one should 'speak gently of the erring' we will be content with mentioning this fact. The railway is in the wrong place. It is midway between the two parts of the peninsula from which traffic can be furnished and far enough away from both to make it of very little value to either. Some people say that the road ought to be electrified, but that would not make it much better. What the Saanich Peninsula needs is a belt line, in sight of the water for all, or nearly all, the way round. Such a line would be the most beautiful scenic railway on the North American continent..."

Time would clearly demonstrate the truth in these remarks, for in a few more years there would be two railway lines competing with the V&S, along the eastern and western sides of the Saanich Peninsula. Whether, or not, there would be competition for the V&S did not seem to be of any immediate concern. It was anticipated by the management of the railway that the improvements under way would lead to increased patronage and greater profits and this would indeed prove to be the case over the next few years.

In March 1908, the company announced that a new ferry barge was expected to be ready for service by May for the long-proposed run between Sidney and Mud Bay. Earlier in the year, a contract for construction of the car ferry barge had been awarded to Sloan Brothers, of Seattle. Apparently, the Great Northern had not forgotten the episode when the Victoria City Council had earlier declined to award their $15,000 subsidy, so the company was not about to see any subsequent work go to the capital city or its workers. The barge would be 160 feet long with a beam of 32 feet and draft of 10 feet. It would have a capacity of six cars.

No immediate arrangements were made but another tug would also be needed for the new service. The Mud Bay barge slip was to be located near White Rock and gave the VTR&F and V&S connections with the Great Northern, the Vancouver, Victoria and Eastern, and the Vancouver, Westminster and Yukon lines on the Mainland.

The Great Northern was also looking at other approaches to making the V&S and VTR&F an operational and financial success. In April, Louis Hill made a visit to Victoria. "Could the Great Northern secure sufficient electric power," said Hill, "it would doubtless favourably consider the scheme of electrification of the Victoria Terminal Railway and Ferry Company, from this city to Sidney."[2] When asked about his company's plans for Vancouver Island, Hill was cautious and indicated that other than the new ferry barge service and line improvements, there were no other

Vancouver, Westminster and Yukon Railway's second No.1 in service on the Mainland section of the VTR&F, circa 1904. She was renumbered to Great Northern No.477 in 1907 and returned to Great Northern's subsidiary Spokane Falls and Northern in 1908.

improvements contemplated and that the Great Northern would not make any future moves to extend its system or interests in the area. Clearly, the Great Northern was growing more cautious about investments without some sign of improved patronage and profits, and would complete only the changes already announced. While the works under way were a sign of hope for beleaguered patrons of the VTR&F, there were other interesting developments on the local railway and industrial scene.

The *S.S. Strathcona* which had briefly served the Sidney and Nanaimo Transportation Company, until blowing a cylinder head in 1902, had been tied up for a number of years at Spratt's wharf in the upper harbour at Victoria. In May 1908, it was announced that she would be sold to a Vancouver company for use in the Skeena River trade. That area was growing in importance because of planned construction of the Grand Trunk Pacific Railway line across central British Columbia to the port of Prince Rupert.

The reason for the reported sale of the paddlewheeler was soon changed. The *Strathcona* was fitted up as an excursion and freight steamer to run between New Westminster and Chilliwack on the Fraser River run. She was wrecked in Nicomen Slough a few years later. Her career had been short and marked by misfortune.

Misadventure, too, seemed to be a part of the VTR&F/V&S story and another chapter had been written only two months earlier with an incident involving one

Frederick Howarth. This Victoria resident, known more for his bravado than good sense, decided to make a flying leap onto the pilot of the VTR&F passenger locomotive as it mounted the grade running up from the Market Building in Victoria to Blanshard Street. Howarth was quietly standing at the corner of Blanshard as the engine approached at a moderate rate of speed. Without thinking, he made a flying leap for the pilot and missed. Howarth was unceremoniously thrown back onto the road. A passerby phoned the police, who rushed to the scene expecting to pick up a dead man. Fortunately, although bruised, little more than his dignity was dashed. When asked why he had done such a stupid thing, Howarth could only reply that it had seemed like such a simple feat. There were other less fortunate happenings in Victoria that year.

In April, the previously mentioned Victoria brick plant, just off Douglas Street, was burned. The loss was estimated at $10,000 and the company was covered for only a quarter of that amount. Insufficient water pressure and the long distance to the nearest fire hydrant complicated matters and the fire demon was victorious. The loss would be considerable for local workmen thrown out of work, but the brick plant at Sidney would, in the short term, profit from the destruction of its Victoria rival.

The clean lines of locomotive No.3 are evident in this World War One era shot at Sidney. The engine appears to be fitted up as a coal burner. Coal replaced cordwood in the locomotives during the middle years of the War.

On May 15th, it was announced that the Sidney Brick and Tile Company at Bazan Bay had completed installation of its brickmaking machinery and was about to commence operation. Five carloads of up-to-date equipment, from Chicago, and consisting of pugmill, moulds and other plant machinery, had been moved over the V&S barge slip and Sidney trackage. The new industrial facility, capable of turning out up to 48,000 bricks in a single day, was served by a spur line. Covering an area of 40 acres in the area between Bazan Bay and the present Pat Bay Highway, it was soon working to full capacity to fill the market void created by the loss of the Victoria plant. The initial work force of 35 men was increased and the company even put up a large boarding house to accommodate staff. It became a major shipper over the

The Sidney Brick Plant

V&S and operated for many years. Competition from the rival Victoria firm was eventually restored and the two companies competed for local and regional customers, from points as far away as Prince Rupert, for many years.

To improve its image, the VTR&F promoted its park adjoining the railway station at Sidney, with its magnificent sandy beach and fine views of the Gulf Islands and Mount Baker, as a local camping spot. They succeeded in attracting a large number of visitors who, more often than not, arrived aboard the cars of the VTR&F.

In spite of relatively low freight traffic levels at times, the operations of the Great Northern barge service at Sidney were reaching farther afield than just the Saanich Peninsula. During June, the Great Northern ferry barge moved six carloads of rails over the VTR&F, from Victoria to a new logging railway under construction by the Victoria Lumber and Manufacturing Company, of Chemainus, at Union Bay, 100 miles to the north of Sidney. Traffic along the line seemed to be holding up fairly well and the improvements announced by the company earlier were well advanced.

Manager Frank Van Sant of the VTR&F visited Mill Bay to arrange a supply of 50,000 new ties for installation along the Peninsula line and by June they were distributed along the line ready for installation. Rebuilding of the transfer and ferry wharf at Sidney was urgently needed to prevent a major mishap. One engine had already fallen through the structure a year earlier and the work was long overdue. Many loads of new ballast were daily leaving the Bazan Bay pit for points along the line from Sidney to Victoria. With a renewed roadbed, better wharf and a new ferry barge, the facilities of the railway were being greatly improved.

The years 1907 and 1908 were significant for the VTR&F and the subsidiary V&S Railway. There had been brickbats and public indignation over the imperfect service provided by the V&S up to that time. Breakdowns and wrecks had continued to plague the struggling railway line, and in spite of the difficulties the parent Great Northern Railway was making a concerted effort to remedy as many of the outstanding problems as possible with careful regard to keeping the expenditure of capital and operating funds to a bare minimum.

10

THE THIRD STATION, 1908-1910

More Improvements and Changes

As part of its improvement package for the VTR&F/V&S, the Great Northern moved one of its own locomotives to Victoria during the summer of 1908. It is not absolutely certain which locomotive this might have been, but we find a clue in the simple drawing of a child from the Children's Page of the Victoria *Daily Colonist* of July 12, 1908. The drawing clearly shows what must have been a Great Northern locomotive. It may have been that company's No.206. Clues of this type try the skills of the historian but the identity of the locomotive must, for the time being at least, remain in the area of conjecture.

Hearn and Wilkie, in their fine *Cordwood Limited*, believe it to have been Great Northern's No.141, a lightweight 4-4-0 or "American Standard" type locomotive, that briefly served as the Victoria and Sidney Railway No.4. This engine was found to be too light for the job and was quickly returned. It was later replaced by Great Northern 4-4-0 No.290, but it seems clear from the above that more than two Great Northern locomotives may have served the V&S over the years.

Whatever the identity of the first Great Northern locomotive sent over, it is absolutely certain that the traffic over the Saanich Peninsula line had increased to the point where another locomotive was needed to help out the older V&S engines.

The new car ferry barge, the *Sidney No.2*, had been launched at Seattle, Washington, in July. She only reached the saltchuck on her second attempt, the first resulting in a hang-up on the ways 40 feet from the water's edge. This minor problem was resolved the next day. A much greater concern was the requirement for the company to pay customs duties on the vessel before it could enter service in the Canadian coasting trade.

The *Sidney No.2* reached Victoria in mid-July and after the payment of $4,500 in duties and the granting of Canadian registration, it was finally able to enter service. She was badly needed on the Sidney-Mainland run to enable the company to service a much increased trade that had developed in previous months.

It was during this same period that one of the legendary incidents in the history of the Victoria and Sidney Railway occurred. Patrons at Keatings, who provided an increasing business for the railway, had been agitating for a station. The company decided that its Royal Oak Station, which served far fewer patrons, could be moved north over the line to Keatings to appease the local populace. It was resolved that the day for the transfer would be July 27, 1908.

Left:
This is not a shelter for milk cans or a lineside outhouse - it was the passenger station at Mark's Crossing. Only four feet square, it was featured in a 1910 newspaper article about complaints by local citizens.

C. J LOWE: AGE 10

The Royal Oak station, 16 by 28 feet in size, had been at that location since the beginning and was not about to be moved without incident. The first part of the problem was to manoeuvre it aboard a flatcar for the ride north over the V&S line. This proved to be the easiest part of the exercise. The move itself was an entirely different matter.

Back in construction days, T.W. Paterson had stretched available funding by building a grade somewhat narrower than would be acceptable on a regular standard gauge railway - only eleven feet wide as opposed to the usual twelve. The drama got under way in the morning, after the first train of the day returned from Sidney to Royal Oak with a flatcar to pick up the station building. After loading was accomplished, for a very short time it looked as if all would go well, but when the unusually wide load reached the first telegraph pole along the side of the right-of-way, the problems really began. After the telegraph pole had been removed, the first stump was encountered, and then another - and another!

As the train proceeded, the exasperated crew left behind a detritus of discarded poles, fenceposts and stumps and the day dragged on. Even the odd building that was too close to the line had to make way.

The work of moving the station only a few miles seemingly took forever and the departure of the afternoon run from Sidney to Victoria was kept long overdue. Finally, the stubborn station building was set out at Keatings and, at ten o'clock in the evening, the "afternoon" train from Sidney, filled with hungry and agitated passengers, wheezed into the Victoria Market Station. It had been one of the longest days in the history of the Victoria and Sidney Railway. In July 1908, there had been two forest fires in the Elk Lake area, probably caused by sparks from locomotives. But, the movement of the station from Royal Oak to Keatings led to a far hotter time for the railway company. It seemed that no matter how hard the company tried to set things right, the more frequent were the misadventures attending its haphazard operations along the Saanich Peninsula.

In spite of the difficulties, the Great Northern and the VTR&F were not ready to concede defeat. At the end of July, the Great Northern formally took over the holdings of the Vancouver, Westminster and Yukon Railway between New Westminster and Vancouver. At the same time the company's Vancouver, Victoria and Eastern line had been completed eastward from Cloverdale as far as Sumas and trains of the Northern Pacific Railway were now able to run into Vancouver over VV&E rails.

These changes led to the eventual transfer of some of the old VW&Y rolling stock to Vancouver Island and a combined baggage coach from the line was soon regularly running between Victoria and Sidney. The Great Northern also sent to the Island one of their four-wheeled "bobber" cabooses, No.0244, which served the V&S for a number of years.

W.S. Butler's store and the Keatings Crossing railway station, after its move up from Royal Oak.

The efforts of the Great Northern to improve its facilities were beginning to have some effect. Gross railway revenues for the year ending on June 30, 1908 had been up fully 50 per cent over the previous year, and while there were increased capital expenditures as well, the company ended the year with a surplus of $9,038.12, as opposed to only $2,961.77 a year earlier. (See Appendix C for details of financial performance.)

Meanwhile, there were still problems with the City of Victoria, who wanted the VTR&F to vacate its station facilities in Victoria's downtown Market Building which faced onto Cormorant Street.

Moving From the Market Building

At the beginning of September 1908, VTR&F President A.H. McNeill (who also happened to be the local legal counsel for the Great Northern Railway), made an inspection visit to Victoria in company with local manager Frank Van Sant. They met with city officials and the result was to be a new terminal facility for the VTR&F in Victoria - this would be the third station.

The *Daily Colonist*, of September 12th, announced that there were to be "New Terminals For the V&S Railway." The article also recapped the legal situation then existing between the VTR&F, the V&S, and the City of Victoria:

> "Just what arrangements the city will consent to depends to a great extent on what the outcome of the negotiations relative to the agreement entered into a few years ago whereby the company agreed, among other things, to build and run a ferry service from Port Guichon to Sidney. The city granted the company the Market Building or a portion of it for offices, and granted a bonus of $15,000 a year. The company made application to the city for the first year's bonus but this was refused, the city maintaining that the company had not lived up to its agreement to build a new ferry, an old boat having been fitted up and put on that service, and also claiming that in other ways the company had violated its agreement. After lengthy negotiations which brought forward no result the city instituted action in the courts to set aside the agreement and the action is now pending. Some months ago the council decided to enter into negotiations not only with the V.&S. company but with the E.&N. Railway Company with a view to arriving at an amicable arrangement concerning all the differences. The points at issue with the latter company have been arranged but the V.&S. troubles have been in status quo. It is expected that another conference with the council will take place when matters will be satisfactorily adjusted and final announcement concerning the new terminal plans will be made."[1]

Some changes were necessary, not just to settle ongoing differences between the City and the VTR&F, but to meet the requirements of greatly increased freight traffic over the line. The next few years were to be the best the VTR&F and the V&S ever had. The investment in new vessels, plant and equipment was starting to pay off for the railway company.

Affairs between the company and the City did not go well at first. The VTR&F appeared willing to move from its Market Building location, but it didn't want to go any farther away from the city centre than a proposed new station site on Blanshard* Street. Not only was the City opposed to the site, it was still planning to proceed with litigation against the VTR&F. There were other objections as well that would take careful resolution.

Many residents along Blanshard Street, between Fisgard and Hillside, were still angry about the disruptions caused by construction of the Market Building extension and some of the damage cases against the railway had yet to be settled.

In mid-September, a protest petition, containing the signatures of 96 Blanshard Street residents who were against the proposed new location, was submitted to Council. The problem could not be resolved and persisted.

During October, further negotiations began in the case of the City of Victoria vs the VTR&F and V&S, collectively referred to as the "Victoria Terminal and Sidney Railway." They were to drag on for months, with no real progress. Meanwhile, business along the railway line was still holding up and improvements of track and roadbed were completed. Finally, on May 28, 1909, the *Daily Colonist* was able to announce that the City had come to an agreement with the railway company, the details of which were:

1. That the company vacate the Market Building.
2. That they forego their claim to a bonus of approximately $25,000 due under terms of the original Victoria Terminal Railway By-Law.
3. That the V&S improve its service.
4. That the V&S undertake to bring freight from eastern manufacturing centres direct to Victoria over the Northern Pacific and Burlington Road, thus eliminating the necessity of traversing the roundabout route via St. Paul.

* At this time the street name was spelled "Blanchard." Today, in the 1990s, it is spelled "Blanshard."

5. That the company shall be given permission to establish a new depot on Blanshard between Fisgard and Cormorant Streets.

This agreement resulted in the dropping of pending charges previously entered by the City. While the matter finally appeared to be resolved, there were still dissatisfied residents living along Blanshard who did not want a railway yard in the middle of their street. They would do their best to see that there was no such settlement between the City and the railway company. The dispute then dragged on for several more months.

By this time the deal outlined above was slightly amended. The VTR&F would abandon the Market Building provided that it was allowed to use a portion along the west side of Blanshard Street, between Fisgard and Herald, for track purposes, including a freight shed. The company was willing to leave a width of 60 feet unobstructed at that point. It was also proposed that the company put on a gasoline powered engine and that freight cars from the Great Northern and Burlington lines should be ferried over the Straits and brought into the city over the V&S line. There was a snag on this point because the railway's charter required it to operate only with steam locomotives. This problem would be overcome and a gasoline powered motorcoach introduced some years later.

The company had already purchased Lots 703 and 704, adjoining its holdings on Blanshard Street, for the purpose of carrying out these arrangements. After some discussion, Council decided to accept the deal, but once again the residents along Blanshard Street objected. They were even prepared to seek a court injunction to prevent the scheme taking place.

Allowing the company to use Blanshard Street would turn one of the best residential sections into a "backyard, where freight would be stored, teaming be done," stated Mr. Jackson, a local resident, "and the whole result in a depreciation to neighbourhood property values."[2] So the matter remained unresolved, the patience of both the City and the railway being severely strained. Both parties could agree, but not the residents.

This northbound mixed train departs Victoria in 1909 with Locomotive No. 1. The house at rear was at the corner of Blanshard and Pioneer (North Park) Streets and was demolished in 1965.

The next idea put forward was for the VTR&F to buy out owners who felt they would be detrimentally affected by the new railway facilities. The railway was not keen on this idea. They put further pressure on the City to settle, by offering to forego any future claims against the City for the bond interest guarantee that the town had been paying since the inception of the railway. It was a good deal but nothing would be done until the residents were also satisfied. This led to more revisions of the agreement and finally, at the end of November 1909, it appeared that all parties affected by the move of the terminal facilities had come together. Under this final draft, the VTR&F would:

1. Remove from the Market Building and take up its rails on Fisgard Street.
2. Erect a suitable station at the corner of Blanshard and Fisgard Streets.
3. Dedicate a street in the rear of its station.
4. Remove its present line on Blanshard Street to the westward and lay two tracks instead of one.
5. Give up all rights or claims to the Market Building.
6. Release the City from all obligations in respect of the subsidy amounting to about $350,000 in the future.
7. Release the City from all claims from arrears in respect of the subsidy amounting to about $22,000.
8. The company in conjunction with the V&S Railway would provide for the transportation of cars of the VV&E Railway from Sidney to the VV&E Railway on the Mainland.
9. The company to make traffic arrangements with the Northern Pacific Railway so that freight may be delivered in the city via Sidney.
10. The railway to run an extra train, giving three trips a day instead of the two then scheduled.
11. The company to pay the City the cost of the legal action.

The City of Victoria was to:

1. Close a portion of Blanshard Street as a thoroughfare.
2. Release the company from all obligations to provide railway ferry steamship service.

The terms of the agreement appeared to be a victory for the City and resulted in considerable cost for the two railway companies and their parent, the Great Northern Railway. It seems improbable that the railway companies would have entered into such an agreement if business had not been good, but it was doing well enough to justify the costs of relocating its Victoria terminal facilities for a third time in 15 years. The problem of dealing with the recalcitrant landowners along Blanshard Street would be left for city officials to solve.

It appeared that the City would move quickly to implement the agreement by submitting a by-law for ratification by local ratepayers, but as the months passed and the by-law did not appear, it was apparent that the Council was concerned about the reaction of residents along Blanshard Street. They still regularly complained. The matter dragged into 1910, and although the VTR&F announced its intention to secure a permit for the construction of its new facilities, nothing concrete seemed to be happening.

In February, the City announced that it would prepare the by-law after all, for submission to the voters. They did so and it was passed by Council. Again, legal action was threatened by the local Blanshard Street residents. The City received a letter from Messrs. Pooley and Luxton, solicitors for Mr. William Jackson of Blanshard Street:

"Gentlemen:

"On behalf of Mr. William Jackson, who is a ratepayer of the city, living on Blanchard Street, we hereby give you notice that after the expiration of ten days from the date hereof, he intends to apply to the Supreme Court of British Columbia to quash the 'Blanchard Avenue Closing By-Law, 1910,' passed by your council on the 7th March inst. on the following grounds:

1. That the said by-law is not passed in the public interest, but is part or parcel of a scheme to grant or lease to the Victoria Terminal Railway and Ferry Company the portion of Blanchard Avenue purported to be stopped up by the said by-law, or to grant to the said railway company the exclusive privilege and right of using the same as a railway depot or for railway purposes.

2. That no such right or privilege can be granted to the said company unless and until same is embodied in a by-law submitted to the electors of the city entitled to vote on by-laws to contract debts and has received the assent of not less than three-fifths in the number of those who vote upon the by-law.

3. That no such by-law as last mentioned has been submitted to the said electors or passed.

4. That the said by-law is not passed bona fide in the exercise of any powers contained in the Municipal Clauses Act.

5. That the stopping up of the said portion of the said street and the granting of the proposed privileges to the said company will not only reduce the width of Blanchard Avenue to 50 feet or less, but will also create a nuisance to the surrounding residents.

6. On such other grounds in law as our client is entitled to object to the said by-law."

POOLEY, LUXTON AND POOLEY

"P.S. - Please take notice that we are also instructed by other ratepayers and residents to take similar proceedings in respect of the said by-law."[3]

The Third
Victoria Station

The VTR&F was growing increasingly anxious about these developments and decided to take the matter beyond the City of Victoria and local ratepayers. They petitioned the Provincial Government to grant them a lease on Crown owned lands in the area. That would permit them to proceed with their terminal plans, thereby implementing the agreement with the City. This application was to be heard at the end of June, but the mere threat was apparently enough to induce the Blanshard Street landowners to reach a financial settlement with the VTR&F. Finally, after more than eighteen months of wrangling, the matter was resolved and the Railway Company was able to make plans for the relocation of its Victoria terminal facilities.

On August 11, 1910, the *Daily Colonist* announced that the Railway Company's plans for the new depot included warehouse and terminal facilities to be erected on Blanshard Street. These were to be ready for occupancy by October. The construction contract was awarded to Messrs. Dinsdale and Malcolm, at a cost of $17,500. The new concrete and brick station building was also to be the VTR&F's corporate headquarters. The passenger station itself, 30 by 60 feet, was expected to be completed by the following January. The terminal grounds took up the full block between Fisgard and Herald Streets and the complaints of the local residents, soothed by a financial settlement of undisclosed magnitude, was quieted. In further consolation, the fine character of the new railway buildings were said to be a credit to the neighbourhood.

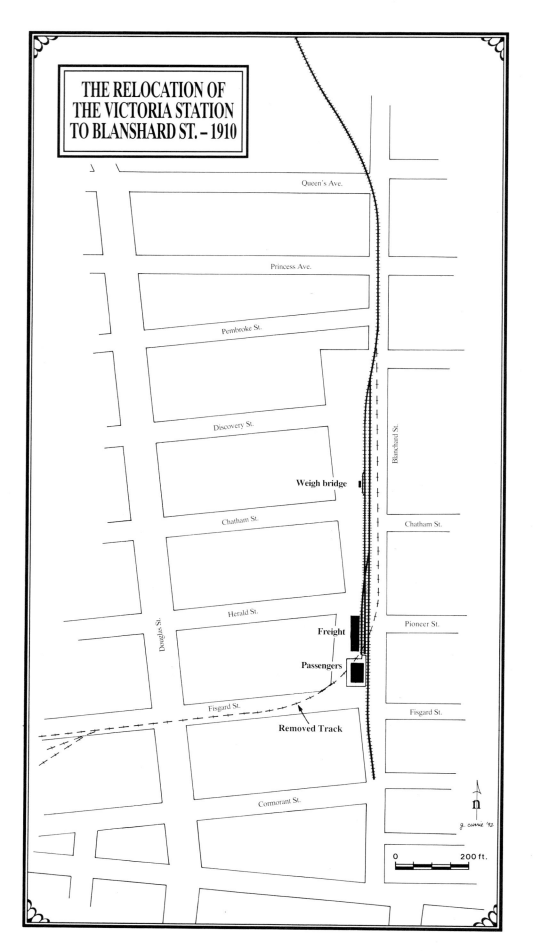

THE RELOCATION OF
THE VICTORIA STATION
TO BLANSHARD ST. – 1910

Queen's Ave.

Princess Ave.

Pembroke St.

Discovery St.

Chatham St.

Herald St.

Fisgard St.

Cormorant St.

Blanchard St.

Chatham St.

Pioneer St.

Fisgard St.

Douglas St.

Weigh bridge

Freight

Passengers

Removed Track

g. currie '92

0   200 ft.

Co-incident with the announcement of new station facilities, the locally titled Victoria Terminal and Sidney Railway announced an improved service between Victoria and the Sidney terminus of its line.

Even as the protracted battle between the City of Victoria, the Blanshard Street ratepayers and the VTR&F was getting underway, the operations of the Victoria and Sidney Railway and its Victoria connector, the VTR&F, were showing a dramatic improvement over previous years. Freight and passenger traffic were both on the increase as a result of the improvements made to the local plant and services. To June 30, 1908, the number of passengers carried was up by 2,400 over the previous accounting period and freight tonnage was up by 10,621 tons. Clearly, and in spite of all the difficulties, the Great Northern was trying to make something of its Vancouver Island connections. However, this was done with a close eye on finances and would continue only as long as the expenditures were offset by increased business.

In September 1908, there was heavy freight traffic coming into the capital city daily. Track improvements undertaken earlier in the year were about complete. The pace of summer traffic, though increasing in magnitude, followed the familiar pattern of earlier years with the increased excursion traffic during the summer, special trains for political conventions such as the annual Conservative picnic at Sidney, and the usual specials for the Saanich Agricultural Association's annual fair.

Both the Victoria and Sidney and the Esquimalt and Nanaimo railways anticipated increased traffic during the fall hunting season. This was the last year for such traffic on the V&S, as the municipality of Saanich was taking steps to limit the use of firearms within its boundaries.

In November, the city was favoured with a brief visit by none other than J.J. Hill. It turned out to be more pleasure than business and Hill soon left after briefly conferring with local officers of the company.

The Saanich Peninsula was a garden of rural charms, still pristine in many sections, and one of the scenic treasures of Vancouver Island. The green rolling hills and quiet meadows, set against the backdrop of snowcapped Mount Baker to the east, made the rail journey out from Victoria to Sidney a scenic delight. There had been many changes since the early years when wolves were actually seen gambolling in the woods near Swan Lake, but bears, cougars and deer were still a common sight.

From time to time, the V&S did additional business with the City of Victoria's waterworks at Elk and Beaver Lakes. Sidney was increasingly prosperous with the construction of the Converse and Brown Shingle Mill, in the spring of 1909.

The Sidney Island Brick and Tile Company, on the island of that name, was creating even more freight traffic for the V&S. The plant, promoted by J.L. Skene and George Courtney, was turning out 40,000 common bricks a day and employing a staff of 30. It commenced operations in June 1909.

There were events of a tragic nature as well. One accident victim along the line, in April 1909, was the horse belonging to the owners of Saanichton's Prairie Inn. This unfortunate nag was neither the first nor the last such creature to die under the wheels of a V&S locomotive.

Again there was talk of competition for the V&S on the Peninsula, in the form of either an electric railway or a branch of the new Canadian Northern Pacific Railway, which was constructing its mainline across the province. This competition would come in time, but the Victoria Terminal and Sidney Railway continued to improve its facilities and increase revenues.

The railway, unfortunately, was still frequently in violation of its schedules, which seemed to the local citizenry to be little more than a flexible guideline as to when the train might be along. Public complaints were frequent. Captain Clive

Phillipps-Wolley, whose work was well-known in the United Kingdom and elsewhere, was one of the Victoria and Sidney's harshest critics. His thoughts on the V&S were contained in an article in the Victoria *Colonist* "Sunday" magazine of June 27, 1909:

> "...The peninsula from Victoria to Sidney is, I suppose, about 20 miles in length with an average breadth of five miles. (I am only attempting to speak in very round figures) and is traversed by two excellent roads and one eccentric railway, tried and found guilty by a long-suffering public and sentenced to electrocution unless it immediately mends its ways.
>
> "Poor old railway! We have all of us cursed it until even Andy almost grew angry. Andy, the boss and buffer, who has stood between an offending company and a long suffering public for many years, until we would hardly change the V.&S. for the C.P. Railway if the loss of Andy was the price of the change; but, after all, our local C.P.R. (Creeping Paralysis?) has served its turn and done its work in the rough and ready way of pioneers, dumping its cars into the sea and fishing them out again with a locomotive and a kedge anchor and it has killed nobody as yet.
>
> "Peace to its memory!..."[4]

For the second year in a row, the highlight of the 1909 summer excursion season was the Conservative picnic. But, the politicos faced strong competition from the annual grocer's picnic, which included a day's outing and sporting events in the park near the Sidney station. The V&S ran four special trains for the August event.

In November 1909, a storm washed out bridges and caused suspension of service along the Esquimalt and Nanaimo Railway. It was suggested that perhaps a connection might temporarily be made with Nanaimo by running the steamer *Iroquois* between Sidney and Ladysmith, to make connections with trains at those points until traffic along the E&N line could be resumed. It was a novel suggestion, but not likely to receive favourable consideration by the CPR who were owners of the E&N and competitors of the Great Northern and its associated Victoria Terminal and Sidney lines on Vancouver Island.

The poor horse belonging to the Prairie Inn was not the only collision victim that year. On December 11th, Joseph Bole was driving his employer's team across the tracks on the West Saanich Road when the rig was struck by the evening passenger train. One of the two horses was killed.

All was not doom and gloom, however. Freight shipments held up well, right through the fall and into the winter of 1909, even though a blockage of service on the Great Northern line in Washington State interrupted onward shipments to Vancouver Island. The GN line had been closed by snow and flooding at a number of points between the Pacific Coast and the U.S. Midwest.

One of the most serious, was the washout of Great Northern Railway lines between Blaine and Seattle. Service over the line to the Liverpool and Blaine ferry slips was held up from the end of November for over a week. The first cars, six in all, did not reach Victoria via Sidney until December 15, 1909. Regular traffic was restored - a daily train of six to eight cars coming in over the Sidney bargeslip for movement into Victoria.

The Victoria Terminal Railway and Ferry Company had purchased the *S.S. Victorian* in January 1903. Its conversion to a combined rail and passenger vessel, in a local shipyard, was to have been the company's way of satisfying its agreement to build a ferry in Victoria. The City of Victoria had not been satisfied, would not pay the subsidy, and the two parties had been in dispute over this and other matters from that time on. That led to the cancellation of the scheduled runs of the *S.S. Victorian*,

Right:
This six keg consignment of ale, from Victoria's Silver Springs Brewery, weighed 1400 pounds and was consigned to Donovan and Martineau of the Sidney Hotel.

End of the
S.S. Victorian

Triplicate.

Victoria Terminal and Sidney Railway Company

British Columbia,

Victoria, B. C. *Aug. 3* 1909

Received from *The Silver Spring Brewery, Limited.*

the undermentioned property in apparent good order addressed to

Donovan & Martineau

Sidney

to be sent by the said company subject to the conditions stated on the other side, and which are agreed to by this shipping note, delivered to the company at the time of giving this receipt therefor.

No. of Pkgs.	Species of Goods.	Marks.	Weight lbs.	Paid On.
6	13½ Ale		1400	

Agent, V. T. & S. Ry. Co.

General Conditions of Carriage.

It is agreed and understood that the Victoria Terminal & Sidney Ry. Company of British Columbia will not be responsible for goods or packages of any kind conveyed upon their Railway, unless receipted for by a duly authorized agent of the Company. It being further expressly agreed that the responsibility of the Company shall cease at this Company's stations, at which said goods or packages are to be delivered; and this Company agrees to carry said goods or packages only subject to the following conditions :

This Company shall not be responsible for the loss or packages, the contents of which are unknown; or for any goods missent, unless they are consigned to a station on the Railway; for leakage of any kind of liquids, breakage of any kind of glass, carboys of acids, or articles packed in glass, stoves or stove furniture, castings, machinery, carriages, furniture, musical instruments of any kind, packages of eggs, or for loss or damage on hay, straw or any articles whose bulk renders it necessary to transport it in open cars, or for damage to perishable property of any kind, occasioned by delays from any cause or change of weather, nor for any loss of weight of grain, or coffee in bags, or rice in tierces; nor for loss of nuts in bags, or lemons or oranges in boxes not covered by canvas, or for damage or loss by fire, unless it can be shown that such damage or loss occurred through the negligence or default of the agents of the Company. It is further especially agreed, that for all loss or damage occurring in the transit of the said goods or packages, the legal remedy shall be against this Company only in case the said goods or packages shall be in the custody of said Company at the happening of such damages, it being understood that the Victoria Terminal & Sidney Railway Company assumes no other responsibility for the said carriage or safety than may be incurred on its own road. All goods and packages subject to charge for cooperage or other necessary repairs.

VICTORIA, B. C.

Victoria Terminal & Sidney Railway Co.

from Sidney to the Mainland, in 1904. Throughout the next four years, she languished at quayside in Victoria.

Early in 1909, the *Victorian* was sold to the Best Steamship Company, a U.S. firm, for service between Bellingham, Everett and Seattle, Washington. When she was moved into Eagle Harbor, Washington, for repairs, the money ran out and the work was never completed. It was said that the Best Company had $35,000 tied up in the repair when they ran into financial difficulty. Perhaps the old girl needed more work than first thought. Soon she was plastered with litigation and her fate uncertain.

Finally, it was all over. In January 1910, the once proud *Victorian* was purchased by Hall Brothers, a Puget Sound shipbuilding firm. Her engines were taken out for use in a storm schooner and she was broken up. It was a sad ending for a fine ship that never seemed to have had quite her share of luck. The VTR&F and parent Great Northern had run the service strictly for freight cars after 1904, leaving the trans-gulf passenger trade to the Canadian Pacific Navigation Company. It was a prudent choice. One wonders how the *Victorian* might ever have competed against the CPN, which had runs from Victoria to both Vancouver and New Westminster. By 1909, it was clear to the Great Northern that the best course was to try to upgrade the Victoria Terminal and Sidney rail service and increase its barge trade, thus concentrating on the best opportunities for financial success.

The Victoria Terminal and Sidney Railway in 1910

In spite of concerted efforts to improve customer service and increased facilities for the carriage of traffic in 1908-09, the Victoria Terminal and Sidney began 1910 with many strikes against it. Trains were still frequently behind schedule, and the lack of adequate station facilities along the line was a constant annoyance to patrons of the passenger service. As if this was not enough, the railway began the year with the tragic death of a young man just off the steamer *Iroquois* on his way into Victoria.

Walter Richard Palmer, the 23-year-old son of R.M. Palmer, had been visiting friends in the Gulf Islands and had just stepped off the gangplank of the *S.S. Iroquois*. He reached up for the grabiron on the side of the coach to swing himself up onto the top step of the passenger car. Making his move too late, he was caught between the corner of the car and the side of the platform on the ferry dock, falling down into a space only a few inches wide and being rolled along between the coach and platform. The unfortunate young man was rushed to St. Joseph's Hospital at Victoria but died shortly after arrival from crushed ribs and massive internal injuries. The "Cordwood Limited" had claimed another victim.

Another accident occurred within months, but this time it involved employees. On July 16th, the afternoon freight run of the V&S was on its way to Sidney. Along the rambling right-of-way the locomotive swayed first left, then right, moving steadily through the kneehigh grass that lined the rural trackage. It was just after 4:00 p.m. The train had reached and passed Saanichton and two crew members were enjoying the ride, and the view, from the top of a wooden boxcar. Unnoticed, a heavy overhead wire sagged in the heat of the warm afternoon sun. Trainmen Foster and Wake stood up for a better view of the track ahead. Suddenly, they struck the wire and Wake was thrown completely clear of the train, landing on the trackside and sustaining serious injuries. The wire also struck brakeman F. Foster square in the mouth, badly lascerating his lips and gums.

Picking himself up, Foster quickly stopped the train and led the crew to the aid of his unconscious companion. The train made double time the rest of the way to Sidney and Wake was transferred to the care of the Sidney Sanitarium. It was a close call for both men, but both lived to tell about it.

By August 1910, the weather had become hot and sultry. An occasional fire was breaking out along the trackside. The worst of these occurred in the third week of August, when a blaze broke out along the tracks near the City of Victoria's water flume line. For a time, the flume was endangered, but through the untiring efforts of the railway's track gang, the fire was extinguished. It had caused considerable anxiety, as the water flume at this location was paralleled by one of the largest wooden trestles on the Victoria Terminal and Sidney Railway. Destruction of the bridge would have suspended operations on the railway for weeks.

Wooden structures, such as the above bridge just south of Beaver Lake, were a constant worry to the railway management and in the summer of 1910 the Great Northern Railway's Chief Bridge Carpenter, Mr. J. Harmon, arrived to inspect all the structures along the line from the Sidney wharf and barge slip to the Victoria terminal. The Victoria Terminal and Sidney was trying to appear as a good corporate citizen, but weren't prepared to spend more than a minimal amount on repairs and upgrading.

Even though freight traffic was on the increase, passengers were increasingly frustrated by the lack of adequate station facilities and slow schedules. The freight seemed to have priority and humans a distant second. As the summer of 1910 passed into fall, these complaints were building to a climax.

W. McMillan and grand-daughter Freda Rook pose under the aqueduct at Colquitz Creek during a family visit in 1910. V&S railway bridge is visible through aqueduct support structure.

On September 7, 1910, a group of Saanich Peninsula citizens entered a complaint against the railway with the Provincial Government. The petitioners cited breaches of the Victoria and Sidney Railway's charter obligations, and demanded immediate government action against the company.

The City of Victoria also joined the list of complainants and invited the Municipality of Saanich to do the same. All parties united to submit a memorandum, asking the Premier and provincial government to take action against the railway. A joint committee, with participation from City Council and local ratepayers, was set up and moved to censure the railway for its lack of action in regard to service complaints.

The complaints against the Victoria Terminal and Sidney were finally placed before the Provincial Government. A committee of local citizens, municipal and provincial politicians attended the conference. The substance of the complaints was that the railway company's service fell far short of that expected of a public common carrier.

Vice-President Brown, of the VTR&F, attempted to defend the road, citing the fact that the railway had never been a paying proposition and, for that reason, the company did not feel justified in any large expenditure in new plant or facilities. Brown felt that up to $60,000 would be required to put the VT&S line in top condition and the company just did not have the funds.

Brown further pointed out that the company was trying to do the best it could with what was available to them. He announced that two passenger trains and a separate freight train were to be run daily between Victoria and Sidney. It had been standard practice for trains to consist of both freight and passenger cars.

The case against the company was neatly summarized by Mr. John Dean, who had long advocated a better train service. Dean penned two separate letters to the Premier and provincial Executive on August 10 and 14, 1910. Copies were summarized in the *Daily Colonist* of September 8th:

The Railway Arraigned

"August 30, 1910 —

To The Hon. Premier and gentlemen of the Executive: This delegation appeals to you to enforce the provisions of the British Columbia Railway Act with respect to the Victoria and Sidney Railway and that portion of the railway belonging to the Victoria Terminal Railway and Ferry Company, located on Vancouver Island for the following reasons:

1. The City of Victoria and the provincial government pay to the Victoria and Sidney Railway Company in subsidies $9,000 and $6,000 respectively; have already paid $262,500; and may be required to pay $112,500 more. The acceptance of this money involves an obligation to the public which this company has failed to recognize, while on the contrary, it has imposed upon the public beyond the limits of endurance and the bounds of common decency, in the manner following:

    (a) By continuing to use antiquated engines incapable of doing the work required, often stalling, causing vexatious delay to passengers.

    (b) By not providing sufficient passenger carriages to accommodate the people desiring to travel thereby.

    (c) By forcing people to travel on the freight cars and to stand in the aisles, on the platforms and steps of the coaches, utterly regardless of section 95 (Railway Act), which provides for the safety of passengers.

    (d) By utterly failing to run their trains on time thus causing great loss of valuable time and irritation to all concerned.

2. Under The Act...the British Columbia Railway Act, sub-section 2 of section 41 of which Act says: 'the trains shall start and run at regular hours, to be fixed by public notice and shall furnish sufficient accommodation for the transportation of all such goods and passengers as are within a reasonable time previous thereto offered for transportation.

3. Sub-section 7 of section 41 says: 'No baggage, freight, passenger or lumber cars shall be placed in the rear of the passenger cars, and no agent shall direct or knowingly suffer such arrangement.

4. It is common knowledge that there is continual flagrant violation of these sub-sections.

5. According to an audit made on behalf of the provincial government, covering a period from April 1895 to June 1901, inclusive, 6 years and 3 months, the railway showed a profit balance of $79.80 after having allowed a charge to expenditure account of interest, amounting to $8,930. The audit also shows a liability balance due on construction account of $25,085.11. It also shows that there were 1,250 one hundred dollar shares issued, on which only 10 per cent had been paid. According to the Railway Act, these shares were liable for an additional 90 per cent, a total of $112,500.

"According to a by-law of the City of Victoria, adopted on the 20th of July 1892, the interest and balance due on construction above referred to should have been paid by the shareholders. Section 4 of said by-law reads as follows: 'Any sum or sums of money which may hereafter be paid by the corporation under this guarantee shall be a first charge upon the undertaking, tolls and property of the company, subject only to the said bonus, and to such division thereof as between the government of British Columbia and the said corporation and the acceptance of the benefit of this by-law by the said company shall be deemed conclusive evidence of the assent of the above company to all terms of this by-law.'

"Payment On Shares

"Now, if these charges on construction account, amounting at that date to $34,019, had not been paid out of earnings and the company had been sued for them, the city having a first charge upon the undertaking, tolls and property of the company, the shareholders would have to pay it which clearly shows that it was wrong to pay it out of the earnings when there was $112,500 subject to call on unpaid shares.

"The question arises: whether it is not the duty of the province and city to insist on these shares being fully paid and refund made to them of their proper proportion of $112,500 plus all excess on earnings ever since the last audit was made in 1902.

"Therefore, in view of what appears to be a wrongful diversion of the earnings, and the fact that the earnings have more than doubled since the last audit, we ask that an exhaustive audit and analysis of the company's affairs should be made to ascertain if it is just and right that the subsidy should be paid by the city and province. For it is quite clear to those familiar with the railway that whilst the earnings have more than doubled, the running expenses of the road have been at a standstill.

"We venture to express the opinion, after an exhaustive consideration on this matter, and the conviction is forced on us, that under the terms on which this bonus is given, there is no inducement but a virtuous one for a railway corporation to give a good service, or to earn more than enough to pay bare running expenses, unless they could earn in excess of the subsidy, for it is readily seen that it is easier (though disingenuous), to play the mendicant and accept the bonus, than it is to earn it and relieve the donors by catering to the public with a good service. The apparent inattention to the upkeep of the concern as a whole can only be ascribed to a desire that it shall not be worth more on the expiration of the bonus than the face value of the bonds, shutting out the province and the city from recovering any of the bonus.

"Transient travellers characterize the railway as a 'joke,' a 'farce.' To those who have occasion to use it often it is an insult to their intelligence and self respect, whereas, if developed to its full capacity, it would greatly appreciate the value of the Saanich Peninsula, add greatly to the trade of this city, be a credit instead of a reflection on the province, and contribute to the convenience and profit of all concerned and at the same time relieve the city and province from the burden of the bonus.

"This presentation of the matter is on behalf of the ratepayer patrons of the railway. The committees from the councils of Victoria, Saanich and North Saanich will each place their views before you.

(signed) JOHN DEAN"

The submission went on with specific details of the complaints against the railway. The engine was said to often stall on the upgrade leading to Royal Oak, or even on leaving the Victoria terminus along Fisgard Street, showering the neighbourhood with sparks.

The passenger cars consisted to two semi-modern coaches, one semi-modern smoker and baggage car combined, and three flatcars. The latter were said to have been converted into passenger cars by:

> "...forming a pen as in the ordinary way for cattle by nailing rails all around to the stakes and placing wooden benches around the sides and ends, with two rows down the middle lengthwise, with provision for access from one side only, the space between the floor and the benches and rails ranging from 10 to 12 inches. A good sized child could easily fall through. The top of the railing is as near as maybe three feet above the floor of the car; over this a roof, which answers very poorly for the purpose for which it is intended, for the soot, sun and dust find easy access. Communication with any other car for water or any purpose whatever is had by climbing across the rails across the end of the said flatcars.

> "It is seldom that fresh drinking water is provided. For months the water tank in one of the coaches could not be used on account of the faucet being broken off; and to harmonize, one of the seats in the middle of the coach has been without a back. The drinking cups are usually dirty and repelling."[5]

A V&S passenger train, complete with "cattle cars," prepares for the southbound run from Sidney to Victoria on a festive occasion. The V&S had three flatcars fitted up for carrying passengers which were the subject of much public criticism.

The arraignment document continued with a description of the so-called "stations" along the line and even included photos of the structure at Elk Lake - a mere 4 feet by 4 feet. Dean cited what he called "the callous indifference to the public convenience" and demanded that provisions of the Railway Act concerning the running of trains on regular schedules be enforced. The railway company had worked to improve its services over the previous years, but did so on a proverbial "shoestring" with most improvements dedicated to a better and more profitable freight service. Somewhere along the way, the convenience of the passengers had been given short shrift. The dispute between the City and the VT&S Railway was not over and would drag on for several more years. In the meantime, poor service was not the only problem vexing the company.

Although an agreement had been arrived at between the City of Victoria and the railway company to remove the railway station from the Market Building to the new site on Blanshard Street, months had elapsed since passage of the enabling by-law. No work had been undertaken to relocate station facilities to the new location.

The New Railway Terminal

All attention seemed to be directed towards the railway company's poor service and facilities, in the autumn of 1910, but there was one bright spot on the horizon. It was finally announced in mid-September that they would be vacating their quarters in the Market Building, tearing up the Fisgard Street trackage, and moving to Blanshard Street.

The contract for erection of the new station and freight sheds was awarded to Messrs. Malcolm and Dinsdale and work began that very same month. It was anticipated that it would be possible to occupy the new premises, estimated to cost about $25,000, by the end of October but work dragged on for some time. In spite of slow progress, Manager Frank Van Sant of the VTR&F forecast the move into the company's new quarters by the end of November. While this was happening, there was correspondence underway between the City of Victoria and the Great Northern. In November, Mr. W.W. Broughton, general traffic manager of the GNR, wrote to Victoria's City Council expressing the hope that what had been done in the way of improving services "will make your people feel that proper consideration is being given to the matter."[6] Lamentably, the City and the Victoria Board of Trade considered that all actions taken by the Great Northern to improve service on the VT&S Railway were inadequate.

The removal of track from Fisgard Street and the preparation of the new terminal facilities was well advanced, when the company was able to move into its still-uncompleted quarters on Blanshard Street, during the second week of December 1910. The old dispute with the City of Victoria seemed to be endless, but at least the City and railway company could end the year having relocated the terminal facilities as had been desired by both parties for several years. It had even been done without the anticipated legal action of local Blanshard Street residents. The VT&S Railway could only hope for a better year in 1911.

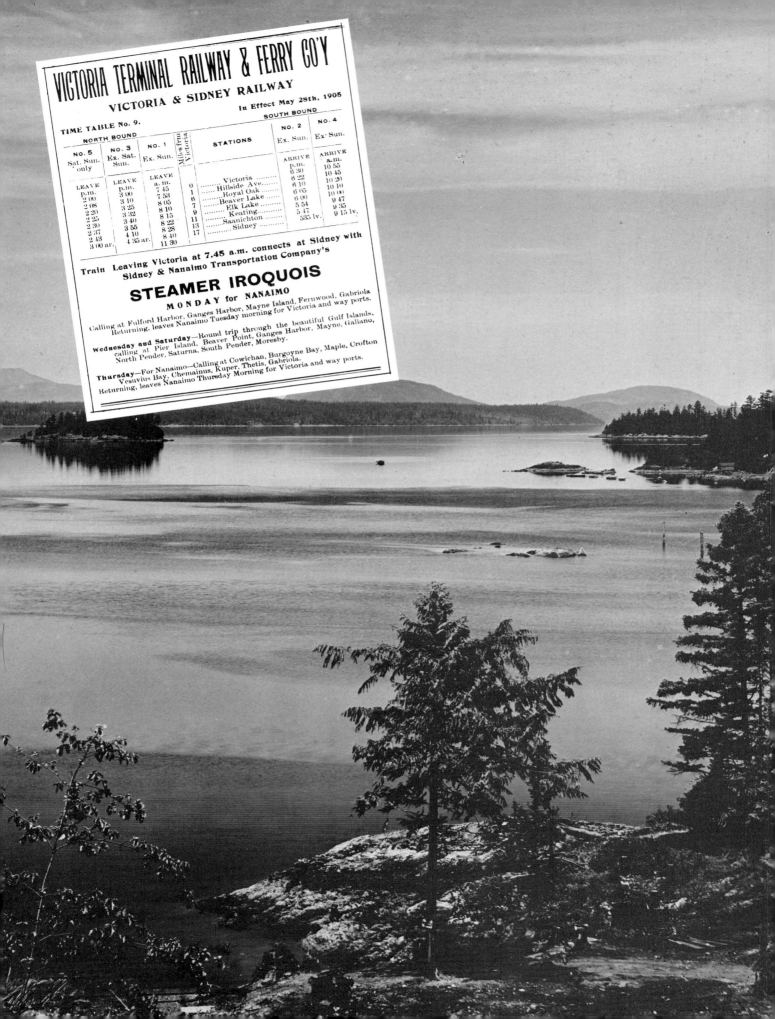

VICTORIA TERMINAL RAILWAY & FERRY CO'Y

VICTORIA & SIDNEY RAILWAY

In Effect May 28th, 1905

TIME TABLE No. 9.

NORTH BOUND			Miles frm Victoria	STATIONS	SOUTH BOUND	
NO. 5	NO. 3	NO. 1			NO. 2	NO. 4
Sat. Sun. only	Ex. Sat. Sun.	Ex. Sun.			Ex. Sun.	Ex. Sun.
LEAVE p.m.	LEAVE p.m.	LEAVE a.m.			ARRIVE p.m.	ARRIVE a.m.
		7 45	0	Victoria	6 30	10 55
		7 53	1	Hillside Ave.	6 22	10 45
2 00	3 00	8 05	6	Royal Oak	6 10	10 20
2 08	3 10	8 10	7	Beaver Lake	6 05	10 10
2 20	3 25	8 15	9	Elk Lake	6 00	10 00
2 25	3 32	8 22	11	Keating	5 54	9 47
2 30	3 40	8 28	13	Saanichton	5 47	9 35
2 37	3 55	8 40	17	Sidney	535 lv.	9 15 lv.
2 43	4 10	11 30				
3 00 ar.	4 35 ar.					

Train Leaving Victoria at 7.45 a.m. connects at Sidney with Sidney & Nanaimo Transportation Company's

STEAMER IROQUOIS

MONDAY for NANAIMO

Calling at Fulford Harbor, Ganges Harbor, Mayne Island, Fernwood, Gabriola. Returning, leaves Nanaimo Tuesday morning for Victoria and way ports.

Wednesday and Saturday—Round trip through the beautiful Gulf Islands, calling at Pier Island, Beaver Point, Ganges Harbor, Mayne, Galiano, North Pender, Saturna, South Pender, Moresby.

Thursday—For Nanaimo—Calling at Cowichan, Burgoyne Bay, Maple, Crofton Vesuvius Bay, Chemainus, Kuper, Thetis, Gabriola. Returning, leaves Nanaimo Thursday Morning for Victoria and way ports.

11

LAST YEARS
OF THE *S.S. IROQUOIS*

The steamer *Iroquois*, under the ownership of Captain Sears and his partner, Munro, had been an essential element in the development of the Gulf Islands during the first decade of the century. With her shallow draft, the *Iroquois* could enter places where larger steamers were unsafe. Equipped for the carriage of both passengers and freight, she formed a vital link for Gulf Islanders on their way to and from Victoria or Nanaimo.

The *Iroquois* ran on a daily schedule, throughout the year, making calls at points as far north as Nanaimo twice weekly. Runs were made to various Gulf Island points on alternate days. Each summer the company operated weekend passenger excursions from Sidney. It was an ideal getaway trip for city residents wanting to spend a day on the water with family and friends amid breathtaking scenery.

The beauty of the Gulf Islands, a myriad of islands from Gabriola in the north, to Sidney Island, in the south, was well known to Victorians and residents elsewhere on Vancouver Island ninety years ago. The Islands' greatest advocate was Phillipps-Wolley, who lived on Piers Island, just off Swartz Bay, a few miles from Sidney. He wrote frequently about their beauty and his words from the *Daily Colonist* of Sunday, July 11, 1908, evoke nostalgic memory:

> "It takes an hour, even by the Creeping Paralysis (V&S Railway) to get to Sidney, whence any of the Islands may be reached by launch or boat, and should the railway be electrified, with terminus at Schwartz's Bay, there seems no reason why a man should take more than an hour between his island and his club, but very few of our people have that instinct for partial seclusion which accounts for the existence of the splendid country homes of England, and therefore there are still one or two islands on the market...
>
> "The disadvantages of the Islands are these: if you are an invalid likely at a moment's notice to be in the need of a doctor, they are perhaps too far from the telephone...This is the first drawback. The second is that under present conditions it is not easy to find a working man, or a maid, who being anxious to remain one, will give up the seductions of Government Street and the opportunities offered by a large town for the quiet and seclusion of an island farm...
>
> "Beyond these drawbacks, both of which can be overcome, I know of none, except that you cannot take a friendly interest in your neighbor's quarrels with his wife; you cannot smell

Left:
This shot of Saanich Inlet from Brentwood Bay, circa 1913 and taken by famed photographer Leonard Frank, shows the beautiful scenery which was enjoyed by passengers on the *S.S. Iroquois*. Inset is 1908 Timetable.

with accuracy what he is going to have for dinner; and you cannot on a moment's notice secure another man for bridge...

"Here the S.S. Iroquois calls with the mail on Mondays and Fridays. Under ordinary circumstances the captain will also call for passengers by request on Tuesdays and Thursdays...

"So far it should not be difficult to obtain evidence for what has been said in favor of the islands of the Gulf of Georgia. It will be somewhat more difficult to make men believe that there is a very considerable difference between the climatic conditions upon them (at least upon the smaller islands) and those of the immediate adjoining mainland. Lying as they do behind Vancouver Island, sheltered by it and each other, and yet not overshadowed by any high land, they are veritable sun traps, and this they show in a variety of ways, e.g. by the early arrival of humming birds and other summer emigrants and the earliness of certain blossoms and vegetable products; moreover (and this is not altogether an advantage) the showers which one sees falling around Cowichan generally pass without falling upon these islands...

"Looked at from the outside as you pass these islands, they seem to be heavily timbered with pines growing upon rocks, which in most cases come down to the water's edge. With many of them this rocky front is but the raised edge of the saucer, the hollow of which contains rich soil overgrown in most cases with easily removed alder, and in all of them the ridges of rock contain between them deposits of rich soil admirably adopted to cultivation...

"In conclusion, to those who are not afraid of their own company, varied by almost daily visits by their neighbors, and if necessary a weekly trip to town, I would recommend an inspection of this island district, because it is the most beautiful in British Columbia, because the land is cheaper than any of the same quality in British Columbia, because for fruit and flower growing it is the equal to the Channel Islands, because the bays are full of fish, which saves the fishmonger's bill, and the game can be preserved, which saves the butcher's bill; because the dry, sunny land and ample beaches, full of small crustacean life, make these islands ideal poultry farms, and because the limited number of them must someday, when the demand arises, make them almost priceless."

Right:

The S.S. *Iroquois* **cruises the inland sea near Bedwell Harbour. Some of the passages were so narrow that the passengers could almost reach out and touch trees on the shore.**

The *Iroquois* was the best known vessel along the string of small ports from Sidney in the south to Nanaimo in the north, and a familiar feature in Wolley's world. She was a well kept, if somewhat ungainly-looking vessel; narrow, stubby and standing high out of the water. She was the pride of her owners; Sears and Munro knew that they had a good financial thing going.

Sometime after the partners took over the vessel in 1903, they had a falling out, the reason for which is unknown. The two men hardly spoke to each other, each wanted to buy the other out, but neither was willing to sell his share. In spite of this, Sears captained the ship and Munro acted as purser, an unusual arrangement continuing for some years. Their vessel was well patronized and a financial success.

In the early years, the Islands of the Gulf of Georgia, were poorly charted and unmarked rocks or shoals could suddenly appear where none were thought to exist. Many of the small coasting steamers of the day were hung up to dry on some rock or beach and tugboats did a fair salvage business. Indeed, there was hardly a ship that could say it had never been on the rocks or in trouble more than once. The *S.S. Iroquois* was no exception.

In spite of the skills attributed to local mariners, the lack of good navigational aids and the vagaries of wind and wave led to unexpected surprises, even on runs through the sheltered waters of the Georgian Archipelago. Such was the case on October 23, 1908. While the *Iroquois* was on her regular Monday trip north through the Islands to Nanaimo, Captain Albert Sears was on shore for the day and a Captain Anderson was in command.

The ship was running slowly through a thick, menacing fog that hung over Northumberland Channel. Nanaimo was somewhere ahead. Anderson reached out with his senses, listening, looking into the leaden mist. The *Iroquois* was running dead slow now, her wake almost imperceptible on the smooth water. The peasoup fog seemed to swallow up even the faint glow of the ship's inadequate navigation lamps.

Nanaimo could not be too far ahead. There was just the turn to port at the upper end of Northumberland Channel and then the run into the dock - if only Anderson's senses could tell him when to make the turn, in the fog and gathering darkness. It was nearing six o'clock in the evening and the little steamer was late. Even the low throb of her engines seemed to die on the still air. Moving ghostlike through the mist, the *Iroquois* carried on, but the lights of Nanaimo were missing, lost in the impenetrable wall of gloom.

A crewman, positioned on the bow, failed to notice the approaching shoreline until it was too late. Crunching along the gravel bottom, the *Iroquois* ground her way onto Jack's Point at high tide. The water rolled in smoothly over the stern and ran through midships. With a plaintiff burst of steam from her submerged boiler, the *Iroquois* heeled over on her side.

Anderson, unlucky as a navigator, was fortunate in evacuating the thirteen passengers in the ship's lifeboats. After a short pull they were landed at Nanaimo. The thirteen hogs in the hold were left to fend for themselves. While many swam to safety, two were drowned, the only casualties of the foundering. A telegram was sent to Albert Sears in Victoria and the B.C. Salvage Company's tug *William Jolliffe* was dispatched, in company with the old *S.S. Maude* as a tender.

The salvage vessels started north from Esquimalt in a dense fog and were forced to lay over off Gordon Head. The next day, as the *Jolliffe* passed Canoe Island in Porlier Pass, the crew were hailed by the tug *Burrard* out of Vancouver. She had gone hard ashore in the same fog that had stranded the *Iroquois*. The *Jolliffe* answered the

These newspaper pictures show the grounded vessel at Jack's Point, Nanaimo, prior to salvage.

distress call and the *Burrard* was hauled off with little difficulty. It was to be a profitable trip for the B.C. Salvage Company.

Running late, the powerful *Jolliffe* and her tender finally reached the stranded *Iroquois* on October 27th. She lay on her starboard, three-quarters submerged, the low seas lapping at her charthouse. From the passenger salon to the stern, she was under water. While valued at $20,000, and insured for $10,000, the rescue would cost $5,000. Thirteen times two was an unlucky number for Sears and Munro but augured well for the salvors.

Diver McHardy was lowered into the *Iroquois*. He sealed up all openings below the waterline with canvas patches held in place by boards. It must have been a daunting task for a hardhat diver, even in such shallow water. Some of the openings were eight to ten feet wide. The rescue of the *Iroquois* was as much a feat in carpentry as a marine salvage. Sealing the steamer below the waterline took 17 hours and included the removal of two hog carcasses! For McHardy, it was all in a regular day's work. There is no indication of whether any overtime pay was awarded. A bonus would certainly have been in order.

With the patches in place, the *Maude* was towed into position alongside the *Iroquois*. With her pumps moving 1,400 gallons of water a minute, she floated the *Iroquois* in little more than an hour. The steamer was towed into Nanaimo for unloading and the *Jolliffe* took her down to Victoria the next day.

The *Iroquois* had been no stranger to the ways. Sears and Munro took her out of the water annually for refit - usually done at Turple's Ways, in Victoria - after the close of each summer excursion season. Sparing no expense, the little steamer was always kept in good mechanical condition.

The *Iroquois* was cleaned up and back on her normal run by November 5th, but somehow her luck was running out. A year later, in September 1909, she lost her propeller off Ganges Harbour and had to be again towed to Victoria for repairs. Her next mishap would be her last.

The *S.S. Iroquois* had made over 2,000 trips from Sidney through the Gulf Islands in the years between 1900 and 1911. Although she had seen a few anxious moments and mishaps, nothing could have prepared the ship, her crew, or the local community for the events of April 10, 1911.

At 8:30 in the morning, as the little "Creeping Paralysis" of the Victoria and Sidney Railway made its way through rural Saanich on the way to the ferry landing at Sidney, the weather was changing. The sky had been overcast at breakfast time in Victoria, the wind only moderate. Farther out along the Peninsula, the trees swayed back and forth furiously in the southeasterly wind blowing up the channel between James and Sidney Islands.

Among the train passengers that morning were Captain George Woollet and Mrs. Woollet, who travelled nervously at the best of times. The Captain knew that she was not looking forward to their trip home to Mayne Island that day, as the train pulled off the mainline onto the dock. The Woollets disembarked along with the other passengers.

Looking about, Capt. Woollet did not like the appearance of either the weather, or the way that the *Iroquois* seemed to be loaded for the trip. Discreetly, advising a friend to join them, the Woollets climbed back aboard the train and went onward to the Sidney station - the trip home could wait another day. It was a good decision.

The remaining passengers hesitated on the wharf for a few moments, but Captain Sears, leaning out of the wheelhouse, told the crew to board them so he could get under way. It was a blustery day, to be sure, but Sears had been out in far worse weather than this. As the gusts increased, the vessel began to bang against the dock, increasing Sears' desire to get away before the ship or dock were damaged.

The Foundering
of the *Iroquois*

The ship's freight had been loaded during the previous night by deckhand Prosper David and was examined by the Mate and Captain before the departure. There were ten tons of nitrate fertilizer in sacks stowed forward; a large quantity of rice, stowed near the Chief Engineer's quarters; 20 cases of pig feed and 15 tons of mixed freight. Twenty bales of hay and a ton of bar iron were lying forward on the passenger deck. The only ballast on board was a small quantity of coal in the ship's bunkers. None of the cargo was tied down. The departure, as described by Sidney Roberts to historian T.W. Paterson, was still clearly remembered sixty years after the event:

> "Capt. Sears was at the pilothouse window, looking out, with one hand on the wheel and the other on the lever which rang the bell in the engine room. You see, they didn't have a telegraph on her, just a wire down to the engineer with a gong.
>
> "When she was ready to go, Sears'd pull the lever, the bell'd jingle - that was standby. When the stern line was let go, he'd ring twice - two bells for reverse - and she'd swing her stern out, away from the wharf. Then she'd slacken the spring line. When she's swung out far enough, they'd let the bow line go and back right out. One bell after reverse was stop, another ahead. That is the way she left the wharf for the Gulf Islands every time."[1]

The *Iroquois* was setting out in the storm. Top-heavy and with her cargo improperly secured, she pulled away from the dock. Purser Munro looked at one of the passengers, and said "If the cargo shifts, we're lost."[2]

As the steamer proceeded, the gusts seemed to increase, snapping off whitecaps and hurling them sideways against the side of the ship. White clouds scudded across the lead-grey sky and the waves came high and close together.

The government and V&S wharves at Sidney, circa 1905, with the *S.S. Iroquois* tied up at the end of the T-shaped wharf. The present Sidney wharf is just north of this site.

"When we were about to make the entrance to Canoe Channel, the wind struck us on the beam, and, together with the seas, gave the vessel a slight list. Her cargo then shifted to the lee side and when the Purser informed me of this, I (Captain Sears) sent the First Mate with the deckhands below to try to right her. While they were below I put her to the wind, but soon it was found that she would not right herself. I immediately headed for Roberts Bay with the hope that she might reach shore before she went down. We had not gone far, however, before she commenced to settle rapidly.

"When I saw that it was impossible to make the shore I ordered one of the lifeboats launched and in this I put the three ladies who were aboard, and six of the men passengers. They, however, seemed to be unable to manage the craft and as she rode in a trough of the heavy seas she swamped. Most of those who were aboard her were able to regain a hold of the boat. As the Iroquois settled her upper deck broke away and many of the passengers got on this as well as other pieces of wreckage which were floating in the vicinity.

"The other lifeboat came to the surface about twenty feet from where I was on the upper deck. We soon secured it but I discovered that a considerable portion of it had been stove in.

"Then I called for volunteers to leave the upper deck, which was almost overladen with people, and in response the Chief Engineer and three Indians came with me in the badly smashed lifeboat. I did not leave the wreckage until 20 minutes after the vessel sank and I decided that I would attempt to reach the shore and seek assistance for some of those who were imperilled in the icy waters of the Gulf...

"When I left the boat there was a large number of passengers on the upper deck, but most of them had on lifebelts and I did not think that they were in any immediate danger. I told them that they would be as safe on the wreckage as we were in the boat and that is the reason that I called for volunteers to man the vessel to go ashore for assistance."[3]

The Captain, Chief Engineer Thompson and three Indian deckhands came ashore at Armstrong's, near Sidney. After they stumbled ashore, the Captain was advised to go home and get some warm clothing - there appearing to be nothing else he could do. Later, he would be severely judged for having done so.

The Rescue

In the meantime, horrified spectators on the Sidney dock were moving into action. Seventeen-year-old Sidney Roberts, a local bank employee, watched the *Iroquois* founder. He ran into the bank with the morning mail and threw it at the teller, yelling "The Iroquois's gone down."[4] As Roberts ran past the Sidney Hotel, the manager there passed him a bottle of brandy and told him to head overland to Curteis Point to see if he could help anyone from the wreck who might land there.

George Brethour and Jim McArthur made for the scene in Brethour's launch. Watching the drama unfold from Sidney Island, a number of native canoes immediately put out into the rough waters. It was a magnificent effort and the Indians and Brethour were later credited with having saved many lives. While the rescue effort was underway at sea, a number of passengers and crew made it to shore by themselves. Engineer Thompson, deckhand Prosper David and Harry Hartnell landed at the Armstrong ranch and were assisted by the tireless Mrs. Armstrong who soon revived them.

The home of Captain Curtis was quickly converted for use as a makeshift hospital, or morgue, if Dr. Gordon Cummings' struggle to revive the victims failed. Eight had been rescued by Brethour and Armstrong and the native canoemen accounted for others. In the crowded drawing room, H.S. Moss and John Bennett lay huddled on the floor shivering in their wet underwear. They were gradually recovering from the effects of hypothermia - which was to kill so many of the passengers and crew. Passenger Joe Phillips lay wrapped in blankets nearby while the doctor worked feverishly over other prostate victims, returning life to some and sadly acknowledging that it was too late for others. (See Appendix D for list of victims and survivors).

The Brethour launch set out again in search of more survivors but when it returned at 3:40 in the afternoon, only dead bodies, nine in all, were brought ashore. All business in the little community of Sidney ceased for the day and the shocked citizens clustered along the dock waiting for news. The exact toll of the dead and missing was still not known. Finally, on Wednesday, April 12th, the casualty toll was officially set at 21 dead or missing. It was the end of an era for the Gulf Islands and the day that Sidney moved from carefree youth to sobre maturity. Even the war years ahead would not have quite the effect on the local people that was occasioned by the loss of the *S.S. Iroquois* on that blustery spring day. For most of the survivors it was the end of the ordeal, but for the unfortunate Captain Sears it was only the beginning of a long and difficult time.

Undoubtedly lengthy debates occurred and many sorrows were drowned at the Hotel Sidney following the *Iroquois* disaster.

In the days and weeks that followed, Captain Sears was forced to endure a number of legal proceedings. An experienced sailor, with 27 of his 46 years spent at sea, Sears was in danger of losing his career, his certificate as a Master Mariner, and his personal reputation. Evidence given by various witnesses at the inquest held in Sidney the next day and, adjourned until a week later, seemed to confirm that the cause of the foundering was the shifting of the unsecured cargo stored on the forward deck. Albert Sears had made the same run more than 1,600 times, frequently in rough weather, but his luck had run out.

After submitting to questioning by the coroner, Sears asked permission to make a personal statement. His first instinct was to protect himself against the strong allegations made against him for not participating any further in the rescue effort: "I wasn't in condition to put out in a boat," he said, "I see the paper puts me down for

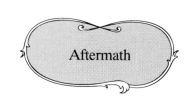

Aftermath

a murderer and everything else. I had been an hour in the water when I landed. I had confidence in the ship. The wind was against the tide. All the windows were closed and there was no danger until the cargo shifted."

The coroner and jury made particular mention of the heroic actions of the three Cowichan Indians, who had put to sea in their open canoe, at great personal risk, to save the lives of three passengers. Grateful citizens later took up a collection for the native heroes. The inquest was then adjourned and the victims laid to rest over the next few days.

The toll of dead and missing was high and all the more appalling in that spectators on the dock had watched helplessly while the *Iroquois* struggled through her final moments. The inquest alone was a trial for Sears and Engineer Thompson, but the public was demanding a full investigation of the sinking.

On April 17, 1911, the *Victoria Times* announced that Albert A. Sears had been charged with manslaughter after a preliminary police investigation. The Federal Government in Ottawa promised a full inquiry. Sears was placed under arrest and bail fixed at $30,000. He appeared in court to answer the charges on April 20th. After bonds were posted on his behalf, he was released.

The Sears manslaughter trial opened in the Assize Court in June 1911, and after less than five minutes deliberation, the Captain was found not guilty in the death of John Brydson, one of the unfortunate victims of the foundering. Apparently, the summing up of the case by Judge Morrison of the Assize Court had a significant effect on the jury members. It was strongly sympathetic to Captain Sears.

The Judge had cautioned the jurors that the proceeding was a criminal one and that they should concern themselves only with the question of whether or not the Captain had acted without lawful excuse in the performance of a legal duty. An error in judgement on the Captain's part was not to be construed as just reason for a guilty finding. More than a simple error had to be shown. "Now," said His Lordship, "what facts of the evidence show him to have been wicked or careless?"[5] Sears had endured an inquest, a preliminary hearing and a manslaughter trial, but his ordeal was still not over.

Admiralty Court Findings

The Admiralty Court held an inquiry into the actions of Captain Sears and Engineer Thompson, during September 1911, and, while they found the harsh comments on his conduct after the wreck were not justified by the evidence, Sears nevertheless was deemed to have failed to perform his duty in rescue work and in the stowage of cargo. The court's findings are worthy of inclusion here:

> "After hearing the evidence of a great number of witnesses in the course of the hearing, which occupied eleven days, the court has reached the following conclusions:
> 1. That the disaster was caused by the fact that shortly after leaving, the ship became subject to a heavy beam sea which made her roll violently and owing to the improperly distributed weights...her stability was impaired to such a degree that it rendered her recovery impossible...We are unable to accept the explanation offered by the Master that the loss of the ship was occasioned by her being damaged by a dislodged pile before leaving the wharf; the evidence not being sufficient to support such a theory.
> 2. The result of the ship heeling to such extent was rendered more dangerous by final submersion of improperly protected apertures, that is to say, the windows on the main deck, which due to their faulty construction, being merely ordinary drop window sashes glazed with common glass, were useless to keep out or prevent for any appreciable time the inrush of water.
> 3. With respect to the boats, after an inspection of them in the

light of evidence, we did not find them to be wanting in either number or cubic capacity, but they were not built 'whaleboat fashion' as required...by the Inspection Rules...

5. There does not appear to have been any proper means of communication between the wheelhouse and engine room...

7. Finally, with respect to the officers, the court finds that:

(a) The Mate, John Isbister, was incompetent and responsible for the negligent and improper stowage of cargo inasmuch that although he had ample time to stow and secure it so as not to impair the stability of the ship...failed to perform his duty in this respect and neglected to do so...his certificate should be and is hereby suspended for six months.

(b) That William Thompson, the engineer, left the engine room of which he was the officer in charge, while the engines were still in motion, before circumstances warranted his doing so...His conduct all through the disaster seems to have been on the principle of 'everyone for himself,' to use his own words to the purser, and therefore his certificate should be and is hereby suspended for a period of nine months from this date.

(c) With respect to Albert A. Sears, Master, while no fault is to be found with his conduct after he reached the shore from the wreck, and the harsh comments made about him in that respect were not justified by the evidence, yet he failed to perform his duty in either personally making a more determined effort to rescue the people in the water, or alternatively in staying by the wreck to the last, and sending the Mate to their assistance. Also, in addition to his general responsibility as regards the stowage of cargo, he assumed responsibility that morning for the negligent and improper stowage thereof by not having ordered any other alteration after inspecting the same than the placing of a dunnage grating under some of it.

Also, he failed in his ability as a seaman and master of the vessel in allowing the boats in their damaged and unseaworthy condition to leave the wreck when they could have remained attached to and under the lea of same, with considerable prospect of safety.

In such circumstances and in view of the deplorable consequences of his failure as aforementioned, the court feels, after considering his conduct in the most favorable light possible, that it would not, in the public interest, be just or safe to allow him any longer to retain his Master's Certificate, and therefore the same is hereby cancelled."[6]

Eighteen months after the tragic loss of the steamer, along with 21 passengers and crew members, the final chapter was written on the *S.S. Iroquois*. On November 5, 1912, William Tzouhalem, Bob Klutzwhalen and Donat Charlie, all of the Cowichan Band, who had been clamming when they witnessed the sinking, were presented with gold medals for their heroism in rescuing three of the *Iroquois* survivors. That recognition was due in part to the efforts of Mr. Justice Martin, who commended the heroes at the time of the Sears manslaughter trial and later in correspondence with the federal government.

The gold medals were presented by F.H. Shepherd, MP, in a moving ceremony at the Duncan Agricultural Hall. In an ironic twist, Shepherd made the presentation with the comment that, "The bravery of these men has shown that the Indians on this Coast could be every bit as brave as whitemen, and that they (apparently) possessed the same love of life as the whiteman." [7]

Today, the warm summer evening excursions and the day-to-day business of moving people and goods between Sidney, the Gulf Islands and Nanaimo on the *S.S. Iroquois*, are a distant memory. The ship's hull was located by divers in the 1970s and her screw, along with some smaller artifacts were recovered - all that remains, save the memories and a few faded photographs.

In the months following the wreck of the *Iroquois*, passenger revenues declined noticeably on the Victoria and Sidney Railway. Steamer service from Sidney to the Islands was restored, in January 1912, when the Canadian Pacific Navigation Company inaugurated a new Gulf Islands schedule utilizing the steamer *Joan*.

While that service was renewed, the arrival of competition in the form of the B.C. Electric Railway Company's Saanich interurban line would soon add an even greater burden to the struggling little Victoria and Sidney Railway. Along the 16 miles of rusting, weedbound track between the capital city and the Saanich Peninsula terminus at Sidney it was business very much as usual.

Divers salvaged these souvenirs from the wreck of the *Iroquois* during the 1970s. The propellor stands at Iroquois Park in Sidney. The earthen and glassware are from the Sidney Museum.

12

COMMERCE, CONFLICT AND COMPETITION, 1911-1913

The Same Old Situation - Still

The years preceding World War One were the most prosperous in the history of the Victoria and Sidney Railway and the Victoria Terminal Railway and Ferry Company. The freight business was steadily improving and passenger revenues were up substantially, despite the poor condition of the passenger equipment and the railway line between Victoria and Sidney.

The ferry connection with the Great Northern system on the B.C. Mainland was the source of most of the increased freight shipments. The tug and barge service ran on an as-required basis, rather than a regular schedule. Barge connections were made at Liverpool, Port Guichon and Blaine, Washington.

In addition to Sidney, Great Northern rail barges also called at ports along the east coast of Vancouver Island as far north as Union Bay. The combined railway and ferry services were money making propositions for the Great Northern.

Unfortunately, the V&S roadbed, plant and rolling stock was receiving only minimal maintenance and public complaints about the line continued as before. The situation on the mile-long VTR&F track from Hillside Avenue to the Blanshard Street Station in Victoria was equally as bad.

To further complicate matters, the City of Victoria was increasingly concerned about continuing payment of its interest guarantee on the V&S Railway's bonds. At $9,000 per year, plus interest on interest, it was a significant figure. Yet, the City was not getting the kind of railway service it deserved in view of its financial support.

Not only were Victoria and Sidney patrons unhappy about dilapidated passenger cars, rundown engines, poorly ballasted roadbed, lack of decent station facilities and little attention to published schedules - as municipal and provincial ratepayers, they were ironically providing a $15,000 annual premium to subsidize this less than adequate service. Unless there should be some prospect of increased income from the V&S, well above the annual interest guarantees of $15,000, there was no real incentive for the V&S, or its parent, the Great Northern Railway, to do anything other than provide the minimum service possible. That is, unless some other form of incentive or persuasion could be found to force improvements to be made on the local Saanich Peninsula service.

Inadequate service had begun under the administration of T.W. Paterson. The situation remained unchanged during the brief period of Victoria Terminal Railway and Ferry Company ownership. It continued under the ownership of the Great Northern Railway when it gained control of the former companies, by purchase of outstanding stock in 1902.

Left:
This little "crummy" or "bouncer" as she was often called, was loaned to the V&S by the Great Northern and was involved in the fatal accident of August 11, 1911 (see p.164). Caboose No.0244 was apparently rebuilt and used on the freight trains until the Great Northern withdrew its equipment in 1917.

Legal action had already been initiated by the City of Victoria against the VTR&F in a statement of claim filed on April 20, 1907. The matter dragged on in the courts for more than two years. On June 12, 1909, the Chief Justice of the Supreme Court gave his decision in the case, requiring the VTR&F to vacate the Market Building, move to new facilities on Blanshard Street, and make other improvements (see Chapter 10). However, the VTR&F and the Victoria and Sidney Railway were really two separate companies.

Most of the changes, required of the VTR&F in the 1909 court decision, had been implemented in one way or another, but the stingy Great Northern Railway continued to restrict maintenance expenditures on its other Vancouver Island subsidiary, the Victoria and Sidney Railway. Any changes it did make gave priority to enticing freight prospects rather than emphasizing better and more comfortable passenger accommodation.

Unfortunately, nothing had been done to compel the V&S to resolve the issue of the bond interest guarantees by the City of Victoria and the Province.

The rolling stock was still shabby and run-down, the locomotives were in bad shape and station facilities between Victoria and Sidney were all but non-existent. The railway had lost its lucrative Gulf Islands ferry connection in the spring of 1911. Soon it would face freight and passenger competition on the Saanich Peninsula from both the British Columbia Electric Railway and the Canadian Northern Pacific Railway.

Tragedy at Elk Lake

The sadly deteriorated condition of the Victoria and Sidney was, once again, brought forcibly to public attention on August 8, 1911 when a tragic derailment occurred on the line.

R. Lane was the night watchman and engine hostler for the V&S but occasionally made a run out to Sidney for the company when the regular brakeman was off. It was one of those warm, languid summer days when the air hung heavy, the breeze was non-existent and the waters of Elk Lake lay as flat as a mirror. Even the green leaves of the Red alder trees and Broadleaf maples hung limply in the still air.

Lane had agreed to go out to Sidney on the morning run, after working all night in the roundhouse. Although tired, he was enjoying the view from the cupola of the little four-wheeled "bobber" caboose of the V&S as it bounced its way towards Royal Oak. From time to time, Lane exchanged pleasantries with Conductor Walker who was riding in the cabin of the caboose below.

There was the usual run at the Royal Oak hill. That sometimes took more than one try, but this day they made it on the first attempt. The nine-car train was made up mostly of empties. The train topped the hill at Royal Oak, ran over the bridges at Snyder's Ravine and Colquitz Creek, swung into the woods at Beaver Lake and headed towards the highest part of the line.

There was always a fine view from the rock cut along the west side of Elk Lake and Lane probably enjoyed it as much that day as he had on numerous other occasions. From the grade at the rock cut, the calm lake water reflected the surroundings of the adjacent marsh and forestland. It was a pretty picture. All seemed well, and the siding at the north end of Elk Lake was just coming into sight. Then something went terribly wrong.

As the engine entered the trackage at the makeshift station, the 4-wheeled "bobber" suddenly leaped from the track and rolled downward toward the lake, smashing the little cupola from the roof of the caboose. Lane was thrown from his high seat and landed under the wreckage. Beyond human help by the time the rest of the crew reached him, his body was laid reverently aside, and the rescuers turned their attention to Robert Walker.

Conductor Walker, who was also on board the caboose, was badly cut and shaken but not seriously injured. Derailments on the V&S were an everyday occurrence - death was not.

The demise of Lane had a sobering effect on his fellow trainmen. Unfortunately, it did not create a ripple of concern in Great Northern headquarters at Seattle, or St. Paul, Minnesota. Nor did it result in improvements to the roadbed or equipment of the V&S line. The tragedy seemingly went unnoticed even in high bureaucratic places. Neither did it seem to phase or deter the long-suffering public who regularly rode the V&S trains to and from Victoria and Sidney.

The dramatic increase in ridership on the V&S during the 1911-12 period was due to a local Saanich Peninsula real estate boom that brought many new settlers into the area. Some were lured by good agricultural land, then readily available in Saanich. Others were hoping just to reside there and travel to work in Victoria over the new Interurban Line of the B.C. Electric Railway which was expected to begin public service in the summer of 1913. New subdivisions were replacing farms in many parts of South Saanich. The southern end of the Peninsula was starting to become more urban than rural in character. The V&S was doing as well as could be expected under the circumstances. Unfortunately, public dissatisfaction and the unresolved issue of the old $300,000 bond interest guarantees by the City and Province were still combining to create increasing difficulties.

This seagull's eye view of the Saanich Peninsula dates from about 1914 and shows the V&S as well as the new British Columbia Electric Interurban line.

Watch Sidney Grow!

S I D N E Y

WHARF

SAW MILL

FERRY SLIP

PROPOSED LINE TO SIDNEY

V. & S. RY

SAW-MILL

BRICK & TILE FACTORY

DOMINION GOVT. EXPERIMENTAL FARM

BAZAN BAY

SHINGLE MILL

B.C. ELECTRIC RAILWAY

VICTORIA

VICTORIA HARB

g. currie '92.

The City and the Province of British Columbia had paid out a great deal of money on the interest guarantees and the bonds were about to mature in 1917. Whoever held the bonds at that time would be in for a great expense as no sinking funds had been put aside since 1892 to provide for payment of the $300,000 debt. If nothing was done to recover the payments made in guarantee of the bond interest before the maturity date in 1917, there would be no hope of recovering monies the City and Province had paid out. Clearly, something had to be done - and quickly!

Above:
Promoters had high hopes for the growth of Sidney. This drawing was part of an advertising campaign in the *Colonist* in 1911.

The next opportunity for the City of Victoria to act came at a meeting of the Dominion Board of Railway Commissioners at Vancouver in late August, 1911. As guarantors of the bond interest, the City and the Province were entitled to first consideration if, and when, the V&S Railway began to operate on a profitable basis.

The City was sure that the railway had made some money over the previous year or two. They claimed that they should be paid $22,000 plus the 1911 bond interest guarantee of $9,000, and asked to be relieved of any further bond interest payments. In return, the City offered to relinquish its claim to the $170,000 it had stood as bondsman through the non-profitable years of the V&S. It was a costly idea, but one which would at least minimize the City's loss. The City Solicitor's report was written up in the *Victoria Daily Times* on September 2, 1911:

> "We issued a writ for the payment of a sum of $170,000, interest on the bonds of the Railway, which the City guaranteed in 1892, and of which between $4,000 and $5,000* has been paid, with 6 ½ years still to run. The City issued a writ, and the Attorney-General, on behalf of the government, served notice - the government having guaranteed ²/₅ and the city the remaining ³/₅. There is now owing to the government the sum of $100,000 and the city $170,000. At the conference, the officials of the Great Northern, who are now coming in, pointed out that last year the road was not earning enough to pay operating expenses and pay the interest on the bonds. For the past three years, however, they admitted that the road has earned something over and above the cost of operating, that aggregate earning for the three years being computed at $40,975.
>
> "The Attorney-General, through an audit, says he has information which leads him to believe that considerably more than the amount named in the company's statement has been earned. The proposition, as agreed by the legal advisors of the respective parties, was that the use and benefit of the railroad to the province and city be recognized, and that it be understood that we do not say anything about the payment of the interest during the years in which they did not make any profit over and above the cost of operating and maintaining the road, and also that it was only fair to assume that when the road was making money the city was entitled to the first charge upon everything over and above operating expenses.
>
> "This the Great Northern has agreed to do, and the amount will be ascertained by an examination of the company's books..."

But talk was cheap, and the City of Victoria knew that pressure would have to be brought to bear on the Great Northern officials in far-away St. Paul, Minnesota, if there was to be any concrete result. While this matter was being pursued, the City decided to add further pressure through the province's Minister of Railways.

On October 6, 1911, a list of 15 complaints was submitted to the Hon. Thomas Taylor, Minister of Railways. These complaints did not concern the V&S directly, but related to a number of problems with the Victoria Terminal Railway and Ferry Company in the heart of the city. This was an opening manoeuvre. It would be followed by complaints against the V&S itself, resulting in a detailed engineering examination of the railway by the Minister.

However, these tactics by the City seemed to have little effect. The winter of 1911 passed and nothing further was done. It was not until June 1912 that there was any real action towards a solution, when Louis Hill, new President of the Great Northern, and Traffic Manager Costello of the same road, arrived in Victoria to confer with Premier McBride.

The Great Northern officials had a long audience with the Premier and while most of the discussion concerned the construction of the Great Northern's subsidiary

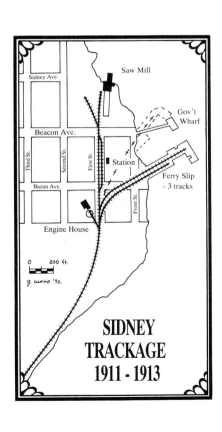

SIDNEY
TRACKAGE
1911 - 1913

* Presumably, the reference to "$4,000 to $5,000" meant retirement of the original principal.

Vancouver, Victoria and Eastern Railway on the Mainland, the subject of the Victoria and Sidney Railway also came up.

"From my discussion with Mr. Hill," said the Premier, "you may say that it is highly probable that within the next few weeks some very important development work will be undertaken by this concern."[1] Beyond that, the Premier had little to divulge. The *Colonist* of June 7, 1912 went on to say that "It was rumoured, immediately upon his (Hill's) arrival, that he was here in connection with a proposal to sell the Victoria and Sidney line to the Canadian Northern, but it was impossible to obtain any confirmation of this statement."[2]

Hope had been brief, a solution seemed no nearer than before. One positive announcement was that Mr. L.C. Gilman, Assistant to the President of the GNR, would come to Victoria later in the year to try to work out a deal with the City and the Province. Premier McBride had more to say on the matter in a speech on provincial railways, which was reported in the *Daily Colonist* on July 13, 1912:

> "As to the Victoria and Sidney line, which is controlled by the Great Northern, I am unable to report that I received any assurance from him (Louis Hill) that there would be at once any considerable improvement of the line....The latest reports from the government go to show that the road is paying, and considering the fact that we can expect a tremendous settlement on the Saanich Peninsula we may expect it to pay even better. But I received no promise from Mr. Hill that the road would be improved. The government must go on and see what it can do, and it is proposed that we shall press the thing so that presently you will get a better service and the province a better return for its investment...But so far as this government is concerned - and the Victoria and Sidney Railway is under our control - we intend to have the system give a better service, pay more attention to the patrons, put on modern equipment and, instead of what is worse than a logging road from this beautiful city to the end of the Peninsula, something that the citizens can take pleasure in.
>
> "I do not want this to be taken as any complaint against the Great Northern in general, because we must remember that the company has spent much in the province...At the same time, if they will only right conditions here and hurry along the construction of the V.V.&E., they might stand better with the people of the province..."[3]

The "Cordwood Limited" in 1912. By this date the original third yard track had been replaced by a siding farther south along the line and the weeds seemed anxious to complete their takeover of the property.

More at Stake

There was more at stake than just the Victoria and Sidney Railway. The Vancouver, Victoria and Eastern (Great Northern's main British Columbia property) was, in the spring of 1912, competing with the Kettle Valley Railway for occupation of a right-of-way down the Coquihalla River, from the summit of the Coast Range mountains to Hope. While the federal authority had some jurisdiction in the matter, the Province had the right to grant or deny the right-of-way. The completion of the VV&E and its linkage with the Gulf ferry-barge service would give Victoria direct connection with the booming Kootenays. There was only room for one railway route in the Coquihalla Canyon and the Kettle Valley Railway and the Vancouver, Victoria and Eastern both wanted to occupy it.

The Province of British Columbia might finally have some leverage to force the Great Northern to do something about the lamentable state of the Victoria and Sidney Railway in return for some kind of access to the Coquihalla route. Time would tell.

Coming to an Arrangement

After some further delay, Gilman arrived in Victoria at the end of September to negotiate with the City and Province over the Victoria and Sidney Railway. An investigation of the line by the Minister of Railways in the meantime had shown the rolling stock, roadbed, stations and plant of the line to be in poor shape. Gilman promised that the V&S would submit to the Minister a list of improvements that it would make, as well as indicate what service improvements might be possible. The City waited anxiously for this - the Minister was empowered to order improvements, if necessary.

First Offer to Settle

Gilman also offered to settle the matter of the outstanding bond interest guarantee with the City and to pay $36,000 cash, in full payment and settlement of all claims against the V&S by the City. The Great Northern would then guarantee V&S Company payment of all future interest accruing on the bonds and indemnify the City and Province against any further loss or payment on account of their interest guarantee. Further, the V&S would be put in suitable condition for freight and passenger traffic. Full details of the offer were published on October 2nd:

> "The offer came before the Council in the nature of a report from the Finance Committee recommending its acceptance. Alderman Okell, Chairman of the Committee, pointed out the negotiations had been underway for some time and the City had endeavoured to secure a better offer. While the Great Northern is behind the V&S Company's offer, the Committee believe the offer to be the best that can be secured and gives the City a very favourable opportunity of getting out of a bad bargain. In 1893 the City and the Province guaranteed interest upon $300,000 bonds floated by the V&S, the City guaranteeing $9,000 per annum and the province $6,000. For the past twenty years these payments have been made by the city and province, the company never having been able to make receipts exceeding expenditures, and until that happens the interest charges were to be paid by the guarantors. They (the bonds) mature in 1917. The city has paid in interest charges about $180,000, and with interest on interest a total of $297,541, and the province $198,000, or a total of $495,000, and with the $300,000 bonds the liability of the company is approximately $975,000. The company controls 17 miles of line in very poor condition, but the terminals at Victoria and Sidney are held by other concerns, the Victoria Terminals being owned by the Victoria Terminal Railway and Ferry Company. The company's offer of $36,000 to the city and $24,000 to the government is approximately what the company during the past three years has earned over and above operating charges, and what it should have paid toward the interest charges it allowed the city and province to pay."[4]

The chance of the City and Province recovering their interest guarantee monies was dismal. If they proceeded against the railway in the courts and won, they would have on their hands seventeen miles of dilapidated railway line, with no public goodwill - and by 1917 would have to face payment of the principal on the original $300,000 bonds.

To further complicate the situation, completion of the BCER's Interurban line along the Saanich Peninsula would offer strong competition and take away much of the Victoria and Sidney Railway's traditional passenger traffic.

The Railway's offer to the City wasn't considered to be much of an offer at all by many members of City Council and local ratepayers. In fact, it was so bad that they rejected it on general principle. The local papers pointed out that the offer would give the City and Province less than 50 cents on each dollar they had paid out. The Mayor wanted to accept the bad bargain and get out of the situation altogether. In his power as Chief Magistrate, he asked Council to reconsider the matter. The public were well aware of the situation and Robert Paten, of Saanichton, let the *Daily Colonist* know just what he thought of the V&S Railway in a letter to the editor:

> "Dear Sir,- May I be allowed to express a hope, through your columns, that the authorities will not accept the very inadequate sum offered by the V&S Railway in full settlement of the claims against them.
>
> "...in view of the fact that the Saanich Peninsula is so closely connected with Victoria and is absorbing more new residents and generally progressing more rapidly than any part of the Island, there cannot be any doubt that the railway, today, is, a property of the shrewd gentlemen who direct it, to ever come into the city's possession...
>
> "The effect of the promises made by the company in the past do not justify the public in attaching any undue importance to those forming part of the present proposed agreement, and as the past history of the V.&S. is an unsatisfactory one, from every point of view, it is to be trusted that political and financial wire pulling may not meet with the success it has so frequently obtained, and I trust you will bring your influence to bear, thus ensuring an open and proper consideration of the matter.
>
> Robert B. Paten   Newtoncroft, Saanichton"[5]

Northbound passenger train with locomotive No.1 near Elk Lake in 1913. Today this part of the old grade is a beautiful community hiking and cycling path.

The problems seemed to go on and on. Finally, in November, it was announced that the City would be permitted to audit the books of the Victoria and Sidney Railway, which were kept in the Great Northern Railway offices at Seattle, with a view to coming up with a more equitable settlement. While this matter was being undertaken, there was yet another flurry of complaints against the VTR&F by Blanshard Street landowners against the spotting and unloading of freight cars south of Fisgard Street. These complaints would have to wait until the audit was dealt with.

The City appointed Charles A. Forsythe, Chartered Accountant, to go to Seattle for the audit. Forsythe spent three weeks in a detailed examination of the V&S's finances, receiving full co-operation from Great Northern Railway officials. He submitted his report to Victoria Council, details of which were published in the *Daily Colonist* on December 17, 1912. In summary, Forsythe's findings indicated:

1. The capital stock of the V&S at the time it passed under Great Northern control in 1902 was $223,000 and this amount was subsequently reduced by the cancellation of 1,200 shares formerly held by the original Sidney Land Company but never paid up.

2. The company's profit and loss figures up to August 31, 1912 were:

April 1, 1903 to June 30, 1903,	profit	$403.30
Year ended June 30, 1904	loss	-$4,006.43
Year ended June 30, 1905	loss	-$8,704.87
Year ended June 30, 1906	profit	$1,725.69
Year ended June 30, 1907	profit	$5,932.69
Year ended June 30, 1908	profit	$1,892.06
Year ended June 30, 1909	profit	$10,716.98
Year ended June 30, 1910	profit	$12,594.16
Year ended June 30, 1911	profit	$17,664.72
Year ended June 30, 1912	profit	$3,920.43
July and August 1912	profit	$1,709.82

Gross operating profit from April 1903 to August 31, 1912 (nine years and five months) was $43,848.50. Other adjustments to the company's books, notably for cancelled shares, raised Forsythe's estimate of the profits to $51,093.57.

3. Some payments had been made to parties other than the City of Victoria and the Province of British Columbia, who had first call on any profits.

In spite of the revealed facts, Forsythe concluded his report by saying that the accounts of the Victoria and Sidney Railway had been kept with "scrupulous accuracy." However, any comparison of these figures and those in the Dominion Government Railway Statistics show major discrepancies. Earlier figures submitted by the V&S Company's own auditor showed different totals again. These apparent discrepancies may be simply due to different methods of assembling financial data by the railway company as opposed to the government authority or Mr. Forsythe.

With accurate and trustworthy data in the hands of Victoria City Council it was hoped that a final figure for a settlement between the City, the Province and the Railway could finally be worked out.

The Railway Report of January 1913

The Minister of Railways had ordered an inspection of the line by the Department's Chief Engineer in the autumn of 1912 and the report was released in January 1913, in time to bring further pressure on the railway company. The list of improvements ordered by the Minister were exhaustive (See Appendix E). There was no doubt that the Great Northern, as owner of the V&S, was finally going to be forced to improve the railway.

An out of court settlement was preferable to the City, who otherwise would have to take over and operate the railway itself. "To have foreclosed and taken it over," said the *Colonist* of January 15, 1913, "would have involved the assumption of a liability of $300,000 on account of the principal of the bonds, of approximately $200,000 for betterments, and $45,000 for interest; in all $545,000, for a railway 17 miles long, without any connection with any other road."

Before the final details could be worked out, disaster struck again at the railway. On the morning of February 12, 1913, the Victoria roundhouse burned down. The building was not insured but, as the company was shortly planning to relocate its engine facilities from there, the loss was not as serious as it might otherwise have been.

Its most familiar nickname was the "Cordwood Limited," but other appellations included the "Tinpot Railway" and the "Creeping Paralysis." By all rules of logic and economics, the Victoria and Sidney Railway had been a dismal failure. In spite of it all, the line was still vital for many people living along the Saanich Peninsula and to the merchants of Victoria who used its freight connections.

Full and final settlement of the differences between the City and the Victoria and Sidney Railway was completed in April 1913. In the agreement, the company was to pay the City $49,500 and the Province $33,000, besides promised improvements to its line. It further had to assume all responsibility for future bond interest payments.

For its part, the City of Victoria released the company from all future financial claims. It had taken 21 years, but the City had finally divested itself of any further financial interest in the Victoria and Sidney Railway. From then on it would be strictly up to the V&S and its parent company to meet financial obligations.

The No.1 Locomotive and crew at Elk Lake passing track in August 1912. Crew from left to right are Conductor Lacoursiere, Fireman R. Mellado and Engineer George Duncan. Brakeman R. Halco peers over the weeds at right.

The Improvements of 1913

With the matter of the bond interest guarantees settled, the railway company moved ahead with plans to implement improvements to its line and equipment as ordered by the Minister of Railways. At the end of June, Superintendent Frank Van Sant announced the pending addition of a third daily passenger train and the acquisition of a new gasoline-electric car with comfortable passenger, as well as express, accommodations. It was even powerful enough to handle a freight car or two when required. To reverse the gas-electric at terminals, the company's old 56-foot turntables had to be replaced with new ones 70 feet in length. The new car arrived in Victoria on June 14, 1913 and was placed on the Sidney run a few days later:

GAS-ELECTRIC CAR NOW IN OPERATION

Improved Passenger Service
Over The V&S Railway
Inaugurated Yesterday - New
Schedule Next Week

"Officials of the V&S Railway Co. are in every way satisfied with the performance of the gas-electric motor car which was placed in actual service on the run between Victoria and Sidney yesterday afternoon.

"A trial trip was held on Thursday, which proved that the locomotive may be expected to do acceptable work as the recommendations of the manufacturers, and the results it has given on other similar lines have led the management to believe. As the necessary turn-tables have been completed both at the terminals of this city and of Sidney, the car was pressed into service yesterday, Mr. Van Sant, the local manager, Mr. R.W. Dale, general agent of the Great Northern Railway, and other railway men interested, making the run...

"In connection with the V&S Railway improvement it is stated that the work of improving the roadbed is well underway, about 50 men being engaged at present in the vicinity of Elk Lake. It is expected that the thorough overhauling which it is planned to give the line will be completed in three months."[6]

Great Northern's Gas-Electric car No.2301 southbound at the Elk Lake passing track on June 21, 1916. Freight and passenger trains usually passed each other at this point. The boxcar was used to carry milk shipments.

By August of 1913 things on the railway were really improving. Residents of South Saanich wanted even better service and passenger loadings were up along the line. Frank Van Sant indicated that freight traffic over the line was brisker than it had ever been. Improvement to the roadbed that year cost upwards of $30,000, the entire line being reballasted and the number of ties increased by 25%. Even the bridges were rebuilt and in early 1914 the Great Northern Railway constructed a new dock and barge slip in Sidney, off the end of Second Street, to accommodate the new and larger barges coming into service.

The Victoria and Sidney, from its Sidney terminus to its transfer onto the trackage of the VTR&F in Victoria, had been a disgrace to properly run railways everywhere for most of the 20 years since its construction began in 1892. The equipment was rundown, the engines leaked and wheezed until they hardly had the power to move themselves, never mind the cars. There was not even a working on-line telephone system. The right-of-way was not properly fenced, the ties were too few and many were rotting into the ground. Rails were warped and bridges sagged. Schedules were meant as rough guides for the crews, and "not for public information." In fact, when all the bad things were added up, it seemed nearly impossible that there could be anything good to say about the V&S.

And yet there was. In the face of inadequate maintenance, debilitated equipment and plant, engines and rolling stock in a ruinous state, stations in shambles, the saving grace of the old "Cordwood Limited" for all the years there had been a V&S train was the genuine kindness and good natured caring of the crews for their patrons. Conductor Andy Forbes or Herman Shade would stop the train to let off or pick up passengers or hunters anywhere. Some crew members were even said to do a little shopping for ladies along the line.

The improvements made to the V&S and VTR&F in 1913 were by far the most substantial on the line since its inception. Considering that the company had received a $15,000 annual subsidy in keeping the line exactly as it was, if it were to suddenly

V&S auditor W.M. Thomas was usually stationed in the Great Northern's office at Seattle. Frank Van Sant (right) was the local manager of the V&S and VTR&F. This picture probably dates from about 1913 when the V&S was given a major upgrading.

make large sums of money, it would have to be well in excess of that figure. Otherwise, the scheme was to keep the status quo so that the railway would be worn out and worthless when its bonds became due in 1917. That would ensure extracting the maximum inflow of dollars for the V&S/VTR&F in annual bond interest guarantees and leaving any receiver with a bankrupt, worthless property. Why didn't it happen that way?

The clear answer is found in two items appearing in the Victoria *Daily Colonist* of July 9, 1913. Great Northern's L.C. Gilman finally told it like it was:

THE VICTORIA AND SIDNEY

"There is not very much new in the interview of Mr. L.C. Gilman, Assistant to the President of the Great Northern Railway, which we print this morning, but it is very satisfactory to have an assurance from him that he proposes to do what he can to make the Victoria and Sidney a railway. He also fixes a date by which he expects the line across the Hope Mountains to be completed by 1915, and this will give the Great Northern a continuous route from Victoria to southern British Columbia. This suggests in brief retrospect:

"When what is now the Victoria and Sidney was first suggested, we think it was by Amor De Cosmos, or at least his name was so prominently identified with it that it formed a part of what was known as the 'De Cosmos Scheme,' the idea was that Victoria should thereby be given a connection with the Mainland by way of a car ferry, and thence with Interior points. Later this project was revived by an organization called the Vancouver, Victoria and Eastern Railway Company, under whose charter the Great Northern has constructed a part of its line in southern British Columbia. Several futile efforts were made by the provincial government to secure the construction of this railway. After a time the opinion gained ground that the Hope Mountains presented an insurmountable obstacle to the construction of a railway. This has now been shown not to be the case, and the Great Northern and the Kettle River Valley Railway will come across this range on the same grade. Thus the long talked-of Coast to Kootenay Railway is about to become a reality..."[7]

In a later interview with the *Colonist* on the same date Gilman was quoted as saying:

"Now that the financial problems as between the Road (V&S), the city and the province, have been adjusted satisfactorily to all parties, it is our intention to make the Railway what it ought to be - a very important link in our system, and of much greater service than in the past to the travelling public through the districts served.

"Several gasoline electric engines of the most approved type are to be utilized immediately and a much improved service will be possible. Track improvements of a very extensive nature are now in hand. Just as soon as we have our road through the Hope Mountains completed - which date is fixed for January 1, 1915 - we will link up our service with the Victoria and Sidney line and run trains from this city to points not only reached by the road in southern British Columbia, but to all points on the Great Northern Transcontinental Line."[8]

For a brief time, in the summer of 1913, it seemed as if the troubled old V&S and its partner, the VTR&F, were about to finally realize the greatness forecast for the railway system so many years earlier. The old De Cosmos scheme and the later Victoria and Sidney Railway scheme were both essential links in the dream of a Coast

Victoria & Sidney Ry.

TO

Rogers Crossing

Royal Oak

Beaver Lake

Elk Lake

Keating

Saanichton

Mount Baker Park

Experimental Farm

Sidney

VICTORIA & SIDNEY RAILWAY

GAS-ELECTRIC MOTOR CAR SERVICE

TIME SCHEDULE
Effective November 16, 1913

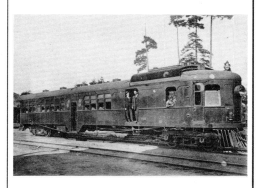

Victoria & Sidney Railway

TIME SCHEDULE

Effective November 16, 1913

NORTHBOUND		Except Sunday	Except Sunday	Daily	Sunday Only
Leave	VICTORIA............	8.00AM	10.45AM	5.00PM	10.00AM
	ROYAL OAK..........	8.20AM	11.05AM	5.20PM	10.20AM
	BEAVER LAKE......	8.25AM	11.10AM	5.25PM	10.25AM
	ELK LAKE.............	8.35AM	11.20AM	5.35PM	10.35AM
	KEATING..............	8.40AM	11.25AM	5.40PM	10.40AM
	SAANICHTON.......	8.45AM	11.30AM	5.45PM	10.45AM
Arrive	SIDNEY.................	9.00AM	11.45AM	6.00PM	11.00AM
SOUTHBOUND		Daily	Daily	Daily	
Leave	SIDNEY.................	9.15AM	1.00PM	6.15PM	....
	SAANICHTON.......	9.30AM	1.15PM	6.30PM	....
	KEATING..............	9.35AM	1.20PM	6.35PM	....
	ELK LAKE.............	9.40AM	1.25PM	6.40PM	....
	BEAVER LAKE.......	9.50AM	1.35PM	6.50PM	....
	ROYAL OAK..........	9.55AM	1.40PM	6.55PM	....
Arrive	VICTORIA.............	10.15AM	2.00PM	7.15PM	....

to Kootenay railway system. The connection seemed almost at hand, with the pending completion of the VV&E through the mountains to Hope.

As always though, there were a number of obstacles to be overcome. These would include the growing incursion of the automobile, better roads and competition from the British Columbia Electric Railway which began in 1913 at the same time as the City and Province were finally extricating themselves from the heavy obligations of the old bond interest guarantee of 1892. And worst of all, the world would soon be locked into a long and deadly war that would affect the whole country. These were the last few years for the V&S, and in spite of a number of positive changes, it would not be an easy time.

The Arrival of Electric Railway Competition

The possibility of a competing line of electric railway along the Saanich Peninsula had been under discussion for a number of years. The lack of a sufficiently large population to support two railway lines on the Peninsula, when the one existing steam line was not doing well by itself, was not considered a deterrent.

The development of the British Columbia Electric Railway's Interurban line in the Fraser Valley had fostered a great deal of agricultural and suburban development there. A real estate boom on the Saanich Peninsula in the 1910-1912 period seemed to confirm that the construction of an interurban line there would also be a success. The possibility that it might have an adverse effect on the Victoria and Sidney Railway was not a serious consideration in an age when it was common practice to build one railway to "kill off" another. In fact, were it not for a lack of sufficient electric power, the BCER would probably have built its Saanich Peninsula line years earlier than it did.

As a prelude to commencing construction of extensions to its Victoria street railway system, the Directors of the BCER announced, in December 1909, that they would develop the hydro-electric power resources of the Jordan River, fifty miles west of Victoria. It was this and the construction of a steam-powered auxiliary plant at Tod Inlet, on the west side of the Saanich Peninsula, that finally gave the company sufficient power to permit construction of their electric freight and passenger line.

Preparatory steps for extension of the railway system were announced on January 1, 1910, when the BCER took an option on a Douglas Street property between Discovery and Chatham Streets for use as a terminal for the new interurban line.

The Directors knew that the prospect of railway development on the Peninsula would be welcomed by local landowners and speculators. The company approached the principal property holders in the area to see what kind of a land bonus they might offer in consideration of the company building the new electric line. The local landowners were supportive and in May 1910, the BCER confirmed their willingness to build the new line at an estimated cost of $500,000. Significantly, this was nearly twice what it had cost to build the V&S twenty years earlier.

This announcement led to a scramble to find out what route the new electric line would take - a detail of great importance to local land speculators and boomsters. As with the Victoria and Sidney Railway in the early 1890s, the BCER considered three routes up the Peninsula from Victoria before selecting their final choice.

The new Interurban line was to run up the western part of the Saanich Peninsula - via Burnside Road from Douglas, to a point out near Rowland's Farm, thence cross country along the route of what is now Interurban Road. The new line had stations at Tillicum, Strawberry Vale, Wilkinson Road, West Saanich Road, thence to Tod Inlet via stops at Heal's Range, Sluggett, Saanich and its terminal at Deep Bay (Cove).

A branch line would run to a resort at Union (Patricia) Bay. This route was selected in November 1910 and the first construction contract for the interurban line was let to contractors Moore and Pethick in September 1911. By the summer of 1912, the

Left:
The gas-electric No. 2301 was featured on this replica 1913 V&S Timetable.

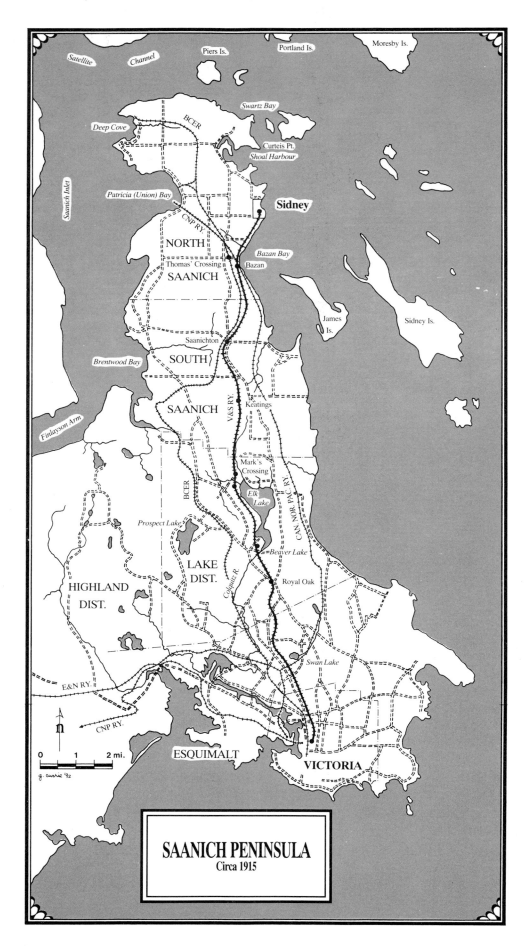

SAANICH PENINSULA

Circa 1915

Moresby Is.

Satellite Channel

Piers Is.

Portland Is.

Swartz Bay

Deep Cove

Curteis Pt.

Shoal Harbour

BCER

Saanich Inlet

Patricia (Union) Bay

Sidney

CNP RY.

NORTH

Thomas' Crossing

Bazan Bay

Bazan

SAANICH

James Is.

Sidney Is.

Saanichton

SOUTH

Brentwood Bay

V&S RY.

Keatings

SAANICH

Finlayson Arm

Mark's Crossing

BCER

Elk Lake

CAN. NOR. PAC. RY.

Prospect Lake

LAKE DIST.

Beaver Lake

Royal Oak

Colquitz R.

HIGHLAND DIST.

Swan Lake

E&N RY.

n

CNP RY.

0 1 2 mi.

g. currie '92

ESQUIMALT

VICTORIA

line was graded and ready for tracklaying and the placement of overhead wiring. Work continued through the winter.

B.C. Electric officially opened the new Saanich Division Interurban line on June 18, 1913. After a leisurely run out from Victoria, a special party which included A.T. Goward, local Manager of the BCER, and Premier Sir Richard McBride, did the honours with a silver spike. It was engraved "Last spike on the Saanich extension of the B.C. Electric driven in by Hon. Sir Richard McBride, Premier of British Columbia on June 18, 1913."

The construction of any other railway line along the Saanich Peninsula could logically be expected to impact the operations of the V&S and the VTR&F, but the timing of the competition's arrival in the summer of 1913 coincided with a major effort on the part of the V&S to improve its facilities and mainland connections. The BCER did take some passenger business away from the V&S that summer, but there was a large Militia summer camp in Sidney that year and both railways benefitted from extra passenger business between Sidney and Victoria. Otherwise, the impact of the Interurban line on the V&S did not really make itself felt for sometime.

Genuine competition had arrived on the Peninsula and there would be yet another railway line within a few years. In the meantime, the world was on the verge of a major war that would dislocate all facets of business and development on Vancouver Island and in British Columbia. With the combined effects of commerce, competition, and now war, the years ahead would not be easy.

These old milk tickets, from the collection of the Saanich Pioneers' Society, were used to prepay farm milk shipments into Royal Oak and Victoria. The photo is a turn of the century farm scene in Saanich.

13

WAR, RED INK AND DEEP SNOW, 1914-1916

The Victoria and Sidney on Its Own

The year 1913 was one of progress and change for the V&S and for the Saanich Peninsula. The real estate boom of the two previous years continued and new subdivisions were springing up from the Victoria city limits, in the south, to the Deep Cove area in the north. There was new home construction at many points along both the line of the V&S and the new Interurban line of the B.C. Electric Railway.

Saanich Municipal Council of 1913 was mandated to improve the local road system through a paving programme. While the paving scheme was not a complete success, it helped to bring closer the day when the automobile, not the railway, would be the primary mode of travel on the Saanich Peninsula.

The programme of improvement promised by the Great Northern Railway for the Victoria and Sidney Railway was still underway and was having gratifying results. This, coupled with the commencement of service on the Interurban line, had done much to help open up the district as never before. Soon, the Canadian Northern Pacific Railway would begin a service along its line from Patricia Bay to Alpha Street in Victoria, adding yet another competitor for the V&S.

For the first time, the V&S was operating without its annual subsidy. In the face of road and rail competition, and with large expenditures paid out for improvements along the V&S line, the financial result for the company at year's end in June 1914 would tell an interesting story.

Unlike the Canadian Pacific Railway, which had a record of public subsidy and handouts unequalled in Canadian history, the Great Northern and its Canadian subsidiaries had constructed most of their Canadian railways without subsidy of any kind. The V&S was one that had been subsidized, but it had begun as an independent line and not as a part of the Great Northern system. The future of the V&S hinged to a large degree on the success of Mainland connections with the Vancouver, Victoria and Eastern and the success of its operations from the Coast to the Kootenays. If the VV&E was a success, it was likely that it would funnel more freight across the Gulf of Georgia and the fortunes of the V&S would improve as well. If the VV&E did poorly, it was a certainty that the V&S would do likewise.

The Great Northern (through the VV&E) demonstrated its continuing commitment to its Vancouver Island subsidiaries in January 1914, when it brought in a new steel car-barge costing $45,000 for use on the Mainland to Sidney run.

The barge could carry twelve loaded cars and would go into service just as soon as a new barge slip could be constructed at Sidney. On a visit to Sidney, President

Left:
This beautiful scene at Rogers' Crossing, with the locomotive framed in snow-covered trees, was taken during the "Big Snow" of 1916 facing west from the opposite side of the tracks as the photo on pages 126-127.

McNeill, of the V&S, indicated that the only holdup would be in obtaining the required authority of the Canadian Department of Fisheries and Marine for foreshore rights for the new Sidney dock. McNeill expected this matter to be resolved quickly but it was to be some time before construction could begin. In the meantime, and in spite of the success of the new gas-electric passenger coach and the thrice-daily service, another "classic" communication from a disgruntled patron of the Victoria and Sidney Railway was printed in a local newspaper:

ACCOMMODATION
ON THE V.&S.

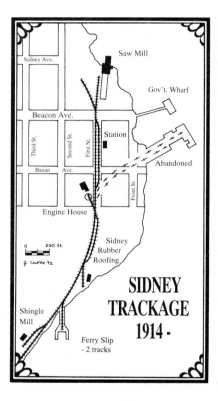

"To The Editor, Sidney Review

Dear Sir,- This subject almost lends itself to the same laconic treatment as that employed by a writer on the subject of "snakes in Ireland" but it does not quite do so. There is apparently an attempt on the part of the management of this line to accommodate its patrons, or it may only be satire, of which it is a delightful example. On the interior of the car in plain letters so that all may read, there is a legend to the effect that the seats are intended to accommodate three people each. Now, I have not a dictionary at hand, but if the word accommodate is looked up, I fancy it will mean something like 'provide for the comfort of.' This these seats certainly do not do. They are ample for two and though three people may squeeze in the end person at any rate is liable to be unseated at any moment by one of those violent oscillations or jerks for which this line is famous.

"What may be regarded as another attempt at accommodation is visible at the Victoria Station. Here there is an apartment that is plainly marked 'Waiting Room,' but it is not obvious what it is waiting for. Usually at railway stations there is a waiting room designated for the comfort and convenience of those persons who may arrive at a station at a time when no train is arriving or departing. But the room in the station in Victoria is securely locked up during a large portion of the day so that it is probably waiting for some other purpose not yet disclosed.

"There is also in many railway stations some provision made for the care of baggage and other parcels which an intended traveller may be glad to deposit pending the time of departure of his train, and it is not unusual for a small charge to be made for this accommodation, which the traveller cheerfully pays for the convenience offered and which in the aggregate probably reimburses the company for any expense involved but in Victoria at the Station the traveller may arrive, as I did on Monday last, with several packages and find all means of communication with the interior of the edifice strongly bolted and barred and as free from human occupation as the wastes of the Sahara Desert, leaving only an open space of platform on which baggage could be placed, where it is exposed to the ravages of wind or rain and to the attention of sundry stray dogs, not to mention the risk of being purloined by any vagrant or thief.

"Surely these small inconveniences cannot be considered to be a part of that advanced civilization of which it is the custom of inhabitants of these parts to brag and boast ad nauseum.

I am. etc.   Charles St. Barbe" [1]

While interesting for its commentary on the operation of the new gas-electric car and the staffing of the Victoria Station, this letter was written to the Editor of the *Sidney and Islands Review*, voice of the Peninsula and Gulf Islands, and, if memory serves, the editor at that time was a gentleman named Charles St. Barbe. (Perhaps the V&S was not receiving enough bad press at the time and so Mr. St. Barbe decided

On August 12, 1914, the No.1 prepares for the southbound run to Victoria with nine cars, her maximum haul for the grades between Sidney and Saanichton. Tank car S.R.R. 21 belongs to the Sidney Rubber Roofing Company. Crew members include, left to right: Conductor Albert Lacoursiere, Brakemen R. Hodgson and Orville Duncan, Fireman Bill Dewitt and Engineer Bill Walker.

The Great Northern Barge Slip

to do his part). Fortunately, local memory was short and there would soon be other topics of complaint to draw Mr. St. Barbe's attention.

The Victoria and Sidney Railway had matters of far greater concern. Yet another competitor, the Canadian Northern Pacific Railway, was beginning with construction of its Saanich Peninsula line.

There were other important concerns affecting the community of Sidney. The Canadian Southern Lumber Company, which had taken over from the Saanich Lumber Company in May 1912, had lasted only until September 16, 1913, before going into receivership and closing down. The mill was the main employer in Sidney and the loss of its workforce, who moved elsewhere, had a severe impact. The mill was to remain closed for nearly four years and its loss was keenly felt by businessmen and citizens alike.

In August 1914, Dominion Government approval of a foreshore lease for the new Great Northern barge slip was finally received and work began on the new structure. It was located south of and directly in line with Second Street in Sidney. The wharf was 300 feet long and remained a Sidney waterfront feature for many years. It was equipped with moveable aprons and two parallel railway tracks for loading and unloading cars.

War had just begun in Europe and the *Review* cited the construction of the new slip as a clear indication that the Great Northern would not be affected by the conflict. The *Review* was dead wrong in its assessment of the Great Northern Railway and the struggling V&S and its editor could not then have even imagined just how devastating the effects of the War would be on the local community.

The most drastic effect of the declaration of war in August 1914 was that the number of ships available for trade and commerce in the Pacific quickly diminished. All available vessels were moved over to the east coast for use in the massive war trade on the Atlantic. Soon, western lumber mills were shutting down at an alarming rate because of the lack of "bottoms" to export their products.

There were similar effects in all areas of commerce. The buoyant economy of 1912-13 was replaced by recession. Before the war's end in 1918, the community of Sidney and area, with a population of about 600, would have 200 men serving in the military. In rapid succession, the closure of the mill was followed by the brickyard and other local factories. Other businesses operated on a reduced basis before they too closed down completely.

**V&S
1913-14 Results**

**Events of
1914-15**

**James Island Plant
under Construction**

Left Top:
**Canadian National
Railway's Gas-Electric
No.500 competed with the
V&S for the local
passenger trade but was
withdrawn within a few
years. There were not
enough passengers to go
around during the World
War One years.**
Bottom Left:
**The venerable No.1 and
crew pose at Sidney on
August 12, 1914. This was
the only new locomotive
the company ever owned.**

At the end of its operating year in June 1913, the V&S had registered a profit of $25,903. A year later, in June 1914, there was a deficit of $25,399.64. While this appears a dismal result, a more detailed look at the books is in order: During 1913-14, the company spent $81,868.01 on improvements to its property. When this is considered in addition to the loss of the annual $15,000 bond interest guarantee, the company's position was not as bad as one might at first suppose.

Passengers carried were 123,599 in 1913 and 86,179 in 1914 - a substantial decline, probably reflecting the entry of the BCER Interurban line into the Saanich Peninsula passenger business. The V&S moved 45,282 tons of freight in 1913 and that total fell to 28,637 tons a year later. The Railway Company had invested deeply in plant and equipment in 1913. At least $35,000 was spent on upgrading the railway trackage alone. Then there was the cost of the gas-electric locomotive and repairs and improvements to other equipment, two new turntables, etc.

Financially, the company was hurting, but it was trying to improve its performance. Time would soon show how much success those efforts were having.

With the effects of the European war becoming more pervasive, the local Victoria-Sidney economy fell into a slump and business on the railway slumped accordingly.

From time to time, the V&S announced reduced passenger fares so that local citizens could attend the "Dollar Days" bargains put on by merchants in Victoria every six months or so. The original water system in Sidney was owned by the Victoria and Sidney Railway and served both the community and the railway from a well situated just outside of town. In 1915, the company lost its water franchise, though the monetary loss was small.

The old plant of the Bazan Bay Brick and Tile Company was razed that year and 40 or so temporary jobs were created for labourers who loaded the last stock on board scows in Bazan Bay.

The one bright spot on the local industrial scene in 1915 commenced on August 16th, when Canadian Explosives, Limited, began construction work on an immense plant at James Island. This new industry would remain an important factor in the local economy for many years. Manager Grubb set his crews to work with a will and soon buildings were rising on the high bluff overlooking Sidney and the Saanich Peninsula.

Many of the workers daily made their way out from Victoria on the trains of the V&S. From Sidney, the men were ferried across to James Island by Mr. Petersen on his launch *Island Belle*. Most of the clearing and grubbing work was done under contract to the firm of Kwon Lee, who employed 80 Chinese labourers. The new plant also employed large gangs of white carpenters, bricklayers and other skilled tradesmen. The construction project gave Sidney a needed economic lift at a time when local trade was at its lowest ebb.

One of the few plants operating in Sidney was the shingle mill. Its siding was the scene of a derailment on August 25, 1915. "Chuffing" quietly, the little No.1 freight engine was backing onto the siding alongside the mill. Suddenly, she banged to a stop - she had hung up on the switch points and jumped the track.

The boys on the train were used to this sort of thing and with the assistance of the local section gang set to work with car jacks to put her back on the track. The task used up a couple of hours, just long enough to delay the afternoon passenger train on its way out to Victoria.

The crew of the gas-electric car must have chuckled as they watched their less fortunate colleagues digging in the dirt to raise the No.1 as they accelerated smoothly out of Sidney, albeit a bit late, for an appointment in Victoria. Life along the V&S was never without incident and excitement.

One of the more unusual events of the year was a three-day cessation of traffic over the newly constructed grade of the Canadian Northern Pacific Railway on north Douglas Street. A steel bridge was manoeuvred in place over the long rock cut just north of the present Town and Country Mall. The Victoria and Sidney Railway was obliged to run a connecting train to each end of the bridge site and transfer passengers and baggage from one train to another for a three day period.

Throughout the ordeal, Conductor Herman Shade was complimented for the careful and courteous way in which he moved his passengers and their belongings from one train to the other. His longtime colleague, the genial Andy Forbes, had quit the V&S and was by then managing the Market Building for the City of Victoria, and so Shade was left to himself in the task of moving passengers and baggage across the gap.

In spite of the line's tardiness and other inconveniences, the pilot of No.1 was still a great place to pose for photos. Crew members in this scene include Conductor Albert Lacoursiere, Wes Moore and Engineer Bill Walker.

The inconvenience ended soon enough and the gas-electric was soon back on the regular passenger run. This service was further improved by the addition of an onboard mailbox, in November 1915, that allowed patrons to post letters and packages on the daily passenger train.

Construction on the Canadian Northern Pacific Railway's Saanich Peninsula line had been going on since 1913 but was delayed by disputes over the prices to be paid for expropriated lands along the route. These matters were well in hand by 1915 and the day couldn't be far off when there would be a third railway competing for passenger traffic on the Saanich Peninsula.

The Competition Coming

The year 1915 drew to a close on a rather dull note. Business was down, many local men were away in the war, agricultural labour was scarce, and prices were not too good either. Both passenger and freight levels were down on the Victoria and Sidney Railway. It could only be hoped that 1916 would bring at least some change in the situation - and it did!

The Big Snow

Heavy snow began to fall on southern Vancouver Island during the last week of January 1916. At first it appeared to be a typical light snowfall, which would be followed by a week or so of alternating thaw and freeze-up before the white stuff finally melted away. The *Victoria Daily Times* of February 1, 1916, showed a picture of the B.C. Electric Railway Company's snow plough: "Not Often Used In Victoria," the caption read. The sweeper was about to be used as never before.

The snowfall continued and by February 3, both the Victoria and Sidney and the Esquimalt and Nanaimo Railways were completely blocked. Victoria was virtually cut off from outside railway communication for the first time ever. Operations on the V&S had actually ceased two days earlier on Tuesday. The daily passenger train had made it back into Victoria on its first run that day but was stranded at Saanichton on its second run out to Sidney. It would remain there for some time.

The snow was the deepest on record and Walter Bate, who went to work for the V&S as a locomotive fireman later that year recalled that there was six feet of snow on level ground at his family's Saanichton farm. "In some places it was drifted ten feet high," he said.

People were stranded in their houses and farms. The situation at the Brentwood Bay cement plant was so desperate that the company sent its steamer *Marmion* around to Sidney to stock up on essential supplies. At North Saanich, it was much worse than in South Saanich, as the former had no incorporated local government with equipment of any kind to call upon. The people of South Saanich did - not that it did much more good!

The situation at Sidney was so bad that even horses with cutters couldn't navigate in the deep snow. The V&S was doing its best to break its way through the drifts but was equipped only with home-made wedge plows. The engines hooked on a couple of cars at the rear for added momentum and charged the drifts, then reversed and tried again, making but slight headway. Back and forth, back and forth, the battle continued. It was frustrating work and it looked like the only way to clear the line would be to dig it out, foot by foot.

On Friday, February 4th, a train left the Hillside Avenue station in Victoria with the intention of going out as far as possible. Another train had succeeded in opening the line from Sidney south to Saanichton and, perhaps the two just might meet. The unlucky train from Victoria made it little further than Royal Oak and had to turn back. It was said that the snowdrifts in the vicinity of Elk Lake were up to twelve feet deep.

Three days later on Monday, the *Victoria Daily Times* expressed the hope that "trains may be sent out over the V.&S. tomorrow, though it is not likely that the first one will be dispatched. This afternoon there remained only about four miles of track to be opened in the vicinity of Elk Lake. Each side of that the track is clear."

Two days later the paper tells us that "the (V&S) management expect early this afternoon that it would be possible to start the 5:00 p.m. train out today and bring in a train from Sidney. In any event the full service will be in operation tomorrow. Some very heavy work had to be done cutting through snowbanks around Beaver and Elk Lakes."

The first through train from Sidney finally arrived in Victoria on Wednesday, February 10th - the line had been closed to traffic for nine full days. It consisted of an engine with a homemade plough mounted on the front and two boxcars in the rear to give it weight for bucking the snowdrifts. The line clearing scheme had at last worked and the *Sidney and Islands Review* remarked that it had taken "just nine days to think up the idea and put it into execution, and during that time Sidney had the unpleasant sensation of being cut off almost entirely from the rest of the world."[2]

The other railways on Vancouver Island were having the same difficulty with snow and the Interurban line of the B.C. Electric took even longer than the V&S to open, only resuming full service on February 11th.

When spring finally came in 1916 it was no particular relief to anyone. Many of the local men were off at war, most industries were shut down or operating at only marginal capacity and morale in the community was low. Later in the spring, it was announced that there would be a summer military camp established at Sidney and this was expected help the local economy somewhat.

In a burst of patriotism, tinged perhaps with the slightest scent of future monetary reward, the members of the Sidney Board of Trade, with Section Foreman Thomson and his V&S section gang, met to voluntarily clean up the park reserve at the Sidney Station and the *Sidney and Islands Review* afforded full coverage to the event:

V.&S. PARK IS NOW AN IDEAL PICNIC GROUND

Much Attention Given to it Friday Afternoon by Gang of Men

"On Friday afternoon last a number of members of the Board of Trade, assisted by Section Foreman Thomson of the V.&S. Railway, and his gang of men, met by appointment at the park behind the station and proceeded to make it look respectable. It was by no means a small job, as the heavy snowstorms of last winter had brought down tons of small limbs and branches from the tops of the giant firs that stand like sentinels, and in fact are one of the landmarks of Sidney. In the southern portion of the park or just south of where the old spur formerly ran down to the wharf this portion of the park comprises somewhere in the neighbourhood of three acres and the ground was fairly carpeted with the amount of stuff that had fallen from the trees. However, nothing daunted, the men set to work with a will and in a short time several big fires were burning freely and were constantly being fed by those gathering up the litter. Fortunately, there was no undergrowth of any kind in this part of the park and with the number of men working it only required about three hours to clean it up perfectly.

"Meanwhile another gang of men were busy directly back of the station cleaning out the underbrush from beneath the trees there. As it was chopped down by some of the men others gathered it up and dragged it to the big fire started on the hollow made by the old spur. As soon as the gang had finished up on the south side they came over to help the operations here and before five o'clock had arrived it was very gratifying to see the splendid progress that had been made during the afternoon. It is now possible to stand at the station and catch a glimpse of the sea through the cleaned out brush. This particular piece of brush has been an eyesore to many residents of Sidney for years past as they always felt that it could be made into one of the most delightful spots in Sidney, but never before did it seem possible to get an organized movement started to clean it up...

"A cordial invitation is extended to the people of this vicinity to visit the park and see for themselves what can be accomplished by a properly organized movement of this nature such as the committee of the Board of Trade are responsible for making last week, and in extending their thanks to this live and energetic organization the fact should not be overlooked that through the kindness of Mr. Van Sant, Manager of the V.&S. Railway, the members of the Board were very materially assisted in their task by Foreman Thomson and his gang of section men."[3]

That the Sidney park had fallen into such poor shape was a clear reflection of the community's pre-occupation with the effects of the war and the poor economy.

Right:
The new Great Northern barge slip at Sidney was completed in 1914, one of the promised improvements of the agreement of a year earlier.

Below:
Great Northern's 4-4-0 No.290 was loaned to the V&S to replace another, smaller engine. She served the line for some years but was gone by 1916 when Walter Bate started work with the V&S.

Morale was low and the Board of Trade's action in fixing up the park was calculated to raise local spirits.

In spite of the difficult situation in the community, summer would bring at least some relief. The old Militia camp which had first operated in 1913 was again used for military training. The 123rd Battalion, B.C. Bantams; and the 321st Battalion, Seaforth Highlanders, spent their summer training period at Sidney Military Camp before moving into winter quarters and thence overseas. The troops increased passenger traffic on the V&S and the railway ran special trains on Thursdays which departed Sidney at 5:30 p.m. and returned from Victoria at 10:30 p.m., in time for soldiers to be back at camp before curfew. This meant a welcome break for a soldier who was having an otherwise miserable week in basic training.

One warm afternoon, in the summer of 1916, a young Walter Bate, son of a local farmer, was standing on the Sidney station platform watching the freight train come in.

"I was standing on the station platform," Walter recalls. "The guy came up to me and said, 'Are you looking for a job?' And I said, 'what job?' 'Firing an engine.'" Walter had never fired a steam locomotive but he was game. "Oh, well, I could take a chance," he replied.

"I did and we had one engineer who was named George Walton, and his brother, Jack Walton. George was a prince to work under, you know. There was a big bar you'd throw to control your steam, you see (called a Johnson Bar). He would save the fireman all the work he could because if he threw that bar down, the flame would just suck up (the stack).

"It would knock your fire all to hell. So this young fellow George, he was beautiful, you know. I'd open the firebox and say, 'I'm going to put some wood in now.' He'd push the Johnson Bar back so the engine (imitates sound of engine exhaust slowing)...hardly making any interruption in the boiler, and you'd put your

Gas-Electric coach No.2301 was removed from the V&S when the bond issue matured in 1917 to prevent seizure by a receiver. Later sold to the Pacific Great Eastern Railway as the No.104, she is pictured here on that line near North Vancouver.

wood and stuff in, and then when I closed it again, he'd drop the Bar a couple of notches to get the steam up." Firing a locomotive with wood was a real challenge.

Walter Bate passed away shortly after this interview - the last surviving Victoria and Sidney Railway employee. Walter Bate served as a fireman on the V&S until its end and clearly recalled the difficult last years of the railway:

"We got paid by the hour. Fifty cents an hour. No, they didn't pay any overtime. You went out and that was it. You just got the 50 cents for the extra hours you worked but no overtime pay as such." Fifty cents an hour wasn't too bad for a 16 year old fireman and, in the summer of 1916, Walter was just happy to have a job.

In spite of local protests to the Board of Railway Commissioners over high passenger fares on both the V&S and the B.C. Electric, the summer traffic of 1916 was extremely busy, the railway reporting Saturday evening and Sunday trains crowded to the limit and freight business was on the increase as well. The renovated park and local beaches, plus military activity in Sidney, made for a prosperous summer.

But when the B.C. Bantams and the Seaforth Highlanders closed down the Sidney camp and departed for winter quarters in early November, quiet once again settled over the town. The only positive happening seemed to be the presence of a pile driver working on repairs in the yards of the Canadian Southern Lumber Company, which had been closed since September 1913. Maybe it was going to re-open.

This activity was followed a month later with news that the Great Northern Railway had selected the Sidney Rubber Roofing Company to provide material for a number of important Great Northern building projects on the Mainland. Still more hope, but no immediate results. At year-end, rumour was that the Canadian Southern plant had been acquired by the Dominion Government and would be turned into a munitions factory.

Rumours fed other rumours and the local citizenry could only hope that some of them would prove true. It was a reverent yet subdued Christmas in Sidney that year with so many men away and most local businesses shut down. But hope springs eternal and perhaps 1917 would be an even better year than the one that preceded it.

14

THE FINAL YEARS, 1917-1919

By 1917, the Victoria and Sidney Railway and the Victoria Terminal Railway and Ferry Company were in their fourth year of operation without the financial support of the old bond interest guarantees that had been paid from 1892 to 1913 by the Province of British Columbia and the City of Victoria.

The Great Northern Railway, through its subsidiary Vancouver, Victoria and Eastern Railway, had assumed responsibility for all interest payments. As the bonds were due to mature on September 1, 1917, the residents of Victoria, the Saanich Peninsula, and the community of Sidney in particular, were increasingly concerned about what would happen on that date. Would the VV&E pay up the matured bonds, or would it default, leading to the appointment of a receiver and eventual sale or closure of the line? As of January 1917, no one seemed to know. The year ahead was to be filled with many changes and a few surprises for the V&S and its patrons.

The general economic climate, brought on by the commencement of World War One in 1914, had caused hardship for most Canadian railways. Similarly, freight traffic was dramatically reduced on the V&S. The line's shipments from 1913 to 1916 were:

Year ending June 30, 1913:	45,282 tons
Year ending June 30, 1914:	28,637 tons
Year ending June 30, 1915:	16,538 tons
Year ending June 30, 1916:	20,203 tons

For the same four-year period, passenger revenues were also down, though not as dramatically. While some passenger business was lost to competition from the B.C. Electric, after it commenced operations in the summer of 1913, the effects were mitigated somewhat by the continued influx of new settlers into the area after the 1910-12 real estate boom. The central location of the Victoria and Sidney Railway through the Peninsula, and its established clientele in areas away from the new Interurban line, also helped the V&S to maintain reasonable ridership, even under the poor, wartime economic conditions. Passengers carried on the V&S for the 1913-16 period were as follows:

Year ending June 30, 1913:	123,599 passengers
Year ending June 30, 1914:	86,179 passengers
Year ending June 30, 1915:	55,264 passengers
Year ending June 30, 1916:	50,987 passengers

Left:
In 1934 the trackage, taken over by Canadian National Railways in 1919, was warped, weed-grown and abandoned after closure of the Sidney Sawmill. The rails were taken up a year later.

The introduction of the gas-electric coach by the Great Northern, in 1913, had given the V&S its best annual passenger total ever. (The two years preceding 1913 were the second and third highest.) The completion of the Interurban line, the spreading influence of the automobile and wartime austerity did not do as much damage to the Great Northern's (VV&E's) plans as might have been expected. The dramatic drop in passenger traffic between 1913 and 1915 would appear to be due more to the cutback of excursion traffic and casual travel through the war years than any other factor.

The Great Northern's aspirations were for the Victoria and Sidney and the VTR&F to become the extreme western end of the VV&E Railway in British Columbia and the Great Northern's transcontinental system. In the literal sense, this did happen, but the failure of the VV&E to succeed in establishing an effective Coast-Kootenay railway service had a detrimental effect on traffic levels on the Gulf ferry service and over the V&S.

No one was even guessing what was going to happen when the Victoria and Sidney Railway bonds matured and became due for payment on September 1, 1917. But, it would take a miracle to keep the railway running for very long after that date. In spite of this pessimistic forecast, there were businessmen in Sidney who still needed the services of the V&S, or at least some railway connection; businessmen who would fight hard to keep the existing rail service. Actions taken by them during the early months of 1917 served to make this very clear.

The Sidney Sawmill, the first industry in Sidney, made its initial revenue by selling ties and timber for construction of the Victoria and Sidney Railway. After that time, in the mid-90s, it had operated only sporadically. Despite the best efforts of well qualified lumbermen, it was not able to stay in business for very long. That anyone would actually come along, in the war year of 1917, with enough gumption to get the place going again, and really turn it into a money maker, would be a minor miracle! But, perhaps a man like G.H. Walton could pull it off.

The Sidney Sawmill
Re-Opened

The saws had last fallen silent in September 1913, but caretaker W. Warne had kept the machinery well maintained so that, even after four years, the mill could quickly be restored to running order. Rumours that the mill might re-open had been circulating for some months in Sidney. In mid-February 1917, the *Review* was pleased to relate that Mr. Warne, Mr. G.H. Walton, of Victoria, and a couple of engineers had been investigating the Sidney mill and had liked what they saw.

Walton decided to put the machinery back in working order and begin operations as soon as possible. Before the end of the month, carpenters and millwrights were sent out from Victoria to begin the task of making the plant ready. The saws made a trial run on April 12th. The first boom of two million board-feet of logs arrived at the mill on April 26th and the new Sidney Sawmills, Limited, was in business. Two carloads of lumber were shipped later that same week.

Manager Walton was well aware of the competition he faced. A key element in his plan, to place the mill in a strong competitive position, was not only to maintain the existing V&S railway connection with Victoria, but also to obtain a connection with the line of the new Canadian Northern Pacific Railway (CNPR) and have subsequent access to their ferry-barge slip at Patricia Bay. The latter would enable the Sidney Sawmills to tap business along the entire Canadian transcontinental railway system.

In May, the local press announced that various steps were being taken to bring the Canadian Northern Pacific Railway into Sidney:

WILL INVESTIGATE
THE SIDNEY WHARF

"...A very interesting report was received from the Railways Committee (of the Sidney Board of Trade) giving an account of the various steps being taken to bring the C.N.R. into Sidney. Why this line should have missed coming in is known only to the directors. Truly, the ways of railway corporations, as of men, are strange. In connection with this matter another deputation paid a visit to Victoria on Monday last and had a further interview with the Honourable John Oliver, Minister of Railways for the province and he advised on the question of what should be done in order to bring about the desired end. Mr. D.O. Lewis of the C.N.R. and Mr. Van Sant of the V&S Railway were also interviewed and as a result communications are now taking place with the Board of Railway Commissioners which it is hoped will prove successful in procuring for Sidney direct connection with the Mainland and the Prairies."[1]

The Sidney Rubber Roofing Company was a major shipper over the V&S line through the World War One years. The railway tracks ran under the conveyor at the far left of photo. Large tank in upper right was for storage of rubber used in roofing material.

The Canadian Northern Pacific Railway had completed its railway connection between Patricia Bay and Victoria and, on April 30, 1917, inaugurated a twice-daily passenger service. On June 7th, the members of the Sidney Board of Trade met with the Board of Railway Commissioners at Victoria. The delegation was led by G.H. Walton and Mr. Mayhew, Manager of the Sidney Rubber Roofing Company. They petitioned for a rail connection with the CNPR:

"The Great Northern opposed the application and it will be news to the local industries to hear that their representative made a statement to the Commission that they were quite able to handle all the business offered in Sidney and another reason given was that the C.N.R. would get nearly all their (V&S) business."[2]

Sidney Rubber Roofing Co. Sidney V.I. BC

However, on June 7, 1917, the Board of Railway Commissioners issued an order for a connecting line, to be made between the Victoria and Sidney Railway and the Canadian Northern Pacific Railway, at a point where the two lines crossed, south of Sidney. The Board of Trade had won, but not without argument from both railways involved in the matter:

> "A.V. Pineo, acting for the Minister of Railways, explained the necessity for a connection in the interests of the many industries at and near Sidney for the benefit of which it was necessary that a crossing should be put in which would enable cars to be transferred into and out of Sidney from the C.N. Pacific mainline at that point.
>
> "A plan was put in by Mr. F.C. Gamble, Chief Engineer of the Department of Railways.
>
> "Mr. Warren of the C.N. Pacific advanced the war and the difficulty of getting steel as the reason against an Order being issued now. It was problematical whether there was the business offering to justify the cost.
>
> "Incidental to the discussion, Sir Henry Drayton (Chairman of the Board of Railway Commissioners) asked how the crossing was protected. Mr. Gamble replied that there was a flagman but the company was under an Order to put in a mechanical interlocking system of de-rails. A.H. McNeill, K.C. said this was to be done as soon as the line was operating.
>
> "It is operating now but there is no mechanical interlocking system there,' said Mr. Gamble.
>
> "Then you are operating illegally under the Order,' remarked Sir Henry to Mr. Warren. On this point the Board issued orders that the company file plans within 30 days for the system ordered.
>
> "Mr. McNeill, on the other point made a claim that the V&S could get cars for shippers over its lines at Sumas, New Westminster or Vancouver.
>
> "The Chairman observed that the C.N.R. had no cars to spare at the present, a situation that the Commission had heard complained of all across the Dominion.
>
> "Representatives of the Sidney Board of Trade stated the case for the industries and informed the Commission that the C.N.R. had promised all the cars needed...
>
> "The Board ruled that the transfer track should be put in near the diamond, where it would get the protection of the interlocking system. The Order was for the benefit of the C.N. Pacific, which must put in the track at its own expense, filing plans within 30 days. The Chairman observed however, that there was a general shortage of steel and the track could not be put in until such time as this was available."[3]

The steel shortage resulted in months of delay. The first cars from the CNPR (absorbed later by the Canadian National Railway) did not enter Sidney over the new railway connection until December 1917.

During that year, there had been a number of other developments of importance taking place in Sidney and Victoria that directly affected the V&S.

After their experience during the "Big Snow" of 1916, the V&S was determined that its line would be kept open in any future snowfall. Again, in 1917, there was a heavy snowfall on the Peninsula, but, fortunately, it was not as severe as in the previous year. This time the V&S kept its line open from the beginning, by running a steam locomotive with wedge plow out to Sidney an hour ahead of the regular passenger train. This had the desired effect and the gas-electric made its usual runs from Victoria to Sidney and return throughout the snowfall without interruption.

In May, the company installed their first telephone in the Sidney station. The company was making some effort to improve service, within the financial realities

The Victoria and Sidney Railway - 1917

imposed on it by reduced freight and passenger traffic, and the ever-increasing competition of the automobile. But still, the biggest worry of all was - what would happen on the September 1, 1917 maturity date? That fateful day was drawing ever closer.

The V&S Bonds Mature

The ultimate date came - and passed. The Great Northern reacted, by quickly removing all of its leased equipment from the V&S and VTR&F lines, so those could not be seized for payment of outstanding debts. The *Victoria Daily Times* gave lengthy coverage to the Victoria and Sidney Railway case in its issue of September 5, 1917:

BONDS OF COMPANY HAVE NOW MATURED

Future of Victoria and Sidney Railway is Threatened

Train Replaces the Gasoline Motorcar

"The future of the Victoria and Sidney Railway, which for 25 years has operated on the Saanich Peninsula is now veiled in great uncertainty. The struggle to make ends meet in the sparsely settled territory in competition with two other lines has brought the matter to a crisis, the next move resting with the bondholders of the company, whose interests are represented by a trust company in Montreal.

"The company had a clear field in its earlier years but was a losing proposition...the Government of British Columbia and the City of Victoria, who had in 1892 guaranteed the interest at two and three per cent respectively on the $300,000 worth of bonds issued in that year, had to make the interest for a term of years. Then in 1913 an agreement was reached which extinguished their interests to the Vancouver, Victoria and Eastern Railway, as the holding company in this province for the Great Northern.

"The company, which had made the Blanchard Street Depot a few years earlier under the authority of a separate company known as the Victoria Terminal Railway and Ferry Company, put on a gasoline motorcar in 1913. It only had three months service before the completion of the Saanich Interurban line of the B.C. Electric Company began, and the V&S has continued to lose money, about $15,000 per year, it is understood, up to date. Added to its other difficulties, in April the Canadian Northern Pacific Railway Company commenced its Patricia Bay service in practically the same territory as the V&S line.

"The bonds matured on Saturday last and since that time the officials have been waiting for some action to be taken by the bondholders. It is presumed that if the controlling company, the Great Northern Railway, will no longer come to the relief of the company, it will pass with the ordinary course of law into a receivership. However, there is no specific information on that point yet...

"The gasoline car has been withdrawn and sent to the United States for repair and officials have no knowledge when it will be returned, as the cost of the vehicle has been steadily increasing.

"Meanwhile, the company is operating the train service which prevailed before the gas car was brought into service in 1913.

"People along the line of the railway are particularly anxious to know what the future holds in store for the line and to Victoria citizens the matter is one of considerable interest."

Apparently, the bondholders in far-off Montreal were in a quandary about what to do with the Victoria and Sidney Railway. No receiver was appointed, nor was there any immediate indication as to what other steps might be taken. Business for the V&S just continued, as before, under its locally appointed management.

If the pending rail connection of the V&S with the Canadian Northern Pacific Railway could be completed, the fortunes of the Sidney Sawmills, Limited, might improve. Consequently, the V&S might actually start making money. The mill's prospects did improve when the Board of Railway Commissioner's order, requiring the CNPR to build a transfer track to the V&S so that cars could be moved to and from Sidney over the CNPR, was implemented.

This new connection meant an increase in revenue for the V&S. They could collect switching charges and actually move the cars to and from the CNPR interchange track. At the same time, the V&S would lose some revenue - by the non-shipment of many of these same cars over their own barge system to the Mainland. The transfer track was to be constructed at Station 122.00 on the V&S line, at a point 2.3 miles from Sidney.

Meanwhile, on September 20th, the *Sidney and Islands Review* announced that Kirk and Company, of Victoria, were to inaugurate a motor truck freight service between Victoria and Sidney. Kirk was prepared to pick up and deliver at any point on the Saanich Peninsula. This new service cut deeply into V&S freight revenues of local origin.

The situation looked bleak for the struggling V&S. Nevertheless, the company made improvements to its Sidney ferry barge slip at the end of September and, while rumours of the line's closure were circulating, the local management officially stated that there was absolutely no truth to them: "The V&S will be found doing business as usual at all times and can be depended upon to give their patrons every possible attention. Both the passenger and freight service will be run on the usual schedule and an effort will be made to facilitate the handling of both," said the company to the *Sidney and Islands Review* of October 4, 1917.

The Sidney terminus of the V&S after takeover by the Canadian National Railway. The boxcar stands near the intersection of First and Bevan. The building on the left, then Kelly's Feed Store, is one of the few remaining today from the V&S era.

The Canadian Northern Pacific was some months behind the projected opening date for its transfer track with the V&S at Sidney. It was not until December 30th that the first cars were switched into the Sidney mill over the interchange. The first shipment of lumber was several carloads destined for lumber dealers in the Prairie Provinces.

This connection would become the major revenue earner for the Canadian Northern Pacific on the Saanich Peninsula, with up to 700 cars annually being moved in and out of Sidney over the V&S/CNPR interchange.

In January 1918, the Sidney Board of Trade, as part of its continuing campaign, prepared a report for submission to J.C. Mackintosh, the newly-elected federal Member of Parliament:

The picture below, taken a few hundred yards south of scene on opposite page, shows the remaining trees in Bazan Park as of 1932. The siding here served the Sidney Rubber Roofing Company after the third track was removed from the main station yard.

"Sidney is situated on the northeast coast of the Saanich Peninsula and is a town of 600 inhabitants. Nearly 200 of its manhood have left during the past three years for Overseas. At the outbreak of the war, like many more places throughout the Dominion, it received a serious setback industrially; its mill, factories, canneries and brickyard all closed down. However, during the past 18 months a strong revival has set in for not only have the old industries re-opened, but new ones are being established, so that there are now operating in the district and giving employment to a considerable number of men a large lumber mill, a rubber roofing plant, a kelp products plant, a clam and fruit cannery, a salmon cannery and a shingle mill and there are excellent prospects of a paper felt factory being established...

"The town is served by three railways, the Victoria and Sidney Railway, operated by the Great Northern Railway Company; the Canadian Northern Railway Company (sic) who also have a connecting and running right over the V&S, and the B.C. Electric Railway Company, 1 1/2 miles away..."[4]

The Sidney Sawmill, under the capable superintendence of G.H. Walton, was by May 1918, cutting an average of 100,000 board-feet of lumber per day. When Walton first opened the mill, he had immediate changes in mind to make it capable of an even larger cut, should it be warranted. But, the demand for lumber and timber was so brisk that he had to make do with the existing equipment to supply his customers. After waiting for an opportune time, he was able to effect the necessary improvements. The additions and alterations cost $20,000 and the mill's growing fortunes were frequently chronicled in the *Sidney and Islands Review*, such as the following article of May 2, 1918:

"The millsite covers an area of about eight acres, which affords good barge shipping and log holding facilities. The sawmill- wide and roomy - is equipped with heavy duty machinery - 60-inch double circular headsaws; fast carriage, made by William Hamilton and Company, Peterborough, with oscillating twin engine drive, capable of handling timbers up to 80 feet; heavy loaders; edger with mechanical 'spotter'; automatic trimmer; four side timber sizer; and P.B. Yates Machine Company resaw (10 inch); live rolls, quick action transfers, etc. In connection is a modern lath mill, with a capacity of 35,000 pieces per day and a well lighted filing room with all the latest equipment.

"Ample power is one of the features of the plant. The boiler house contains a battery of Jenckes Company boilers - two 18 feet by 72 inches and two 16 feet by 66 inches. These furnish steam to one 300 horsepower engine operating the headsaws, one 250 horsepower engine running the edger, and one 325 horsepower twin engine taking care of the rest of the machinery. There is also an electric light engine with capacity sufficient to operate the yard arc lights as well as the mill systems.

"A large planing mill distant 100 feet westerly contains two McGregor-Gourley and two S.A. Woods Machine Company planers and matchers; also sticker and resaw. Three dry kilns nearby are of the West Coast type and take care of the mill output in good shape. There are two large dry sheds for finished lumber, one of which has just been erected.

"The timber deck at the rear of the sawmill, (served by a spur line from the Great Northern Railway) usually holds an impressive assortment of big sticks awaiting the arrival of cars for loading. These timbers range in size from 8 by 8 inches to 24 by 24 inches, the lengths varying up to 80 feet. A powerful crane recently installed permits of even the largest timbers being handled easily and quickly when loading is in progress. A smaller timber deck on the waterfront is served by a light gauge railway track between the sawmill and planing mills; here cargo and barge shipments of lumber, etc. are loaded, an electrically operated crane being provided for that purpose. A second G.N.R. spur line serves the planing mill, dry sheds and yard. A considerable area of the latter is planked, which facilitates the handling of loaded trucks. Conveniently situated is a small building containing the electric trimmer saw for working on broken lumber.

"H.C. Winston, who took charge as superintendent last October is handling the plant in a way that backs up his reputation as a successful mill man. Mr. Winston, who was with the Campbell River Lumber Company for 12 years, not only erected the firm's plant at White Rock, B.C. and ran it till last fall, but also built and started up most of the half-dozen shingle mills formerly operated by that company under various names. Prior to coming to British Columbia, Mr. Winston was with the Atlas Lumber and Shingle Company at McMurray, Washington."

Left:

The old V&S No.2 was not as well suited for the railway as the No.1 because of her light weight and poor traction. Here she switches at the Sidney Sawmill in the late 1890s.

Right:

The Sidney Sawmill became a financial success during the war years under the capable management of Mr. G.H. Walton and during the 1920s shipped up to 700 carloads of lumber per year before its closure during the Great Depression.

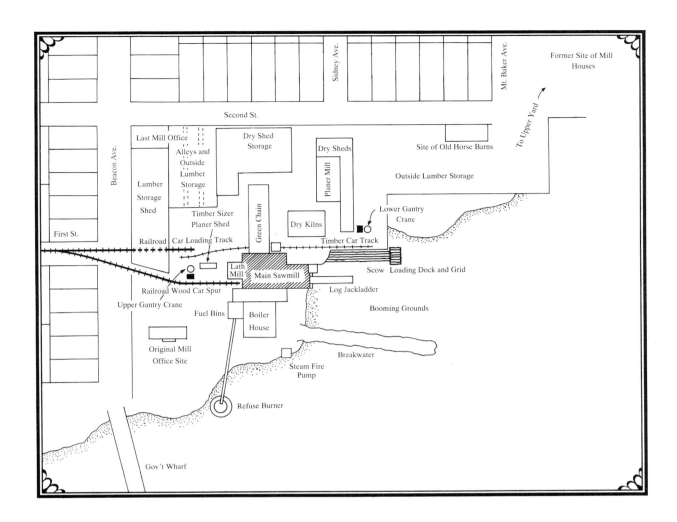

Former Site of Mill Houses

Sidney Ave.

Mt. Baker Ave.

To Upper Yard

Second St.

Site of Old Horse Barns

Last Mill Office

Dry Shed Storage

Dry Sheds

Alleys and Outside Lumber Storage

Beacon Ave.

Planer Mill

Outside Lumber Storage

Lumber Storage Shed

Green Chain

Dry Kilns

Lower Gantry Crane

First St.

Timber Sizer Planer Shed

Railroad   Car Loading Track

Timber Car Track

Lath Mill

Main Sawmill

Scow Loading Dock and Grid

Railroad Wood Car Spur

Log Jackladder

Upper Gantry Crane

Booming Grounds

Fuel Bins

Boiler House

Original Mill Office Site

Breakwater

Steam Fire Pump

Refuse Burner

Gov't Wharf

Sidney Mills, Sidney, B.C.

Complaining about the V&S had been a major pastime for local correspondents during the many years it had operated. The addition of the B.C. Electric Interurban line, in 1913, and the Canadian Northern Pacific four years later, gave agitators an even wider field. The *Sidney and Islands Review* of July 25, 1918, contained these classic comments:

> "The comment was made one morning last week that the V.&S. train was exactly on time. 'Yes,' was the response, 'it's a very good service - what there is of it!'...
>
> "One feature which impresses the visitor to the Saanich Peninsula is the remarkable network of railway systems with which it is endowed. To have three distinct railways laid down and in operation, is a distinction itself, and that two of them have transcontinental connections is more remarkable still...The point we wish to emphasize and will strike all who make a deeper acquaintance than a mere casual visit to the Peninsula, is the remarkable fact that with all the railway activity, Sidney, the most important centre, is avoided, save by the V&S. It is a pity that such enterprise should not have been made available to the largest settled district, which also has lumber mills, factories and canneries in its midst."

Regardless of the passing of the maturity date for the V&S Bonds and the withdrawal of all Great Northern support, the line was kept running - but only barely. All operating expenses were severely cut. By the autumn of 1918, the company was running only one daily passenger train and a twice-weekly freight train.

Passenger levels on the V&S line declined. Potential patrons, of a more-frequent service, often walked the mile and a half distance to the B.C. Electric station to catch the interurban train to Victoria. Aside from this, the BCER line had little or no commercial importance for the town of Sidney. Its franchise forbade entry there for thirty years.

On October 3, 1918, the *Review* gave a detailed description of the local transportation systems and had some suggestions for the V&S:

> "...This road passes through most beautiful scenery, skirting the coast and opening up lovely views of the Islands. It is a line, which if enterprisingly worked, has manifest advantages and great possibilities...But having constructed their line, the Great Northern rested on their laurels. They drew their grant from a beneficent government, and left the line, as far as passenger traffic is concerned, to operate itself. Occasionally, a few freight cars are rumoured to have been seen passing over it. So much for the benefit Sidney receives from the last railroad undertaking...The extent of the service the public of Sidney and Victoria receive from the S&V (sic) line is limited to one train a day in either direction, with a bi-weekly freight train. Its fares are exorbitant in comparison with other lines - 50 cents for a single fare of 14 miles...
>
> "...The train stops at every station, and occasional halts are made at places not indicated on the map. The whole of the running is accomplished by one solitary engine, which in appearance is contemporaneous with George Stevenson's 'Rocket.' Still, it is a hard worked machine, and it has our sympathy as it is responsible for the whole of the haulage on the road... The journey from Sidney to Victoria means a whole day must be set aside in which to do it, and although the departure from here is timed fairly early, half of the morning is gone when the Sidney Flyer, with clanging bell and clouds of dust, grunts and squeals its way into Victoria and deposits its jaded passengers, who have lost the freshness of Sidney's air by the time they arrive."

The V&S was literally on its last legs, and it was obvious that operations could not continue for very long. Over 70 years later, Walter Bate, when asked about harassment to V&S employees by disgruntled patrons, replied: "People were so used to getting on the train and then getting to town an hour and a half later or something like that. It was taken in stride. They spoke of the old V&S as a joke a lot of times."[5] Asked about the condition of the road, after the Great Northern left it strictly to local control, Bate remembered the situation very well: "The tracks were very rough. You'd go to put in a stick of wood (into the locomotive firebox) and you'd open the door and maybe the engine would lean that way, you know, and you'd miss the door. It was really tough. The boilers were getting shot. You carried 80 pounds of steam and weren't allowed to carry any more than that."[6]

The Victoria and Sidney Railway struggled through its last winter running more by good fortune, and the goodwill of its hard working crews, than anything else. By the spring of 1919, it was almost over. On April 2nd, a Sidney Board of Trade delegation met with Premier John Oliver to discuss the situation. Oliver assured them that regardless of whether or not the V&S continued, or even if the CNPR did not wish to take over operation of part of the line into Sidney, he would somehow facilitate continued rail service to the industries there.

On April 5, 1919, Premier Oliver received official notification from Manager Frank Van Sant that all operations over the Victoria and Sidney Railway would be discontinued after April 30, 1919. The end was at hand. Van Sant had received definite instructions from Great Northern headquarters in St. Paul, Minnesota, and any appeal to higher management was out of the question. The old "Cordwood Limited" had given just about all it had, and now it was done.

An examination of the V&S Railway's operating record, taken from the Annual Reports of the Chief Engineer of Railways and Canals, chronicles the downward spiral of operations through the World War One years. As an example, figures for tonnage of freight originating on-line and off-line from 1913 to 1919 clearly show a decline:

Origination of Freight Tonnage - V&S Railway

Year	Originating (On-Line)	(Off-Line)	Total (Tons)
1913	21,161	24,121	45,282
1914	12,341	16,296	28,637
1915	6,479	10,059	16,538
1916	7,974	12,229	20,203
1917	?	?	31,286
1918	?	?	19,682
1919	12,843	6,756	19,599

(Full details for 1917-18 were not available as wartime austerity measures limited publication of full financial details).

By the end of 1918, incoming traffic had dropped to only one quarter of what it had been in 1913. The 12,843 tons of freight originating on-line during the last year of operations consisted of 5,580 tons of lumber from the Sidney Sawmill and 5,000 tons of miscellaneous merchandise (mainly originating in Victoria). There were shipments of other unspecified on-line commodities which amounted to only 816 tons. Much of this was probably agricultural produce. Shingles and other forest products made up the next largest category of freight at 630 tons. Most of the freight carried on the V&S originated at Sidney or Victoria and shipments from other on-line points were for the most part seasonal. Other categories of freight included grain, flour, petroleum products, etc.

Surprisingly, the cordwood shipments of the early years, which gave the railway it "Cordwood Limited" appellation, were no longer a factor at all. During World War One years, the V&S locomotives burned coal. Walter Bate recalled that at first they used nut coal and then, finally, lump coal. The latter would cause a clinker problem in the firebox of the locomotive if it was not carefully controlled by the fireman.

The company had coaling facilities on the dock at Sidney, where loaded coal cars were pushed up a ramp to facilitate shovelling across into the locomotive tender, an overhead coal bin was established at Elk Lake Siding, and there was a coaling ramp and bin in Victoria.

During the last year, off-line shipments of 6,756 tons consisted mainly of miscellaneous merchandise destined for Victoria merchants. All in all, it was a disappointing showing. In spite of the low figures shown here, the railway was an absolute necessity for the Sidney Sawmill and several other Sidney industries. Something had to be done - and quickly!

The Sidney Board of Trade quickly went into action. They petitioned both the Canadian Northern Pacific Railway and the B.C. Electric Railway to see if either would take over operation of at least a portion of the line - from the CNPR transfer track at Bazan Bay into Sidney. Both of these schemes were mooted over the following weeks. The Victoria Board of Trade gave their support to the Sidney Board of Trade in securing a guarantee for some kind of rail service for Sidney.

Top:
British Columbia Electric Interurban car on the former V&S interchange track at Saanichton. The original equipment for the Interurban was transferred over this track from the V&S during construction in 1912 and 1913. The Agricultural Hall, the large building on the left, is still a prominent landmark.

Bottom:
A car stands on the interchange track at Saanichton. View is from opposite direction of above and was probably taken from the V&S right-of-way. The second, and still standing, Prairie Tavern is seen at centre right.

On April 30th, the V&S made its last run, as reported in the *Victoria Daily Times* of that date:

RAILWAY TO SIDNEY CEASES OPERATIONS

Last Train Will Run Tonight

Negotiations Progress

"The railway service from Victoria to Sidney will terminate when the inbound train on the Victoria and Sidney Railway reaches the city tonight. The Peninsula town will then be left without any communication southward except by the B.C. Electric Interurban line, and jitneys which have recently started operation.

"The V.&S. line for some years past has been a drain upon the resources of the Great Northern Railway, which has recently operated it. The company therefore decided to close down bringing its operations to an end today.

"Premier Oliver took the matter up with the Canadian National Railway officials with the idea that it might operate a service to Sidney. Mr. Cameron, of that company, investigated the matter thoroughly but held out little hope that the project would pay."[7]

Likewise, the Victoria *Daily Colonist* reported on the demise of the V&S in their issue of May 1st:

"The last train to travel over the Victoria and Sidney Railway tracks reached home last night. Sidney is now without direct communication with Victoria, except by jitney. The B.C. Electric Interurban line and the Canadian National Railways operate in close proximity to the town but do not touch it.

"The Canadian National Railway is urged to operate the Sidney line by Premier Oliver, but the proposal was turned down after investigation. It is possible, however, that some later developments may result in the absorption of part of the line by the C.N.R. or the electrification of a spur line from the B.C. Electric into Sidney."

The V&S had struggled to survive in a sparsely populated area that generated only marginal passenger and freight revenues. Many schemes had been tried to improve the system, to put it on a profitable basis, but to no avail. Many wondered why the Great Northern had not abandoned the line sooner than they did.

The last train had run and the V&S became someone else's problem. On May 15, 1919, Mr. John Powell Roberts, of Vancouver, was appointed receiver for the Victoria and Sidney Railway with a mandate to settle up the railway's affairs.

The most immediate problem caused by the shutdown of the V&S was the possible closure of the Sidney sawmill, with its 140-man workforce:

"That the Sidney Mills, Limited, will be obliged to close down if some arrangement is not made in the very near future for the continuance of freight service over the Victoria and Sidney tracks, or at least, over that portion of the tracks lying between the mills and junction of the Victoria and Sidney and the Canadian Northern Pacific Railway about a mile and a half south of the city, was stated by Manager G.H. Walton to a Review representative this morning. The Victoria and Sidney discontinued operations yesterday, and while it is understood that the string of freight cars which is at present being loaded at the mills will be handled by the railway company, no further assurance of any service whatever is given."[8]

For the Sidney Sawmills and other local industries, the problem of railway service was immediate and could not await a resolution of just who was going to operate the line over the long term. For a brief period, the mill crew operated the No.3 locomotive of the defunct V&S to move cars of lumber out to the CNPR/ Canadian National Railways interchange. Meanwhile, the Sidney Board of Trade lobbied the government and the CNR to assume responsibility for operation of the V&S trackage into Sidney. By May 15, 1919, Premier John Oliver, who was also Minister of Railways, was in contact with President D.B. Hanna of Canadian National Railways, urging him to take immediate action to provide a rail service to Sidney.

Several weeks earlier, on a visit to Victoria, Hanna had indicated that the Canadian National might be willing to take over the trackage into Sidney, but would assume no cost in doing so. Now Hanna was hedging - he had legitimate concerns over the condition of the Sidney trackage and the ability of heavier CNR locomotives to operate over it.

Over the
Last Hurdle

Matters were expedited when V&S receiver Roberts officially requested Premier Oliver, in his capacity as Minister of Railways, to grant the CNR running rights over the V&S trackage into Sidney. Armed with the request, Oliver wired Hanna again, urging him to act: "Manufacturing interests in Sidney are suffering greatly from want of transportation." Oliver implored, "Sawmill pays from $15,000 to $20,000 monthly and the Rubber Roofing Company $2,000 in railway freights. Majority of this would accrue to your company if you furnished transportation. Roofing company is at present transporting its output to Victoria by motor truck, and it is likely that both concerns will close down unless you afford relief at once. I feel sure that $500 would make the road safe to operate until a more permanent arrangement can be made. Surely you are not going to let this small sum prevent your obtaining such a good feeder for your road."[9]

Finally, the lobbying was successful and the first Canadian National train ran into Sidney on June 26, 1919, with the company operating by virtue of a Certificate from the provincial Minister of Railways. It seemed that the freight service had been saved, but there was no solution to the loss of the V&S passenger service. A group of returned military veterans proposed to operate a gas jitney service to carry passengers over the line, but the scheme fell through.

The CNR's operating permit for the line was extended for another three months in September 1919. Final settlement of the Sidney railway crisis came in December, when Canadian National Railways bought the Sidney trackage from receiver Roberts for $25,600, including $600 for payment of the last year's taxes on the line.

The tracks from the Victoria terminal to the interchange at Bazan Bay were torn up and the equipment of the V&S Railway was sold off over the next few years. Receiver J.P. Roberts submitted his final report and was discharged in November 1922. The bondholders, in the final analysis, received a total of $67,815 - only 22½ cents for each dollar they had invested - a dismal showing for the 25 year period of the bonds. The stock of the V&S was worthless, but the company still held annual general meetings until final dissolution in 1935.

In the beginning, there had been the dream of a railway and ferry service from Victoria to the Mainland and a connection there with the transcontinental railways and, while that objective was obtained, the V&S was never more than a limited success in financial terms. In 25 years of operation its locomotives ran 720,389 miles and carried 602,693 tons of freight and 1,254,876 passengers.

But in terms of public utility, even running on an irregular schedule as it so often did, it was an absolute necessity for the development of the Saanich Peninsula and the Gulf Islands and the local people would have been hard pressed without it. A generation of people grew up along the line of the V&S and, in its heyday, it was as familiar to Peninsula residents as is the family car today.

History, with the benefit of hindsight gained through the passage of a hundred years or so can often teach us a great deal. The lesson of the Victoria and Sidney Railway, a century after its inauguration, is that its greatest service to the community was in the moving of people to and from Victoria and Sidney. If the little line could struggle on, from 1894 to 1919, without an adequate population base, relatively low ridership and low freight revenues, it could today be a resounding financial success, moving passengers from the Saanich Peninsula to Victoria by rail, thus greatly easing the pressure of automobile traffic along the Pat Bay Highway.

There is something to be said for the old "Cordwood Limited" after all. It is an even better idea in 1992 than it was a century ago, in 1892. If public responsibility and fiscal good sense prevail, we will again see passenger rail service along the Saanich Peninsula in the not too distant future.

The old Victoria and Sidney Railway is mostly memories and faded photographs now, but a walk along the old grade by the west side of Beaver and Elk lakes quickly transports one back to those long-ago days when the woods echoed to the whistle of the old No.1 and the squeal of steel wheels on steel rails heralded the arrival of the twice-daily train.

The old grade is silent now and the locomotives and cars were consigned to that "Great Roundhouse In The Sky" where steam is always up and the trains run only on-time. It was a tough show for the V&S, almost from beginning to end, but the railway is part of our local heritage and we would be as poor without it today as would have the pioneers of the Saanich Peninsula who, for a generation, made it their main mode of travel from Sidney to Victoria.

In 1922 the abandoned No.3 stood forlornly on a siding at Bazan Bay. Unable to find a new owner when the V&S shut down in 1919, she awaits the scrapper's torch.

The Colquitz Creek trestle
of the V&S as it appeared
in 1934. Today a pedestrian
footbridge adjoins this site
at the end of Pipeline Road
in Saanich.

APPENDIX A

EXCERPTS FROM REPORT ON RAILWAY SURVEY AND ESTIMATES
BY JOHN HAMILTON GRAY, C.E.

Victoria, 5th February 1893

To: The President and Directors of the Victoria and Sidney Railway Company

Gentlemen, I beg to submit for your consideration:-

1st.   A Bill of Works showing approximately under its proper classification the cost of each item of construction and supply, necessary for the full completion of your railway between Victoria and Sidney.

2nd.   A specification which should govern the works during their construction.

3rd.   A set of general drawings, which are intended to govern the character of the structures and works proposed; to be a guide to persons tendering and upon which my estimate is based.

Since my incomplete report, after the completion of surveys, in November last, I have been able to compute carefully the amount of work done for the expenditure of $4,200.00 under the head of "surveys."

As you are aware, three distinct preliminary lines were "run" and compared, radiating from a common point some five miles south of Sidney; these have been termed for reference the Easterly, Central and Westerly Lines.

The first or Easterly Line followed the trend of the sea coast, gradually converging toward it from the point "in common" inland, until at Cordova Bay, it was on the salt water and from thence through the depression by Lost Lake to Victoria.

The second or Central and adopted Line, (from the radiating point) follows up Sandhill Creek through a central valley and across the divide, to Elk Lake and along the shore of it and Beaver Lake to their common outlet, from whence it crosses three defined depressions or valleys in an almost direct line to Victoria.

The third or Westerly Line, swung to the west from number 2 before leaving Beaver Lake, made grade into, and followed down the valley of the Colquitz River, (outlet of Elk and Beaver Lakes) for some distance, leaving which it turned Southerly through a small valley to a junction near Victoria with the Central Line.

The question was so thoroughly considered and discussed before location was begun, that it is unnecessary now to repeat the reason that resulted in the adoption of the Central Line; suffice it to say that although the Coast Line for one half its distance, undoubtedly presents less engineering difficulties and was less costly to construct by fully ten per cent, yet the central position of the present line was so superior from a commercial point of view and so much better calculated to serve the interests of the districts, through which the Railway runs, that your choice eventually rested with it.

The Coast and Central routes would be practically of the same length while that by the Colquitz River would be one and one half miles longer, without any compensating advantages over the Central Line, in the matter of grades.

The location of the Coast line was projected only, that is to say, cross-sectioned for its position proper.

The Central Line has been revised and finally located and in miles the total surveys result as follows:-

Preliminary lines	50.0 Miles
Actual location	30.3 Miles
Projected (cross-sectioned)	7.0 Miles

Being a total of about 87 miles of instrument work. The price or cost of survey includes the supply of equipment, both field and office and preparation of two sets of plans for the Government.

I propose after a few remarks upon the general physical features of the country passed through and the engineering character of the work to refer to the Bill of Works in detail.

The character of the country and the attendant works might very properly be classed under two heads viz, the Northerly or light, and the Southerly or heavy. The first or light work extends from Sidney southerly to the eighth mile. Over this portion the grading, in a more or less heavily timbered country, would be extremely light, the total material to be handled throughout this distance aggregating about twenty-seven thousand cubic yards being about twenty-two per cent of the total quantities.

On the rise or ascending grade beginning 1 1/4 miles from Sidney (previous to which the line is level and close to the sea-shore) to the summit leading into Sand Creek, a difference of elevation of 128 feet is obtained in about ten thousand feet or 100 "stations," the grades, varying from 1.65 to 1.00 per 100 feet, the maximum curvature being four degrees or having a radius of 1433 feet.

The heavier work may be said to begin after passing the 8th mile. On the summit or divide between the waters flowing north and south into Elk Lake (8 1/4 miles) the first rock "in situ" is seen; falling from this divide and along the shores of Elk and Beaver Lakes to the 11th mile though the grades are easy, owing to the indented and in many cases "bluff" character of the shores, the curvature is continuous and in two instances 10 degree curves are employed, these being the exception to a general curvature of 5 degrees or 1146 feet radius.

The greatest obstacle to a satisfactory location by the Central route is the quick descent from the level of Elk and Beaver Lakes. To follow the ridge which contains or hems these lakes in and which trends to the south-east, would entail heavy works through a broken, rocky country without adequate results. An attempt to lessen the rate of grade by "developing distances" to the north-west failed most signally and did not compare at all favourably with what was done, viz:- To reach the valley by the use of maximum grades on a line or route affording the best and easiest alignment - This descent occurs between the 11th and 13th miles being 140 feet of fall in 8000 feet with a "rest" or level stretch of 1500 feet about three quarters the way down. The grades over this distance are 1.50 and 2.00 feet per 100 feet until the 15th mile is reached, where excepting a short piece of 1.90 feet per 100 feet, the curves being two four degree, one five degree and a six degree near the foot of the grade.

Excepting the short piece of 1.90 per 100 feet rising out of Footes Valley the grades on the remainder of the line to Victoria nowhere exceed 1.50 per 100 feet until the 15th mile is reached, where the steep pitch from the ridge on the north, across the Cloverdale Farm, necessitates the use of the maximum (2 per 100) grade. The curvature throughout the last six miles of the railway is nowhere excessive...

[Author's Note: Space limitations did not permit publication of this Appendix in full. Those wishing to examine the complete document will be able to see it at the Victoria City Archives or at the Saanich Pioneers' Society Museum in Saanichton. Other local museums are welcome to copy this report. The only other part of John H. Gray's report included here is his estimated costs for construction of the railway which follows:]

VICTORIA AND SIDNEY RAILWAY
Approximate estimate of proposed works.
18 miles of single track.

Description of Works	Quantities	Rates	Amount
Clearing, Acres	117	$ 40.00	$ 8,190.00
Close-cutting, Acres	83	80.00	664.00
Grubbing, Acres	5	125.00	625.00
Fencing, Miles	15	750.00	11,250.00
Solid Rock, exc. cu.yds.	7,340	1.65	12,111.00
Loose Rock, cu. yds.	1,100	.80	880.00
Cement, cu. yds.	12,000	.80	9,600.00
Earth, cu. yds.	102,339	.32	32,748.48
Extra haul (distance 600 ft.)	21,500		2,300.00
Underdrains - lineal ft.	300	.25	75.00
Rip rap (cu. yds.)	800	2.00	1,600.00
Square timber (per 1000 b.m.)	400,000	23.00	9,200.00
Round timber (cribbing) (Lineal feet)	1,800	.12	216.00
Piles driven (ft.)	3,000	.35	1,050.00
Flatted timber 12"	14,200	.12	1,704.00
Wrought iron (pounds)	28,000	.09	2,520.00
Cast iron (pounds)	12,000	.06	720.00
Public road crossings (No.)	12	150.00	1,800.00
Farm road crossings (No.)	48	21.00	1,008.00
Ties 7"x6" (2,300/mi.)	41,400	.26	10,764.00
Carriage of rails, (tons)	1,508	2.00	3,016.00
Track laying (miles)	18	300.00	5,400.00
Ballasting (cu. yds.)	33,480	.40	13,392.00
Points and crossings (sets)	22	150.00	3,300.00
Station buildings	5		10,000.00
Wages with 15% added			5,000.00
50# rails (tons)	1,414	35.00	49,490.00
Fastenings (tons)	51	41.50	2,116.50
Bolts (tons)	12	96.00	1,152.00
Spikes 4 1/2x1 1/2 (tons)	31	90.00	2,480.00
Water service			3,180.00
Turntables (No.)	2	1,200.00	2,400.00
Telegraph line (miles)	16	90.00	1,440.00
Signboards (No.)	21		125.00
Roundhouse (No. of stalls)	2	900.00	1,800.00
Equipment			51,000.00
Value of work open to contract			$264,236.98
Expenditure By Company			
Right-of-way purchase			56,495.00
Surveys, preliminary and location			4,200.00
Engineering and superintendence			5,000.00
Expenditure Necessary to Complete			$329,931.98

APPENDIX B

VICTORIA AND SIDNEY RAILWAY CONSTRUCTION AGREEMENT

THIS AGREEMENT made the twenty-eighth day of April One Thousand Eight Hundred and Nintey-Three.

BETWEEN THE VICTORIA AND SIDNEY RAILWAY COMPANY (hereinafter called The Company) of the one part and Thomas W. Paterson of the City of Victoria in the Province of British Columbia, Contractor of the other part.

WHEREAS the company has determined to construct their line of Railway as authorized by their act of incorporation, from the City of Victoria to the townsite of Sidney, in the District of North Saanich in the Province of British Columbia: and being in length a distance of sixteen miles or thereabouts.

AND WHEREAS the Company has in pursuance of its powers and under its act of incorporation issued bonds of the Company secured upon the said line of Railway for the sum of three hundred thousand dollars ($300,000.00) bearing interest at the rate of five percentum per annum payable half-yearly and the principal thereof being payable at the end of twenty-five years from the date of the said bonds, and the said interest being guaranteed by the Government of the Province of British Columbia and the City of Victoria, severally as to two percentum by the Government, and three percentum by the City in pursuance of the Act of the Legislature of that Province, and the By-Law of the Corporation of the City of Victoria.

AND WHEREAS the Company is authorized to issue capital stock of the Company in addition to the amount already subscribed, and is authorized to pledge any stock which under the powers of this Act can be issued for the construction of the railway or any other purposes of the Company.

AND WHEREAS the said Contractor, has agreed to build and construct the said line of Railway as hereinafter provided.

NOW THIS AGREEMENT WITNESSETH that the said Contractor for himself, his heirs, executors and administrators, and in consideration of the money and stock to be delivered to him as hereinafter provided: Hereby covenants, promises, and agrees, with the said Company, their successors and assigns, that he the said Contractor shall and will secure all rights-of-way not already obtained by the company, and forthwith commence and carry on to completion without avoidable delay, and so as to complete ready for active operation by the first day of January one thousand eight hundred and ninety-four: the construction of the said Railway: and to build and complete the same in all respects in accordance with the plans and specifications hereto attached: which are hereby incorporated herewith, and made a part hereof by the signatures of the parties, so far as the same are applicable to and not inconsistent with this contract: that is to say: in case of any conflict between the terms of this contract and the plans and specifications the terms of this contract shall prevail and to the satisfaction of the Company's engineer whose certificate shall be binding and conclusive on the parties hereto.

AND THE SAID COMPANY hereby covenants and agrees to pay the said Contractor the sum of fifteen thousand eight hundred and thirty-three dollars ($15,833.33) for each and every mile of track constructed, and a proportionate sum for each fraction of a mile from time to time as the work progresses, upon a certificate of the Company's engineer as hereinafter more particularly provided and the said Company also hereby covenants and agrees to make and issue to the said Contractor as paid up stock in the said company shares or stock in the said company to the amount of five thousand five hundred and fifty-five dollars ($5,555.00) per mile of track constructed which stock or share certificates shall be made and issued to the said Contractor as shares or capital stock paid in full: from time to time as the work progresses as hereinafter more particularly provided. Payments as aforesaid shall be made as follows:
- Forty-five per cent of the contract price in cash and stock upon the completion of each mile or fraction of a mile of grading to the satisfaction of the Company's engineer. Estimates to be made monthly if required by the Contractor.
- Fifteen per cent of the contract price in cash and stock upon delivery of the rails upon the ground at or near Sidney.
- Twenty per cent of the contract price in cash and stock upon delivery of the rolling stock.
- Ten per cent of the contract price in cash and stock upon completion of tracklaying and ballasting to the satisfaction of the Company's engineer.
- The remaining ten per cent upon completion of the contract to the satisfaction of the Company's engineer.

In witness whereof the said Company have hereunto attached their common seal, and the said Contractor has set his hand and seal the day and year first above written.

The common seal of the Company

was hereunto affixed in the presence

of (signed) James Jeffrey.

        (signed) P.C. Dunlevy, President

        (signed) Robert Irving Secretary

Signed sealed and delivered

by the said Thomas W. Paterson

in presence of (signed) James Jeffrey

        (signed) Thomas W. Paterson

VICTORIA AND SIDNEY RAILWAY
SUMMARY STATEMENT OF EARNINGS

Year End June 30th:	Passenger Traffic	Freight Traffic	Mails & Express	Gross Income & Misc.	Net Income
1895	$ 3,552.35	$ 2,867.22	$ 20.25	$ 6,448.82	$ -4,321.56
1896	9,843.83	11,929.98	244.71	22,018.52	1,667.71
1897	7,911.20	8,360.03	415.20	16,686.43	1,492.00
1898	8,991.30	9,271.60	408.89	18,671.79	3,937.78
1899	8,362.50	9,240.20	409.14	18,011.84	1,348.22
1900	9,167.45	8,346.35	407.17	17,920.97	-141.87
1901	9,703.01	10,281.65	401.61	20,386.27	153.74
1902	11,961.88	11,699.99	400.64	24,062.51	1,466.85
1903	13,300.52	13,324.22	421.99	27,046.73	-7,600.27
1904	13,323.44	12,951.84	453.95	26,729.23	-2,477.00
1905	12,787.57	13,672.05	527.43	26,987.05	-7,420.84
1906	12,583.00	13,755.84	456.85	26,795.69	2,961.77
1907	16,977.31	13,772.15	1,436.54	32,186.00	9,038.12
1908	18,849.38	20,856.46	1,354.10	40,635.95	4,985.14
1909	20,247.18	22,533.79	*571.46	42,927.30	12,599.90
1910	20,793.21	24,465.01	*730.62	46,565.69	19,298.47
1911	25,057.90	29,120.28	143.14	54,321.31	20,611.25
1912	28,359.24	30,709.40	644.99	59,713.63	8,786.13
1913	38,153.48	38,789.88	*2,445.58	76,943.36	25,903.52
1914	30,519.80	24,987.28	*1,297.78	56,468.37	-25,399.64
1915	20,321.38	11,071.15	*679.21	31,679.97	-13,301.15
1916	16,345.46	12,236.49	*3,942.45	31,934.69	4,660.15
1917	25,373.73	18,985.98	*3,063.72	47,027.50	12,383.81
1918	19,205.10	11,655.06	284.74	31,144.90	-3,286.87
1919	11,078.00	12,830.12	581.77	24,080.00	-8,712.01

Notes: 1. All data is from the Annual Reports of the Chief Engineer of Railways and Canals for Canada.

2. Compilation of this data required the perusal of over 4,500 pages of Federal Government reports. It should be noted that similar, separate figures were submitted by the Victoria Terminal Railway and Ferry Company and can be abstracted from the same reports. They are not included here because of their length and because our main concern is with the Victoria and Sidney Railway, the bond interest of which was guaranteed by the City of Victoria and the Province of British Columbia.

3. * means that baggage and express income is included in passenger income for the years shown. Miscellaneous income remains listed under the Mails, Express and Miscellaneous heading for years in which asterisk is shown.

4. The complexity of data in Chief Engineer's Reports made it necessary to combine figures for Miscellaneous Income and Mails and Express in a single column.

5. Copy of summaries of complete financial data will be made available to Saanich Pioneers' Society Museum.

VICTORIA AND SIDNEY RAILWAY
SUMMARY STATEMENT OF OPERATING EXPENSES

Year End June 30th:	Maint Line & Bldgs.	Work & Repair Engines	Work & Repair of Cars	General Operating Expense	Total Expenses
1895	$ 2,551.84	$ 4,073.90	$ 0.00	$ 4,144.64	$ 10,770.38
1896	8,828.49	7,509.61	0.00	7,018.71	20,356.81
1897	2,752.32	6,843.07	274.24	5,378.80	15,194.43
1898	3,018.98	6,222.16	98.97	5,393.90	14,734.01
1899	3,692.64	7,351.26	179.73	5,439.99	16,663.62
1900	5,814.29	6,683.59	201.99	5,362.97	18,062.84
1901	4,867.59	7,457.32	192.10	7,715.52	20,232.53
1902	5,425.17	7,677.82	597.94	8,894.73	22,595.66
1903	10,593.77	9,805.67	705.27	13,542.29	34,647.00
1904	10,135.53	7,718.74	1,448.60	9,903.36	29,206.23
1905	11,054.93	8,825.70	2,751.89	12,075.37	34,407.89
1906	5,523.35	6,038.57	615.48	11,656.62	23,833.92
1907	6,032.75	11,786.20	2,054.77	11,786.20	23,147.88
1908	10,449.83	5,626.53	3,546.44	16,028.01	35,650.81
1909	9,165.38	14,270.56	4,431.81	2,459.65	30,327.40
1910	7,236.59	15,357.25	1,840.68	2,832.70	27,267.22
1911	9,049.85	18,446.08	3,098.33	3,115.80	33,710.06
1912	18,388.49	22,236.84	6,401.07	3,901.10	50,927.50
1913	11,578.46	30,858.86	6,350.77	4,168.97	52,957.06
1914	45,824.07	26,652.62	4,467.79	4,923.53	81,868.01
1915	16,587.55	16,674.10	4,947.17	3,772.30	44,981.12
1916	5,332.97	17,931.33	1,106.15	2,904.09	27,274.54
1917	4,643.60	23,048.59	4,055.58	2,895.92	34,643.69
1918	5,772.97	32,253.59	2,571.71	2,883.50	34,431.77
1919	4,788.94	22,736.72	2,321.77	2,944.58	32,792.01

ANNUAL OPERATING STATISTICS - 1895 TO 1919

Year End June 30th:	Mileage Passenger Trains	Mileage Freight Trains	Mileage Mixed* Trains	Total Miles Run	Total Passengers Carried	Tons of Freight Carried
1895	0	0	11,520	11,520	15,052	4,573
1896	0	0	24,128	24,128	26,917	28,788
1897	0	0	23,808	23,968	18,242	16,646
1898	410	0	23,725	24,135	19,294	18,464
1899	500	0	23,661	24,161	19,573	19,084
1900	0	0	24,240	24,240	21,783	17,051
1901	0	0	24,250	24,250	22,761	18,726
1902	1,780	0	24,130	25,910	26,703	23,255
1903	**6,965	0	25,550	32,515	34,379	21,783
1904	15,156	0	11,268	26,424	41,694	23,633
1905	13,140	2,808	12,224	28,172	46,456	23,037
1906	13,468	0	11,393	24,861	48,980	23,200
1907	12,869	0	11,870	24,739	60,800	19,103
1908	11,837	0	10,146	21,983	63,127	29,724
1909	7,046	152	15,211	22,409	68,428	30,003
1910	6,822	0	15,834	22,656	67,498	35,766
1911	12,699	7,880	9,974	30,551	81,965	34,535
1912	16,135	10,199	5,655	31,989	91,121	34,365
1913	21,169	10,313	416	31,898	123,599	45,282
1914	32,075	9,439	496	42,010	86,179	28,637
1915	33,204	9,755	224	43,183	55,264	16,538
1916	32,339	9,500	336	42,175	50,987	20,203
1917	35,470	7,777	2,413	45,600	81,618	31,286
1918	27,180	7,168	1,264	35,612	53,129	19,682
1919	22,650	7,168	1,055	30,873	29,327	19,599
Totals	322,914	82,159	314,791	719,864	1,254,876	602,963

* The term "mixed trains" refers to trains in which both freight and passenger cars are carried. Until 1902 the V&S ran mixed trains almost entirely.

** 1903 was the first year after completion of the Mainland section of the VTR&F and it was at this time that the V&S began to run straight "freight trains" on a regular basis.

V&S FREIGHT TRAFFIC MOVEMENT
YEAR ENDING APRIL 30, 1919

COMMODITY	ORIG. ON LINE (tons)	ORIG. OFF LINE (tons)	TOTAL (tons)
Grain	258	150 tons	408
Flour	11	0	11
Bit. Coal	4	200	204
Fruit & Veg.	45	805	850
Dressed Meats	2	3	5
Other Meats	0	2	2
Poultry	0	3	3
Househld. Gds/Furn.	14	12	26
Wines and Beer	0	6	6
Cement, Brick, Lime	12	60	72
Other Manufactures	452	800	1,250
Sand	0	40	40
Misc. Merch.	5,000	2,720	5,720
Other Commodities	816	716	1,532
Lumber	5,580	306	5,886
Other For. Prod.	630	150	780
Other Mill Prod.	0	106	106
POL*	19	0	19
Sugar	3	0	3
Naval Stores	0	14	14
Castings, Mach.	0	64	64
Sheet metal	0	18	18
Hay	2	578	580
Recapitulation	12,843 tons	6,756 tons	19,599 tons

* Petrol, Oil and Lubricants.

VICTIMS AND SURVIVORS
OF THE SINKING OF THE *S.S. IROQUOIS*

The tragic events of April 10, 1911 were a shock to Sidney residents and local authorities and it took some days to make a final listing of the dead, missing and survivors. This information was published in the *Victoria Daily Times* on April 12, 1911:

The Death Toll Numbered 21:

Bodies Recovered:	Miss Isabel Fenwick
	Mesach Phillips
	John Brydson
	Jan Bactaren
	Sydney A. Clark
	A.D. Munro, Purser
	Herbert Hartnell, Steward
	Andrew Olsen, Fireman
	Tom Chan Lung, Chinese Cook
	Foo Yet Sim, Dishwasher
Missing:	Miss Edith Fenwick
	Mrs. Evan Houson and Son
	Mr. Prophet
	William Aitken
	George Webber
	Mr. and Mrs. William Green
	P. Green
	D.N. Davidson, Deckhand
	Unknown Chinaman
Survivors:	Miss Margaret Barton
	H.S. Moss
	Henry E. Hartnell
	John Bennett
	Captain A.A. Sears
	John Isbister, Mate
	W. Thomson, Chief Engineer
	Joe Phillips, Deckhand
	Prosper David, Deckhand
	John David, Deckhand

APPENDIX E

DEPARTMENT OF RAILWAYS IMPROVEMENT ORDER

(From Victoria *Daily Colonist*, January 1, 1913)

The decision reached by the Provincial Minister of Railways, Honourable Thomas Taylor, upon the complaint of the City of Victoria, dated August 6th last, against the Victoria and Sidney Railway Company and the Victoria Terminal Railway and Ferry Company, under the provisions of Section 177, Chapter 144, British Columbia Railway Act, 1911, was presented to and approved by the Executive at its session of yesterday and will forthwith be laid before His Excellency, the Lieutenant-Governor. The effect of the Minister's ruling is embodied in a certificate issued by him under authority of Section 179 of the Railway Act, upon the report of the Chief Engineer and Inspector of Railways of the Province authorizing and ordering as follows:

a. The third track, lying between the tracks shown in red on the plan attached to the decree of the Court referred to in the complaint of the City of Victoria is authorized as necessary accommodation;

b. The Railway Company is prohibited from unloading freight from cars standing on the track of the company to the south of Fisgard Street;

c. The changes of the grade from Pembroke Street south on Blanchard Street to the end of the track on Cormorant Street shall be left to the direction of the Chief Engineer of Railways, the changes authorized by him to be carried out to his entire satisfaction;

A Thorough Examination

d. The railway companies herewith referred to shall forthwith cause to be made a thorough examination of their lines by the engineers with a view to the improvement of the alignment and grade throughout and shall submit plans and profiles showing the proposed improvements to the Chief Engineer and Inspector of Railways of the Department of Railways of British Columbia, for his approval, and the Chief Engineer and Inspector of Railways shall, without delay, signify his approval thereof with such changes or alterations as he may consider desireable. The railway company shall thereupon immediately proceed to carry out the work underlined and complete the same before the 30th day of September, 1913;

e. The rails in present use, weighing about fifty (50) pounds to the lineal yard on the line of the Victoria and Sidney Railway and those on the line of the Victoria Terminal Railway and Ferry Company may be retained for the present provided:-

(1) That the number of ties is increased to 3,000 per mile;

(2) That the ties shall not be less than eight feet long, eight inches thick and eight inches wide;

(3) That tieplates of approved pattern shall be placed upon every tie and the bottom of the rail spiked to the former;

(4) That the ties shall be of Douglas fir or cedar, the latter to be used only on tangents, and then not more than six in every 33-foot length of rail;

(5) That the splice or anglebars shall have four holes and shall not be less than 24 inches long, and that every rail splice shall have the required number of bolts and nuts;

(6) That the rail braces either of cast iron or of pressed steel shall be placed on curves;

(7) That the spikes shall be fully and properly spiked to every tie;

(8) That the switches shall be of the split rail pattern on mainline turnouts, on others the switches may be stub end switches;

(9) That rigid frogs may be used except on the mainline turnouts;

(10) That frogs and mainline turnouts shall be of the spring rail pattern;

(11) That guardrails shall be laid on bridges and elsewhere it is considered necessary;

(12) That all frogs and guardrails shall be properly packed, according to Section 205 of the Railway Act, 1911;

(13) That the track throughout shall be properly ballasted, with either broken rock or approved gravel;

(14) That the thickness of the ballast under the ties shall be not less than eight inches;

(15) That all bridges, culverts and cattleguards shall be repaired and strengthened throughout as may be directed;

(16) And that all matters mentioned in the foregoing paragraph shall be carried out to the satisfaction of the Chief Engineer and Inspector of Railways within twelve months from the date of certificate.

Improved Rolling Stock

f. The rolling stock, consisting of locomotives, passenger coaches, mail, express, baggage box and flatcars shall be increased:

(1) By providing locomotives of greater power and efficiency than those now in use, and of the latest approved design;

(2) New and modern passenger coaches, fitted with the latest approved sanitary closets or toilets for both men and women, together with wash basins;

(3) New mail, express and baggage cars, fitted with the necessary and suitable closets;

(4) New box and flatcars, all the number required to operate the railway efficiently and to meet the convenience of the travelling public and the volume of business operating.

All the rolling stock enumerated herein shall be fitted with the most approved safety appliances. All the items set forth in this paragraph shall be completed to the satisfaction of the Chief Engineer and Inspector of Railways within twelve months from the date of this certificate.

g. The wharf and car ferry landing stage at Sidney shall be improved and made safe, the grade of the track leading thereto shall be reduced;

h. The railway company is permitted to retain weighing scales where those are located at present on Blanshard Street, as a necessary adjunct to the handling of freight;

i. The railway crossings at Tomie and Topaz Avenues to be made to conform with those streets when paved and surfaced with concrete and planks, laid to the full width of the pavement to correspond with the work already done by the railway company in the cases of the railway crossings at Kings Road and Bay Street;

j. The track along Rose Avenue shall be raised to conform to the present grade of that street on either side thereof;

k. Temporary level crossings shall be made at Fisgard, Chatham, and Pembroke Streets and these crossings shall be permanently paved hereafter in the same manner as the crossing at Kings Road and Bay Street, as soon as the beforementioned streets have been paved by the city;

l. No railway crossing shall be permitted of the line on Herald Street to connect with Pioneer Street, as a crossing here would be dangerous. Traffic passing to the east from this street must be diverted by way of the street dedicated to the company on the rear of the railway station, to Fisgard Street;

m. Permission is refused to assess the company on the local improvement plan in connection with the paving of the streets along which the railway passes.

VICTORIA AND SIDNEY RAILWAY, VICTORIA TERMINAL RAILWAY AND FERRY COMPANY PLANT AND EQUIPMENT

General

The plant and equipment of the Victoria and Sidney Railway and the Victoria Terminal Railway and Ferry Company were lettered for each individual company. There were relatively few changes in the equipment of the Victoria and Sidney Railway over the 25 year period of its existence. After the Victoria Terminal Railway and Ferry Company was incorporated, some of the equipment was lettered for that railway. Rolling stock from the VTR&F was frequently photographed on the line of the V&S, as was equipment from other Great Northern Railway subsidiary companies on the Mainland. This included equipment from the Vancouver, Westminster and Yukon Railway and the Great Northern Railway itself. It was probably cheaper for the parent company to move equipment around than it was to expend funds on equipment for the V&S alone.

After the Mainland line of the VTR&F from Port Guichon to Cloverdale was sold to the Vancouver, Victoria and Eastern Railway, some VTR&F equipment seems to have taken up longterm residence on the Victoria and Sidney line. For short term requirements (for peak traffic on the V&S) it seems likely that additional equipment was moved back and forth from the Mainland to Vancouver Island.

This makes it very difficult to compile a comprehensive list of all equipment that was used on the V&S. The list here is limited to those items of equipment for which it can be definitely established that operated on the Victoria and Sidney Railway and the Victoria Terminal Railway and Ferry Company.

Summary of Railway Characteristics

A. Victoria and Sidney Railway
- Length of line: 16.26 miles
- Length of sidings: 1.20 miles
- Rails, steel, weighing 50 pounds per yard
- Number of ties per mile: 2,464
- Nature of rail fastenings: fishplates
- Number of level crossings: 13
- Number of overhead bridges: 1
- Number of trestle bridges: 2
- Junctions with other railways: none
- Radius of sharpest curve: 637 feet
- Number of ft. per mile of heaviest grade: 105 ft. (2%)
- Gauge of railway: 4'8"

B. Victoria Terminal Railway and Ferry Company
- Length of line: 18.40 miles from 1903 to 1907
  1.14 miles in Victoria until 1910
  0.99 miles in Victoria until 1919
- Length of sidings: 1.5 miles

- Rails, steel, weighing 56 and 60 pounds per yard
- Number of ties per mile: 2,640
- Nature of rail fastenings: Angle-bars
- Number of level crossings: 31
- Number of overhead bridges: 0
- Number of trestle bridges: 8 (Mainland section)
- Junctions with other railways: 2
- Radius of sharpest curve: 573 feet
- Number of feet per mile of heaviest grade: 26 (0.5%)
- Gauge of railway: 4'8"

Summary Statement of Rolling Stock and Engines

A. Victoria and Sidney Railway

	1895	1900	1905	1910	1915	1919
Number of engines:	2	2	3	2	3	2
Number of Coaches:	1	1	2	2	2	1
Combines	1	1	1	1	1	1
Box and cattle cars:	3	3	2	2	2	2
Flatcars:	15	15	15	15	15	15
Cabooses:	0	0	0	1	1	0
Gas-Electric Coach:	0	0	0	0	1	0

B. Victoria Terminal Railway and Ferry Company

	1895	1900	1905	1910	1915	1919
Number of engines:	n/a	n/a	1	0	0	0
Number of coaches:	n/a	n/a	2	0	0	0
Number of combines:	n/a	n/a	1	0	0	0
Box and cattle cars:	n/a	n/a	0	0	0	0
Flatcars:	n/a	n/a	0	0	0	0
Cabooses:	n/a	n/a	0	0	0	0
Other:	n/a	n/a	0	0	0	0

Roster of Locomotives of the Victoria and Sidney Railway

Road No.	Builder	Builder's Number	Year	Type	Cylinders (inches)	Drivers (inches)	Notes
1	C.L.C.*	445	1893	2-6-0	16x24	50"	1.
2	C.L.C.	196?	1875	4-4-0	16x24	62"	2.
3	Baldwin	?	1882	4-4-0	?	57"	3.
4	Baldwin	10830	?	4-4-0	17x24	63"	4.
290	Pittsburg	443	1880	4-4-0	17x24	63"	5.
2301	G.E.**	3742	1913	CRE-70-Bll	V-8	36"	6.

Notes: 1. V&S locomotive No.1 was purchased new from C.L.C.* (The Canadian Locomotive Company) and served the V&S from beginning to end. This locomotive had received a new boiler in 1914 and, although in need of major repairs, it was sold to United Engineers of Vancouver. The locomotive was resold to the logging firm of Bloedel, Stewart and Welch at Myrtle Point, near Powell River. It was assigned the road number 5. It was used for two year and was then retired and scrapped.

2. No.2 was less suited to the V&S line than the No.1 and was used mainly for passenger service or when the No.1 was not available. It was retired sometime before 1910 and scrapped at Victoria in 1918.

3. This locomotive was built for the Northern Pacific Railway in 1882 and was sold to the Victoria Lumber and Manufacturing Company of Chemainus in 1899 for use on that firm's logging railway. It was found to be unsuitable for that type of work and was sold to the V&S, arriving and making its first run at Victoria June 20,1902.(See *Victoria Times* of June 21, 1902, p.5) It has been indicated that this locomotive was also Vancouver, Westminster and Yukon Railway's first No.1 and photographic evidence seems to confirm that. This would mean that this locomotive was loaned or leased by the VW&YR from the V&S during the period of its construction which did not begin until after the No.3 was already serving the V&S in Victoria. It was presumably returned to the V&S as being too small for mainline work on the VW&YR after that company's short line of railway was completed. The No.3 was abandoned at Bazan Bay siding after the demise of the V&S in 1919 and was cut up for scrap in the early 1920s.

4. This locomotive was originally No.141 on the Great Northern Railway and was renumbered as No.4 when it arrived on V&S trackage about 1907. It was found to steam poorly and to be unsuited to the work demanded of it on the V&S. It lasted only about four weeks before being returned to the Great Northern for use elsewhere.

5. Great Northern No.290 was an oil burning 4-4-0 and arrived on the V&S in the early summer of 1908. She apparently served the line for some years until being withdrawn. The late Walter Bate informed me that this engine was not on the property when he started working with the V&S in 1916. It may have been withdrawn in 1913 when the Gasoline Electric Car was introduced.

6. The Gasoline Electric car No.2301 was built by G.E.** (General Electric) and arrived on the V&S in June of 1913. It served until the Great Northern equipment was withdrawn after the Bonds on the V&S matured and was later sold by Great Northern to the Pacific Great Eastern Railway where it became the No.104.

Other Equipment Notes

a. The first two passenger cars used on the V&S were constructed by the Crosson Manufacturing Company in Ontario. No other details are known.

b. Great Northern caboose No.0244 was used for a number of years on the rear of V&S freight trains and was involved in one fatal accident on the V&S line. This type of caboose was also used on the Mainland section of the VTR&F.

c. A number of locomotives were used on the Mainland section of the VTR&F. Apparently, only one locomotive was ever lettered or owned by the VTR&F. All other engines used came from the Great Northern Railway or from its subsidiaries in the Fraser Valley. The locomotives used on the Port Guichon to Cloverdale run are known to have included Moguls (2-6-0s) No.456,477,480. There are

also pictures of the V&S No.3/VW&Y No.1 (1st) on the line. It is obvious that the Mainland line was run from the general pool of locomotives that the Great Northern Railway and its subsidiaries maintained on the B.C. Mainland.

Other Plant and Buildings

When the specifications were drawn up by John Hamilton Gray, C.E., for the Victoria and Sidney Railway, they included a list of the railway equipment, buildings and service facilities that would be required. Gray's list included the following:

a. Two terminal stations or depots, at Victoria and Sidney and way station and freight houses not to exceed three in number.

b. There was to be a large freight shed at each terminus having a superficial floor area of at least 1,200 square feet.

c. At the way stations a freight shed having a superficial area of about 500 square feet shall be built in conjunction with the station.

d. Section houses shall contain a kitchen, dining room and sleeping accomodation for five and shall not exceed two in number. (These were at Bazan Bay and Royal Oak).

e. Tool houses must not be less than ten feet long and eight feet wide with a height in the clear of eight feet. They shall have two doors, one at each end, with an opening each of six feet. Tool houses shall not exceed four in number.

f. There shall be two water tanks situated at each terminus. (There were actually three, including the one at Elk Lake). Tanks were to be circular and capable of holding not less than 10,000 gallons.

g. Turntables shall be erected at either terminus; these shall be built of wood and iron in accordance with the design provided.

h. If in the opinion of the Engineer a wye is expedient, it may be substituted for a turntable. (This was not done.)

Note: The detailed specifications for the V&S Railway, including Gray's recommendation as to what locomotives and cars should be acquired are more than 30 pages in length and are greatly detailed. A copy may be seen at the Saanich Pioneers' Society archives or the City of Victoria's archives. Copies will also be available to any other interested museums in the region.

APPENDIX G

FIRST AND LAST VICTORIA AND SIDNEY RAILWAY PAYROLLS

1. FIRST PAYROLL

A.F. Forbes, conductor
George Parsons, brakeman
Herman H. Shade, brakeman
F.J. Andrews, brakeman
A.J. Jones, brakeman
Thomas Brownley, brakeman
F. Carpenter, brakeman
D.M. Hasker, fireman and wiper
John Walton, fireman and wiper
George Walton, engineer and fireman
E.G. Hasker, fireman and wiper
C. Irvine, wiper

2. LAST PAYROLL

Herman H. Shade, conductor
W.C. Bate, fireman and brakeman
C. Ching, coach cleaner
John Walton, engineer
George Walton, engineer and handyman
J. Frank, fireman
William Walker, engineer

Note: Neither of these payrolls seems to include station and maintenance of way staff who must have been on the payroll as well. The list of first employees comes from *A History of Saanich Peninsula Railways*, by R.D. Harvey, Q.C., which was published in the Annual Report of the Minister of Railways for British Columbian, 1955. The list of final employees is from the David Wilkie Collection and is credited to the Great Northern Railway. The names of other V&S and VTR&F employees are found throughout the text but so far no complete record has emerged.

APPENDIX H

WALTER BATE REMINISCENCES

Walter Bate was born on the Saanich Peninsula in 1900 and raised on the family farm near Saanichton. In 1916, at 16 years of age, he was hired as a locomotive fireman on the Victoria and Sidney Railway. He worked for the V&S from 1916 until its closure in 1919 and was later employed in construction and as a railway fireman on the building of the Canadian Northern Pacific Railway between Sooke and Shawnigan Lake. Most of his working life was spent as a mechanic for Island Coach Lines. He retired and remained a resident of Sidney until he passed away on March 17, 1992.

Walter was a bright, intelligent man with a warm heart and a fine memory. He was undoubtedly the last living employee of the old Victoria and Sidney Railway or "Cordwood Limited," and his reminiscences about it are an interesting and important contribution to the preservation of local Saanich Peninsula history.

The following are edited portions of an interview the author conducted with Walter during late 1991.

WORKING ON THE RAILROAD

"Well, I was standing on the station platform. A guy said, 'Are you looking for a job?' And I said 'what job?' 'Firing an engine.' I said, 'I've never fired an engine.' Anyway, I said, 'Oh, well, I could take a chance.' I did..."

"I lived on Princess Avenue. I very seldom went up to the station...I hopped on the train just out of the front door. I'd catch the train coming up from the roundhouse. My brother lived there. The night watchman down at the end there, he kept the engines and he'd put a fire in it and get it all laid up for the morning. He would toot the horn as he was coming across Hillside and I'd just hop on the train as it came up in the morning..."

"The passenger train left town at 8 o'clock and then the freight train would leave about eleven o'clock. Sometimes I worked the passenger and sometimes I worked the freight. I liked the freight because you didn't have to be at a certain place at a certain time."

"We'd go out in the morning and there was switching on the freight. We'd go out in the morning and get back about four o'clock and that'd be our day. The passenger train I can't remember. We used to make two trips and then change over on the last trip..."

"We worked on the freight until midnight. Sometimes we wouldn't get back into the shop until midnight. We got paid by the hour. Fifty cents an hour. They didn't pay any overtime. You went out and that was it. You just got the 50 cents an hour for the extra hours you worked but no overtime pay as such..."

"(While working the Sidney picnic excursions) they'd take the train out and drop the passengers where the dance was, then they'd go on to Sidney and pick up another load and turn around on the turntable. That was a helluva job on that turntable. It took three of us to turn the engine. The wheels got drier running around in circles. Once you got it going it was alright. To get it started was terrible...The train would lay over (at Sidney). We'd just go out and join the crowd and have a good time. Everybody knew everybody else."

THE RAILROAD OPERATIONS

"People were so used to getting on the train and then getting to town an hour and a half later or something like that. It was all taken in stride. They spoke of the old V.&S. as a joke a lot of times..."

"I think it was the Roadmaster at the head office in the building (running the trains)..."

"We did most of the engine work at Hillside. They had a little shop there and they used to pull the engine out at night, and...The turntable was right close to the shop - just a round turntable. There was also one at Sidney and we used it for emergencies. But the big shop was out from Hillside. There was two tracks, a hundred yards long on one side, to store the equipment on the side while they were working on the other one in the barns. It was quite a big barn..."

"(The railway barge) came in twice a week. We'd pull it at eight o'clock at night. We'd push back on (the barge) with loads of lumber. We'd also take cars out from Victoria and they'd ship them. We'd pull the incoming cars off the barge first and they'd go on a siding. Then we'd push our cars back on and that'd be it. They had a big siding at Sidney. It was quite a long one with double track there..."

"They got an awful lot of gravel off the beach at Sidney. The Chinese used to load the cars in the daytime and then we'd come along and pull them all at night..."

"(For snow) they just had a V-thing in front of the car - a wedge plow. They'd plow and they'd get stuck and then they'd back up and take a run at it. It was on the locomotive, on the cowcatcher. We used to call it the 'extra cowcatcher.' It was made of steel. The engine used to get going, they'd move about 25 miles an hour and they'd throw snow all over hell. When the snow piled up they'd stop and then back up and take a run at it. I remember in 1916 we had six feet of snow at our place. The horse would get bogged down. You'd dig him out again and finally we'd get to open roads..."

"Coaling up was done at night. We had a big hopper there and I think it was the watchman there working on the engine, helping out. They used to pull a string and open the gate and the coal would come down. I can't remember how they got it up there. I'm wondering if they had a ramp coming off the hillside going into above the hopper...It was up on Hillside, just beyond Hillside and you turned the bend just right in there. And there was a big mattress and bed factory I think there afterwards, when the road was still running..."

"The coal came in at Sidney on boat or barge...they seemed to have small wheeled trucks they'd pull off the barge onto a ramp...we opened a chute and filled our tenders (on the dock). Then we had another one just beyond Elk Lake. There was a large one there. It was a kind of a house built up on stilts and they had this filled with coal and we'd just go swing the door open and it'd come down and fill your tender up. It made a hellofa racket..."

"You get good coal and poor coal. Some of it turns to klinkers so quick. You put a lump of coal in there...and of course coal melts at a certain heat and it spreads out, you see, and the klinker spreads out and then goes down and then you have no heat at all...and you have steam for about ten or fifteen minutes and you look and see the gauge start to go down. There'll be a klinker about so big just red in there. And you'd have to put this bar with a sharp point and break it in half to get it out through the door. It was quite a chore..."

"Lots of time we pulled the lever (to dump the ashpan) when we were going along the track, you know. You're not supposed to but we'd pull the lever and all the things would go out on the track and there'd be sparks all over. We got away with it though. The grade was built up pretty high along there you know, all sand and they didn't cause any fires."

THE EQUIPMENT

"The No.3 and No.1 were the ones that I ran. The No.1 was the freight engine, No.3 was the passenger...big wheels. One of them had very small wheels to give it power and the other one had big wheels for the passenger service. Those are good old memories. It was a long time ago, you know..."

"Of course they had the gas electric. That belonged to another railroad (the Great Northern). They loaned it to us. The gas electric had a front compartment for baggage and mail, about eight by ten (feet). There were post offices at Sidney and Saanichton and Elk Lake. There was also a stop at Hillside but no station then... It was a beautiful machine. It just carried 35 passengers. They could (also) hook cars on behind it. I don't think it could handle more than one but it was as smooth as silk that thing. You wouldn't feel a jerk. It just gradually moved away. It was just like an electric. A gas electric they called it. The gas engines run the turbine that drives the wheels... They kept it (at Victoria) and it run two trips a day or whatever...That was a beautiful machine. I rode in the coaches (behind it) but I was never up in the engine room. It would take off so smoothly, you know..."

"We had a small caboose on the freight. And then they put a longer one on but they only kept it for a while."

SOME OF THE EMPLOYEES

"Van Sant was manager 'til he passed away. I don't remember very much of him. I spoke to him a couple of times when I went in to get a job. But he was very shrewd. Stern and very shrewd and he'd stand and look you over for about five minutes before he answered any words to you..."

"We had one engineer who was named George Walton, and his brother, Jack Walton. George was a prince to work under, you know. There was a big bar (Johnson Bar) you'd throw to control your steam, you see. He would save the fireman all

the work he could because if he threw that bar down, the flame would just suck up (the stack). It would knock your fire all to hell. So this young fellow George, he was beautiful you know. I'd open the firebox and say, 'I'm going to put some wood in now.' He'd push the Johnson Bar back so the engine (imitates the sound) ... hardly making any interruption in the boiler, and you'd put your wood and your stuff in and then when I closed it again he'd drop it a couple of notches to get the steam up."

"But the other son-of-a-gun, his brother, he was hard. He had arthritis awful bad and the kids used to play all kinds of tricks on him. In the engine they'd put stuff on his seat and that. He was miserable all the time but I got along pretty good with him. Only one day, he started giving me heck coming up the Royal Oak hill. He started to pick on me for some reason or other. He threw the Johnson Bar down and of course that knocked the fire all to hell. He said, 'Put some wood in there.' 'No, I'm not going to put wood in there until you push that Johnson Bar back.' 'No, I'm not pushing that Johnson Bar.' So we got just below the Royal Oak Hill and there we were, without steam. He sat there for about ten minutes and finally he gave up. He said, 'Alright, get the wood and I'll keep the Johnson Bar back.' From then on we got along pretty good. But he had arthritis awful bad, you know. The poor bugger could hardly straighten up..."

"And of course losing steam on that long grade from Sidney up to Meadow Farm. That was a tough one, you could have the best wood in the world but when you hit that grade with a good fire and the engineer was a little mad or something, he'd drop that Johnson Bar and increase the stroke of the engine. Well, gosh, there'd be no steam before you got half way up the hill."

"You see, you can't put any wood in because if you opened up the door you'd let all that cold air in, you see, and the steam would just go down. I used to put the odd stick in. I'd have my ass one way and I'd swing the door open and pull it shut quick and the old engineer said to me, 'that was good, son.' He was there (on the right seat in the cab) and I was over here (on the left side). I was left handed so I'd put my ass facing him and he says to me one day, 'I never had a fireman put his ass in my face and I'm not going to start now.' I said, 'you're going to live with it mister.' That's the only way I could fire. So he thought for awhile and then he grunted..."

"I know Herman Shade was the Head Conductor and Jack Walton was the engineer on the passenger and George Walton was the freight engineer. And Bill (Walker), he used to have a home out at Saanichton, the Conductor. His mother was the first nurse in Saanich and she used to tend our homes when anybody got sick and everything else. She did that for years..."

"I believe it was Thompson (one of the section gang foremen). He went to Royal Oak, as far as Royal Oak on this (Sidney) side and then another section boss from Royal Oak to Victoria. He had a family out here at Bazan Bay. He had two daughters and they were nice looking kids too. I used to go out dancing with his daughters. But then finally we just grew apart, after I got a job in town."

"They had pump cars. I can't remember what they were called. They had this handle and with four men on them, you'd go along pretty good..."

"Bill Butler who run the store (at Keatings) was the agent for the V.&S. at Keatings. I think he sold the tickets for the train out of the store. He used to run a stage from the train to the cement works. The cement works was going fairly good then..."

PLACES ALONG THE WAY

"There was (a brick plant) at Bazan Bay...with its own siding. (Also, on the site of the present Mayfair Shopping Centre in Victoria) there was a big one. I can remember them building these square things up and they'd be green - the clay. And there'd be fires lighted and you'd see them changing colour. Then finally when they were finished they were kind of an orange colour. They were making firebrick. The brick kilns were 20 or 30 feet long, eight or ten feet high. I think that Victoria was the big one (plant)."

"I started in 1916 and (the Sidney plant) was still going but I think it went out of business some years after that. They kept on and private people owned it for a long time. But it eventually run out of stuff (clay). The same with the Hillside one. They ran out of clay - that's the only reason they quit..."

"There was a big siding at Keatings. That's where I used to go to school. I used to go there (to the gravel pit). It was after the bend going to Saanichton, on your left as you headed towards Victoria. In fact, one of our boys... see we used to play in there. We used to dig holes and tunnels and go into the bank. One of the boys went in one day and it caved in...and smothered him. There was hell a poppin' over that..."

"There was a spur at Royal Oak and it connected somewhere there to a mill or something...and they did a lot of action there. The creamery was further in towards town..."

"I believe the track went down into the brickyard at Victoria (as opposed to just crossing it on the trestle)...I can't remember. The track came around pretty low there...there was quite a little climb (going south) to get across Hillside, then you started to wind up the grade from Hillside to the terminal. It was just about where the Hudson's Bay is now..."

"They had a big mill at Sidney (Sidney Rubber Roofing). That mill at Sidney was operating at full speed all through the war. The lumber and stuff just poured out of there. During the war little mills also sprung up in backyards, you know..."

"Victoria's station building was quite a big one. Sidney was just a square. All the way out to Sidney they were small and then Sidney was a little bigger and they had a small office in it. The roof overhung about three feet so you could walk underneath, and they piled the freight up along there..."

"Well I guess there weren't any telephones out there (the Sidney Station didn't have a telephone until 1917). I can remember us getting our telephone where I lived in the period around '16 or '17 or so, when the war was on. And we paid $2.50 a month for the phone..."

"(At the Sidney Sawmill) Mr. Walton was quite a man. I didn't know him too well but I know the name quite well. You forget a lot of things after all the years..."

"There was lumber and then there was a lot of stuff going out towards the mill. The mill had to have all this extra stuff sometimes. We'd have about seven carloads sometimes. Seven carloads going out..."

"I can't remember where, but I know there was a big (military camp) around here somewhere. We'd run a special train there back and forth to the city. There was just two passenger cars. And the gas electric would handle two. That grade coming up from Sidney to Spring Meadow Farm was a bad grade..."

"(To get up that hill from Bazan Bay to Saanichton, while hauling freight) it would depend what the load was. Sometimes the car would be loaded with sawdust or something like that. We might have up to seven cars..."

A MEMORABLE OCCASION

"We killed a couple of horses (near the gravel pit spur below Keatings) one night...(Walter had earlier described getting off the locomotive to check on an apparently dead horse. He kicked the horse and it let out a cry and jumped, scaring him badly)...It scared the hell out of me. I never got out (of the cab) again after it got dark. I never got off to go on the ground after that!"

THE LAST DAYS

"I think the gas car was taken away about two months before (the end of the V&S in 1919)..."

"The tracks were very rough. You'd go to put in a stick of wood (in the locomotive firebox) and you'd open the door and maybe the engine would lean that way, you know, and you'd miss the door. It was really tough. The boilers were getting shot. You carried 80 pounds of steam and weren't allowed to carry any more than that. I think one engine carried 120 but that would be the most..."

LIFE ON THE SAANICH PENINSULA

"We used to walk four miles to play basketball. Then we'd walk back. We worked ten hours a day on the baling machine (on the family farm). We'd play basketball for a couple of hours at night, we'd go to a dance, come home for a sleep and go back to work. That was the only thing you had to do in those days. You were brought up to do that and the work was no big deal, you know. We'd put out 32 tons a day (of hay). My chum and I used to pack that hay up eight feet high and stack it. We'd take a bale of hay and swing it on our knee or shoulder...You were hired to do it and it never used to bother us in those days. We'd play basketball after that and baseball on Sundays..."

"(The coming of the railway) was something new. The district was young and growing, you see, so we were getting a railroad and there was a lot of gossip and a lot of talk about it when it started. It gave the people something to talk about. There was nothing out here, just a couple of farms."

"And then the B.C. Electric put a track in just above there. There were three tracks on the peninsula - the C.N.R. the V.&S. and the B.C. Electric. But they were only three miles apart, going out to Sidney and back - three railways! The B.C. Electric went to Deep Cove. They put the track into Deep Cove figuring that it would be a great place for sports and picnics. They ran the track right into there and they had the whole area. We used to have some big picnics there. They'd come out from town..."

"Well that's all there was going. They looked to each other for a good time and they had a good time. I had a good time in my young days. I always found that I had a lot of friends. Even if you didn't know a man he'd come up to you and pat you on the shoulder or something and say 'I'm so and so...'"

APPENDIX I

OLD SIDNEY AS REMEMBERED BY MORAN BRETHOUR

Moran Brethour is the grandson of Julius Brethour, one of the principal backers of the original Sidney townsite. He grew up in Sidney during the 1920s and 30s, worked in the Sidney sawmill, and after a career in sawmilling elsewhere, returned to reside in Saanichton. He is an active member of the Saanich Pioneers' Society. The following sites in Sidney are as he remembers them.

1. Site of original Saanich Canning Co., built about 1905.
2. Site of old original Sidney Trading Co., owned partly by J.J. White and later sold to C.C. Cochran. Post Office was in this building. Later used as part of cannery.
3. Site of cannery warehouse and office, built in 1930s. Razed.
4. Original Sidney Hotel. Burned down.
5. Sidney Trading Co. store built in 1912. Torn down 1979.
6. House built by C.C. Cochran.
7. House once occupied by Sir Arthur Currie when he taught in Sidney.
8. House used by Lind family as a boarding house until the mid 1930s.
9. Bakery building built in 1930s.
10. Site of old Mill office until late 1920s.
11. Last offices and dry sheds of Sidney Lumber Co. built in late 1920s and later Mitchell & Anderson retail store and apartments. Now site of Landmark Bldg.
12. Site of Sidney Mills.
13. Three small stores including Bobby Sloan's Shoe Repair, Cornish Books (in 1930s).
14. Jim Critchley's grocery store.
15. Sidney Post Office 1912-1936.
16. Merchants Bank of Canada, later Bank of Montreal, then Cafes, etc.
17. David Craig's home and blacksmith shop.
18. Old mill boarding house run by Gerke. Torn down in 1920s.
19. Old mill boarding house, later "House of David" then dry shed for retail sales. Torn down in early 1930s.
20. J.J. White home called "Winona".
21. Old custom office when J.J. White was officer.
22. Sepher Halseth (head surveyor at mill) house. Married Ellen Berquist.

23. Sidney Super Service garage built by Earl McKenzie after fire in 1929. Later sold to Fred Wright.
24. Sam Roberts real estate office.
25. Earl McKenzie garage. Burned Nov. 21, 1929.
26. Seagull Inn boarding house run by James Speedie in 1920s and 30s. Later Cafe and bus depot run by Frank Godfrey.
27. George Brethour's home built about 1911.
28. House occupied by Fletcher & North (butcher) in 1920s.
29. Building where Sidney Review was printed for many years in 1920s and 30s.
30. George Brethour's carpenter shop. Torn down in early 40s.
31. Store and leather shop owned by Hearnes and later by Stan and Flossie Anderson.
32. Barber shop in 1940s.
33. V.I. Coach Lines storage shed for buses in 1930s and 40s.
34. Stacey's hall and ice cream parlour.
35. Nelson Fralick home and watchmaker shop.
36. Mrs. Babas Barber Shop in 1930s.
37. House originally owned by Bill Pollard.
38. Sam Fairclough house originally built ca. 1910. Later Sands Funeral parlour.
39. Harry Hooton house.
40. House
41. Clanton home.
42. House built by A.L. Wilson, cannery partner and superintendent. Now Dud Harvey.
43. "New School" built 1919. Now Masonic Hall.
44. Original Sidney school.
45. House
46. F.F. Foneri house. Review owner in early days.
47. Mill houses for married families of staff. Some moved in 1930s up Henry Avenue. One still there.
48. Chinatown. Mostly burned and torn down in mid 1930s.

49. Present post office built 1936.
50. Original Berquist Block. Burned down Jan. 19, 1928.
51. Berquist home and blacksmith shop. House moved and still exists on 3rd St.
52. Stores and old Lesage drug store, 1920s.
53. Simister's dry goods.
54. Halseth's Picture Show until 1920s.
55. Imperial Service station. George Gray, Bill Stacey, Charlie Douma, some of operators.
56. Alfred (Nip) Critchley home. Still existing.
57. Wesley Cowell's butcher shop and home.
58. United Church Manse (Keyworth) still exists as Chiropractic Clinic.
59. Wesley Hall.
60. John Matthew's home.
61. Old House (Moore's home) used in 1918 as school for primary grades due to overcrowding at Sidney school and while new school was being built.
62. Angus Ego pool room later Jack Gilman barber shop and pool room.
63. Hugh Moore's building.
64. Moorehouse home.
65. House
66. Old Sidney Lock-up (2 cells).
67. House occupied by Charlie Woods, cannery foreman in 1920s and 30s.
68. V&S Station. Later moved to 3rd and Bevan for Scout Hall, then to Colwood for proposed railway station but never used. Burned.
69. Matthew's Hall built by John Matthews and later moved. Is now existing Scout Hall.
70. House occupied by Holland the butcher in 1930s.
71. Kellys original Feed Store, later Mounce's Feed (and later Wyatt & Carrington Cafe).
72. V&S Engine House.
73. V&S Turn table.
74. V&S water tank.

75. Original Copeman house (Miss Copeman, later Mrs. Geo. Pearkes) bought by George Cochran in 1911.
76. Provincial Gov't offices and yard in 1940s.
77. Site of old Dance pavillion.
78. Area known as "The Park" in V&S history.
79. Fred William's machine shop and marine ways. Sold to Copeland & Wright in 1920.
80. V&S wharves.
81. Government wharf.
82. Site of old mill burner.
83. Ingamelles Bakery, later Bowcotts. Many years Liquor Store, now Salvation Army Thrift store.
84. Sidney Freight yards and coal sheds.
85. St. Andrews Anglican Church.
86. Dr. Macoun's office (famous botanist). Also headquarters of Alpine Club.
87. Capt. Byers' house. (Old sealing captain, later had taxi boat).
88. The Sidney Theatre built in 1920s replacing old one on Beacon Ave. (No. 54) same owners. Burnt down by Sidney Volunteer Fire Dept.
89. Anchor Bolt for sawmill Derrick guyline. Existing with plaque.
90. Site of sawmill Derrick
91. Booming ground.
92. Mill breakwater.
93. Site of Sidney Rubber Roofing plant (approx. 7 acres).
94. Sidney Roofing dock.
95. Old Great Northern dock. It was rebuilt to start the Anacortes ferry in 1922 and C.P.R. Bellingham ferry in 1923. It was destroyed in the Big Storm of 1929. Ferry accommodation was built at the foot of Beacon on the end of the Government dock.
96. Small Customs house and later bath house for swimmers.
97. Old original arch for travellers. Later moved to Beacon Ave. at head of wharf.
98. Site of old Sidney Water Sports Gala and swim meet (1920s).
99. Old sailing ship used as breakwater.
100. The present ferry dock for the Anacortes ferry.
101. Site of Converse & Brown's shingle mill.

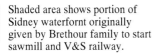 Shaded area shows portion of Sidney waterfornt originally given by Brethour family to start sawmill and V&S railway.

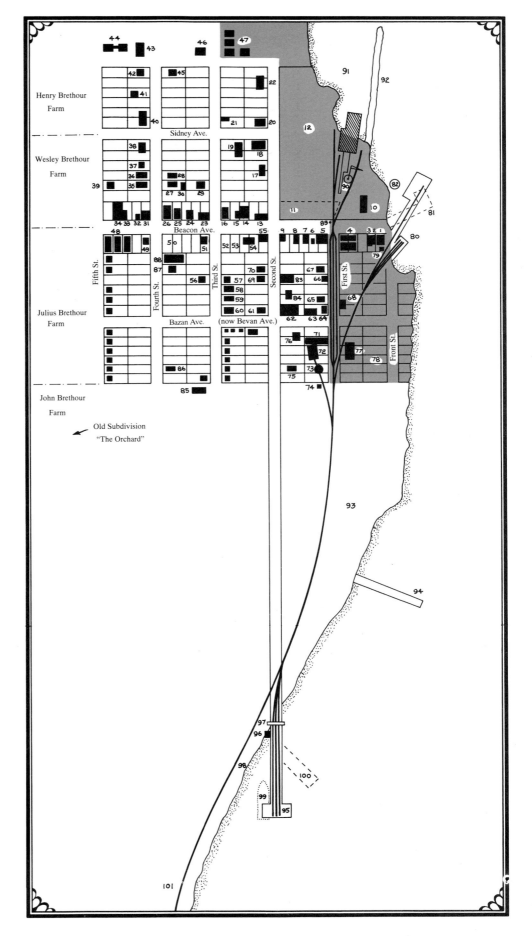

Characters by Affiliation

See Index for location in text.

FEDERAL GOVERNMENT OFFICIALS

De Cosmos, Amor, former Premier and M.P. for Victoria
Drayton, Sir H., Chairman, Board of Railway Commissioners
Jones, Captain, Dominion Department of Marine
Mackintosh, J.C., Federal Member of Parliament
Martin, Mr. Justice, of Supreme Court - commended Indian rescuers
Shepherd, F.H., M.P., presented medals to Indian heroes

BRITISH COLUMBIA GOVERNMENT OFFICIALS

Bullock-Webster, Superintendent of Police
Bunster, Arthur, former M.P.P. (M.L.A.) for Saanich area
Campbell, Constable, Provincial Police
Gamble, F.C., Chief Engineer and Inspector of Railways
McBride, Sir Richard, Premier, British Columbia
Morrison, Judge of Assize Court
Oliver, John, Premier and Minister of Railways
Pineo, A.V., Agent for Minister of Railways
Taylor, Thomas, Minister of Railways
Thomason, Provincial Boiler Inspector

VICTORIA CITY COUNCIL

Barnard, Alderman
Beaven, R., Mayor
Beckwith, Alderman
Grahame, Alderman
Hayward, Mayor
McCandless, Alderman, later Mayor
McGregor, Alderman
Munn, Alderman
Redfern, C.E., Mayor
Renouf, C.E., Alderman
Topp, City Engineer
Vincent, Alderman
Williams, Alderman
Wilmot, C.A., City Engineer
Yates, Alderman

SAANICH LAND COMPANY

Mackenzie, D., Vice-President, SLC
Rounding, S., Secretary of SLC
Tilton, E.G., Secretary-Treasurer, SLC
Wollaston, P., Director in SLC

VICTORIA AND SIDNEY RAILWAY

Anderson, J., General Manager V&S and VTR&F
Bodwell, E.V., Barrister, principal shareholder V&S/ VTR&F
Brethour, J., Provisional Director V&S
Brethour, H., Provisional Director V&S
Cowan, M.H., Vice-President and Treasurer V&S
Gray, J.H., Surveyor and Engineer for V&S
Irving, R., Secretary V&S
McNeill, President VTR&F/V&S
Macauley, W.J., Director V&S
Mackenzie, Captain S.F., General Manager VTR&F/V&S
Paterson, T.W., Contractor, principal shareholder, General Manager
Pemberton, J.D., Trustee VTR&F

Roberts, J.P., Receiver for V&S
Van Sant, F., General Manager VTR&F/V&S

VICTORIA AND SIDNEY RAILWAY EMPLOYEES

Andrews, F.J.
Bate, Walter, Fireman
Brethour, S.
Brownley, T., Brakeman
Carpenter, F., Brakeman
Dewitt, W., Fireman
Duncan, G., Fireman
Duncan, O., Brakeman
Forbes, A., Conductor
Foster, F., Brakeman
Halco, R., Brakeman
Hasker, D.M., Engineer
Hasker, E.A., Brakeman
Hodgson, R., Brakeman
Irvine, C., Wiper
Jenkins, Master Mechanic
Jones, A.K., Brakeman
Lacoursiere, A., Conductor
Lane, R., Night watchman and hostler
Mellado, Shopman, fireman
Parsons, G., Brakeman
Peterkin, R., Fireman
Ross, C., Brakeman
Shade, H., Brakeman, Conductor
Singh, P., Freight handler
Thomson, Section Foreman
Wake, Brakeman
Walker, R., Conductor
Walton, G.C. (George), Fireman, later Engineer
Walton, J., Wiper, Fireman, Engineer
Warne, W., Caretaker
White, J.J., Stationmaster Sidney

SIDNEY AND NANAIMO TRANSPORTATION COMPANY

Anderson, Master of S.S. Iroquois
Cavin, Capt., first Master of S.S. Iroquois
Fraser, Mate S.S. Iroquois
Harrison, Purser S.S. Iroquois
Isbister, J., Mate of S.S. Iroquois
Munro, A.D., Purser and Co-owner S&NTCo.
Paterson, T.W., first President S&NTCo.
Sears, A.A., Master and co-owner of S.S. Iroquois
Watson, A., Builder of S.S. Iroquois at Port Moody

VICTORIA TERMINAL RAILWAY AND FERRY COMPANY

Anderson, A., First Officer of S.S. Strathcona
Anderson, J., General Manager VTR&F
Bodwell, E.V., Shareholder VTR&F
Brown, Vice-President VTR&F
Fell, T., Solicitor for VTR&F
Henry, A.E., Shareholder VTR&F
Luke, Steward of S.S. Strathcona
McGuire, C., Chief Engineer S.S. Strathcona
McKay, Second Engineer S.S. Strathcona
Mackenzie, Captain S.F., General Manager VTR&F

McMillan, J., Civil Engineer
McNeill, A.H., Lawyer and VTR&F official
Mansell, Mate, *S.S. Victorian*
Newlands, L.C., Purser of *S.S. Strathcona*
Paterson, T.W., Advisor to General Manager VTR&F
Riley, Captain, Master of *S.S. Strathcona*
Rogers, J.W., Captain of *S.S. Victorian*
Van Sant, F., General Manager VTR&F
Wood, A.E., President, VTR&F

FERRY COMMITTEE

Baker, E.C., Businessman
Baker, M., Businessman
Beckwith, A., Victoria Alderman
Dunsmuir, J., Member and President E&N Railway
Ker, D.R., Businessman
McGregor, Victoria Alderman
Paterson, T.W., V&S General Manager
Shakespeare, Noah, Chairman of Committee
Wilson, A., Businessman

RAILWAY OFFICIALS (OTHER THAN V&S/VTR&F)

Great Northern Railway:
Bodwell, E.V., Counsel for GNR
Broughton, W.W., General Traffic Manager, GNR
Costello, Traffic Manager, GNR
Dale, R.W., General Agent, GNR
Gilman, A.C., Assistant to President, GNR
Guthrie, A., Agent for GNR takeover of VTR&F
Hill, J.J., President, GNR
Hill, Louis, Vice-President and later President of GNR
Canadian National Railways:
Cameron, CNR official
Hanna, D.B., President, CNR
Lewis, D.O., Official of CNR
Canadian Pacific Railway:
Abbot, H., General Superintendent, CPR, Pacific Division
Shaughnessy, Sir T., Vice-President, President CPR
Van Horne, Sir W.C., President CPR
Other Railways:
Atkinson, I.C., Vice-President, Port Angeles and Eastern Railroad
Courtney, G., Chief Passenger Agent, E&N Railway
Dunsmuir, J., President, E&N Railway
Goward, A.T., Local Manager British Columbia Electric Railway
Hendry, J., President of VW&Y Railway, agent for purchase of V&S, and shareholder in VTR&F
Irving, R., Manager of Kaslo and Slocan Railway (Former Secretary of V&S)
Jaffray, J., Agent for purchase of V&S
Mackenzie and Mann, Railway Contractors

SIDNEY SAWMILLS

Hammill, Partner in original Sidney Sawmill
Hewitt, M., Superintendent of Sidney mill construction
Morrison, E., Manager Sidney Sawmill
Patterson, Purchaser of Sidney Sawmill
Walton, G.H. (Geoff), Manager Sidney Sawmills
White, J.J., Manager Sidney Sawmills
Winston, H.C., Superintendent, Sidney Mills, Limited

BUSINESSMEN AND OTHERS

Bellinger, H., Partner in the Crofton Smelter
Bole, J., Teamster for Prairie Inn
Breen, Partner in Crofton Smelter
Bryden, T., Contractor

Call, J.J., Manager, Sidney Canning Company
Camp, J., Keeper of the Prairie Tavern
Chipman, C.C., Commissioner Hudson's Bay Company
Croft, Henry, Bidder for contract to build V&S
Cummings, Dr. G., Attended victims of *S.S. Iroquois* disaster
Dinsdale and Malcolm, Contractors
Elford and Smith, Victoria Brick Yard
Going, W.H., Member of V&S survey party
Hare, Captain M., Master of the *Mary Hare*
Jones, C.W., Engineer VW&Y Railway
Kirk and Company, Operators of motor freight service
Kwon Lee, Labour contractor
Lyon, W.H., Member of V&S survey party
McBean, A., Contractor
MacDonald, W.J., Victoria businessman
McHardy, Diver at Jack's Point wreck
Mayhew, Mr., Manager of Sidney Rubber Roofing Company
Moore and Pethick, Firm of contractors
Roberts, Sidney, Bank employee
St. Barbe, Charles, Founder of *Sidney and Islands Review*
Skinner, T., British businessman
Skene, J.L., Sidney Island Brick and Tile Company
Sloan Brothers, Seattle engineering contractors
Sorley, T.C., Civil Engineer
Troup, Captain J., Canadian Pacific Navigation Company
White, J.J., Owner in Sidney Canning Company
Wilson, J., Sidney businessman

CITIZENS

Birch, H., Landowner
Brethour, G., Rescuer in sinking of *S.S. Iroquois*
Charlie, D., Native rescuer in *S.S. Iroquois* disaster
Dean, J., Businessman, advocate for better service on V&S
Fox, G., Farmer
Gallagher, C., First fatality on V&S
Hagen, Farmer
Klutzwhalen, B., Native rescuer of *S.S. Iroquois* passengers
McArthur, J., rescuer of passengers from *S.S. Iroquois*
Macdonald, T., Landowner
Marcotte, Farmer
Moses, C., Landowner
Paten, R.B., Landowner
Phillipps-Wolley, Sir Clive, Writer and local Landowner
Reay, C.H., Farmer
Rippon, W., Landowner
Scalthorpe, W., Landowner
Taylor, W.S., Landowner
Thompson, Farmer
Turgoose, F., Farmer and Postmaster
Tzouhalem, W., rescuer of passengers from *S.S. Iroquois*
Winch, P., Landowner

Chronology

October 1879	A.R. Bunster proposes Victoria to Mainland rail and ferry connection from Saanich Peninsula.
1891	Amor De Cosmos proposes Victoria, Saanich and New Westminster Railway scheme - the "De Cosmos Scheme."
April 1892	Victoria and Sidney Railway is incorporated.
August 1892	Work begins on Sidney sawmill.
September 1, 1892	First Annual General Meeting of V&S.

October 1, 1892	Start date for construction of V&S Railway.
November 1892	Bonds to finance railway sold in New York.
December 1892	Sidney sawmill is completed.
March 1893	Tenders let for construction of Victoria and Sidney Railway.
April 28, 1893	Contract awarded to T.W. Paterson to build V&S Railway.
April 20, 1893	City requests revision of railway grade at Elk and Beaver Lakes to protect city water supply.
September 11, 1893	First rails arrive at Sidney on ship *Rathdown*.
October 3, 1893	Locomotive No.1 is delivered at Sidney.
January 1894	Temporary southern terminus established at Tolmie Avenue pending resolution of brickyard dispute.
June 2, 1894	First "official" trip over the V&S line.
April 1, 1895	V&S Company takes delivery of railway from contractor.
November 1895	First complaints of poor service.
December 1895	V&S gets mail contract for Saanich Peninsula.
February 10, 1896	Steamer *Mary Hare* burns at Thetis Island.
July 30, 1896	V&S running commuter trains for workers at Elk and Beaver Lake waterworks.
January 16, 1898	First fatal accident on the Victoria and Sidney.
July 1898	Committee set up to open communication with railways for a fast rail and ferry service from Victoria to the Mainland.
March 9, 1900	V&S is awarded Gulf Islands mail contract.
March 31, 1900	*S.S. Iroquois* arrives in Victoria for fitting up after construction at Port Moody.
April 19, 1900	First joint timetable of the V&S and Sidney and Nanaimo Transportation Company is published.
October 15, 1900	President James J. Hill of Great Northern Railway expresses interest in a Victoria railway connection.
November 29, 1900	"Victoria Terminal Railway By-Law, 1900" is ratified by Victoria ratepayers, assuring the construction of a rail and ferry connection to the Mainland.
January 1901	Plans perfected for combined rail/passenger ferry to the Mainland.
March 1901	Barge *Georgian* purchased by Captain S.F. Mackenzie of VTR&F for Sidney-Liverpool run.
April 13, 1901	Arrangements made for temporary rail barge service from Liverpool (opposite New Westminster) to Sidney.
October 1901	First annual general meeting of VTR&F Company.
November 1, 1901	Terminal Company acquires V&S.
November 7, 1907	Ground broken at Topaz Avenue for extension of VTR&F to Victoria's Market Building.
November 1901	Rails arrive at Liverpool for construction of Mainland section of VTR&F.
February 19, 1902	Puff of Locomotive heard in Chinatown.
February 26, 1902	*S.S. Iroquois* to serve new town of Crofton.
April 17, 1902	Crofton mails to go via V&S and S&NTCo.
May 29, 1902	Arrangements for purchase of sternwheeler *Strathcona* by Sidney and Nanaimo Transportation Company are completed.
June 16, 1902	First car over Great Northern system arrives in Victoria from Chicago.
June 24, 1902	*Strathcona* begins service on Sidney-Nanaimo run.
August 20, 1902	*Strathcona* blows cylinder head and is withdrawn from Sidney to Nanaimo route after only two months service.
September 1902	Announced purchase of the VTR&F and V&S by John Hendry and A.H. Guthrie. (This is the Great Northern takeover).
October 5, 1902	Victoria Terminal Railway and Ferry Company and Victoria and Sidney Railway absorbed into Great Northern system.
January 1903	Victoria city extension is completed after delay in obtaining crossing over Douglas Street.
January 12, 1903	*S.S. Victorian* arrives in Victoria for conversion into a combined rail and passenger ferry.
March 1903	Locomotive No.3 arrives on V&S and enters service.
April 30, 1903	Port Guichon-Cloverdale line of VTR&F completed.
May 6, 1903	Introductory excursion from Sidney to Port Guichon and return on *S.S. Victorian*.
November 26, 1903	Sidney and Nanaimo Transportation Company and *S.S. Iroquois* sold to Sears and Munro.
July 1904	City refuses to make first subsidy payment to VTR&F as in Agreement of 1900 because new ferry was not built in Victoria.
March 17, 1905	Agreement between Victoria and VTR&F is reached. VTR&F to forego subsidy and *S.S. Victorian* to be withdrawn from Sidney-Port Guichon run in favour of a tug and barge service.
April 1, 1905	New short line cutoff from Oliver's, on VTR&F line, and Liverpool is completed.
May 10, 1907	Derailment on Sidney ballast spur and cars in sea.
July 8, 1907	One of VTR&F locomotives returns from rebuilding at Delta, Michigan.
July 14, 1907	V&S has two accidents in one day.
August 14, 1907	V&S train derailed be fallen tree.
August 20, 1907	Locomotive ran off Sidney dock "a few days ago."
November 1, 1907	Mainland section of VTR&F taken over by the Vancouver, Victoria and Eastern Railway.
May 1908	Great Northern constructs new barge in Seattle for Sidney-Port Guichon run.
May 20, 1908	*Strathcona* is sold after six years at quayside in Victoria.
July 1908	Great Northern locomotive No.290 arrives at Sidney for service on V&S.
October 25, 1908	*S.S. Iroquois* sunk in fog off Jack's Point, near Nanaimo.

October 30, 1908	*S.S. Iroquois* floated by salvage tug *William Joliffe* and towed to Victoria for repairs.
November 4, 1908	*S.S. Iroquois* back in service.
April 27, 1909	V&S train kills horse from Prairie Tavern.
May 28, 1909	VTR&F agree to vacate Market Building and move to new station on Blanshard Street.
August 21, 1909	Protests of Blanshard Street owners hold up construction of new VTR&F station.
May 12, 1910	Rumour is circulating that Canadian Northern Railway will build rail ferry connection at Deep Cove.
May 13, 1910	New car ferry to serve the Sidney-Mainland run.
August 26, 1910	Fires along V&S require assistance of Provincial forestry officials and police.
September 8, 1910	V&S service is arraigned.
September 1910	Contract let for new VTR&F station on Blanshard Street.
December 19, 1910	Market Building is vacated.
December 25, 1910	New Blanshard Street station is completed.
April 10, 1911	*S.S. Iroquois* founders off Sidney with loss of 21 lives.
April 1912	City of Victoria brings suit against V&S for recovery of bond interest subsidy funds.
Spring 1913	Temporary transfer spur constructed between V&S and new B.C. Electric line at Saanichton for transfer of Interurban railway equipment and supplies.
May 13, 1913	V&S finally wipes out its debt to the City of Victoria and the Province of British Columbia and Great Northern assumes financial responsibility for bond interest through its subsidiary, the Vancouver, Victoria and Eastern Railway and Navigation Company. Great Northern agrees to bring in modern equipment and upgrade the V&S Railway facilities.
June 13, 1913	Temporary interchange track is removed.
June 16, 1913	Work train arrives on V&S to install longer turntables in preparation for introduction of new gas-electric passenger car.
June 18, 1913	B.C. Electric Interurban line from Victoria to Deep Cove opens.
July 13, 1913	Two new turntables in place at Victoria and Sidney for gas-electric car.
July 14, 1913	New gas-electric arrives at Sidney for service on the V&S.
July 16, 1913	Grading of Canadian Northern Pacific line on Saanich Peninsula about to begin.
October 30, 1913	Promised track improvements completed on V&S.
August 1914	New Great Northern barge slip completed at Sidney.
August 9, 1915	Explosives plant at James Island to open.
September 2, 1915	Rails ready for laying of Patricia Bay Branch of Canadian Northern Pacific Railway.
February 1, 1916	The "Big Snow of 1916" begins. V&S tied up by deep snow for nine days.
Summer 1916	Military camp at Sidney improves traffic revenues on the V&S. Special military trains run from Victoria to Sidney.
November 1916	Work begins in preparation for reopening of the Sidney Sawmill which has been closed since September 1913. Military camp closes.
February 1917	Sidney Sawmill to be reopened.
May 1917	First telephone is installed at Sidney station.
June 7, 1917	Board of Railway Commissioners order Canadian Northern Pacific Railway to construct interchange track with V&S at Sidney.
September 1, 1917	V&S Bonds mature and become payable in full. No apparent immediate action taken by bondholders. Great Northern withdraws its equipment from the V&S.
January 3, 1918	First cars leave Sidney over the CNPR enroute to Canadian prairies with lumber from Sidney Mill.
May 1918	Sidney Sawmills are booming.
July 11, 1918	Captain Albert A. Sears of *S.S. Iroquois* dies.
Summer 1918	Service reduced to a single daily passenger train and freight service as required. The end is near.
April 3, 1919	Government gives assurance of continued service if V&S shuts down.
April 5, 1919	V&S will make its last run on April 30,1919.
April 30, 1919	Victoria and Sidney Railway makes its last scheduled run.
May 3, 1919	Board of Trade wants CNPR to run V&S into Sidney until longterm arrangements for service can be made.
June 26, 1919	Returned soldiers propose motor jitney service over the V&S.
Summer 1919	CNPR takes over Sidney section of V&S on permit authority from Provincial Minister of Railways.
December 1919	Canadian National Railways purchase Bazan Bay to Sidney portion of V&S line as part of their Saanich Peninsula lines.
1919 to early 1930s	CNPR provides railway service to town of Sidney until sawmill closes in the Great Depression.

Numbered Notes

In the interests of readability, numbered notes have been kept to a minimum by citing the source of the note in the main text. Copies of all reference material used for this work will be available at the Saanich Pioneer Society in Saanichton and will be made available to such other local museums and archives as may desire to copy them. In addition, a list of other printed materials used in the preparation of this books is also appended.

Chapter 1

1. V.&S. Railway Charter, April 23, 1892.
2. Victoria and Sidney Railway Interest By-Law, July 20, 1892.
3. Hearn, George and Wilkie, David *The Cordwood Limited*, B.C. Railway Historical Association, 5th Revised Edition, 1976.
4. Victoria *Daily Colonist*, May 15, 1894, page 5.

5. Victoria, B.C., Provincial Archives, Report of the Minister of Railways For 1955, DD 9.

Chapter 2
1. Victoria, B.C., Legislative Library, Dominion of Canada Sessional Papers, Summary Statements, Department of Railways and Canals For Year Ending June 30, 1896.

Chapter 3
1. Victoria *Daily Colonist*, March 25, 1899, page 2.
2. Victoria *Daily Colonist*, April 15, 1899, page 2.
3. Ibid.
4. Ibid.
5. Victoria, B.C., Legislative Library, Dominion of Canada Sessional Papers, Summary Statements, Department of Railways and Canals for 1895 to 1899.
6. Victoria *Daily Colonist*, July 22, 1899, page 2.
7. Victoria *Daily Colonist*, September 22, 1899, page 4.
8. City of Victoria, "Victoria and Saanich Railway Extension Loan By-Law, 1900." Published in Victoria *Daily Colonist*, February 22, 1900, page 7.
9. Ibid., p.7.
10. Victoria *Daily Colonist*, February 27, 1900, p. 4.

Chapter 4
1. Nanaimo, B.C., *Nanaimo Herald*, April 3, 1900.
2. Ibid.
3. *Victoria Daily Times*, August 14, 1900.

Chapter 5
1. *Victoria Daily Times*, October 3, 1900, p.8.
2. *Victoria Daily Times*, October 15, 1900, p.8.
3. *Victoria Daily Times*, October 19, 1900, p.6.
4. Ibid.
5. Victoria *Daily Colonist*, October 16, 1900.
6. *Victoria Daily Times*, November 5, 1900.
7. Victoria *Daily Colonist*, November 8, 1901.

Chapter 6
1. *Victoria Daily Times*, January 11, 1902.
2. *Crofton Gazette and Cowichan News*, July 22, 1902.
3. *The Daily Herald*, Nanaimo, July 12, 1902.

Chapter 7
1. *Victoria Daily Times*, February 6, 1902.
2. *Victoria Daily Times*, August 23, 1902.
3. Victoria *Daily Colonist*, November 29, 1902.
4. *Victoria Daily Times*, January 8, 1903.
5. *Victoria Daily Times*, February 3, 1903.

Chapter 8
1. Victoria *Daily Colonist*, June 3, 1903.
2. Victoria *Daily Colonist*, June 9, 1903.
3. Victoria *Daily Colonist*, June 17, 1903.
4. Ibid.
5. *Daily News-Advertiser*, Vancouver, July 19, 1903.
6. Victoria *Daily Colonist*, October 7, 1903.
7. *The Daily Herald*, Nanaimo, November 27, 1903.
8. Victoria *Daily Colonist*, August 24, 1904.
9. Victoria *Daily Colonist*, June 20, 1905.

Chapter 9
1. Victoria *Daily Colonist*, May 11, 1907.
2. Victoria *Daily Colonist*, April 11, 1908.

Chapter 10
1. Victoria *Daily Colonist*, September 12, 1908.
2. Victoria *Daily Colonist*, March 15, 1910.
3. Ibid.
4. Victoria *Daily Colonist*, (Supplement), June 27, 1909.
5. Victoria *Daily Colonist*, September 8, 1910.
6. Victoria *Daily Colonist*, November 9, 1910.

Chapter 11
1. Victoria *Daily Colonist*, Islander Magazine, August 16, 1970 - Interview - Sidney Roberts, by T.W. Paterson.
2. *Victoria Daily Times*, April 11, 1911.
3. *Victoria Daily Times*, April 10, 1911.
4. Victoria *Daily Colonist*, Islander Magazine, August 16, 1970 - Interview - Sidney Roberts, by T.W. Paterson.
5. *Victoria Daily Times*, June 9, 1911.
6. *Victoria Daily Times*, September 14, 1911.

Chapter 12
1. Victoria *Daily Colonist*, June 7, 1912.
2. Ibid.
3. Victoria *Daily Colonist*, July 13, 1912.
4. Victoria *Daily Colonist*, October 2, 1912.
5. Victoria *Daily Colonist*, October 22, 1919.
6. Victoria *Daily Colonist*, July 19, 1913.
7. Victoria *Daily Colonist*, July 9, 1913, p.4.
8. Ibid, p.2.

Chapter 13
1. *The Sidney and Islands Review*, Sidney, B.C., January 9, 1914.
2. *The Sidney and Islands Review*, Sidney, B.C., February 10, 1916.
3. *The Sidney and Islands Review*, Sidney, B.C., May 25, 1916.

Chapter 14
1. *The Sidney and Islands Review*, Sidney, B.C., May 17, 1917.
2. *The Sidney and Islands Review*, Sidney, B.C., June 7, 1917, page 1.
3. Ibid, p.3.
4. *The Sidney and Islands Review*, Sidney, B.C., January 10, 1918, page 1.
5. *The Sidney and Islands Review*, Sidney, B.C., May 2, 1918.
6. Interview - Walter Bate by author (See Appendix H).
7. *Victoria Daily Times*, April 30, 1919.
8. *The Sidney and Islands Review and Saanich Gazette*, Sidney, B.C., May 1, 1919.

Other References

BOOKS

Akrigg, G.P.V. and Helen B., *British Columbia Place Names*, Sono Nis Press, Victoria, 1988.

Beebe, Lucius and Clegg, Charles, *Mixed Train Daily*, Howell North Books, Berkeley, California, 1961.

Gosnell, R.E., *The Year Book of British Columbia and Manual of Provincial Information, 1897*, Victoria, Queen's Printer, 1897.

Harvey, R.D., "History of Saanich Peninsula Railways," *Annual Report, Railway Department of British Columbia, 1955*, Victoria, Queen's Printer, 1956.

Hearn, George and Wilkie, David, *The Cordwood Limited*, Revised Fifth Edition, 1976, Victoria, British Columbia Railway Historical Association.

Skelton, Oscar D., *The Railway Builders*, Toronto, Glasgow, Brook and Company, 1921.

Turner, Robert D., *Vancouver Island Railroads*, Golden West Books, San Marino, California, 1973.

White, Elwood and Wilkie, David, *Shays On The Switchbacks*, Revised Fourth Edition, 1973, Victoria, British Columbia Railway Historical Association.

NEWSPAPERS AND PERIODICALS

The *B.C. Mining Record*, 1895 to 1913, Victoria, B.C.

The *B.C. Mining Exchange and Engineering News*, Victoria, B.C.

The *Crofton Gazette*, Crofton, B.C.

The *Crofton Gazette and Cowichan News*, Crofton, B.C.

The *Daily Colonist*, Victoria, B.C.

The *Daily News-Advertiser*, Vancouver, B.C.

The *Daily World*, Vancouver, B.C.

The *Nanaimo Free Press*, Nanaimo, B.C.

The *Nanaimo Daily Herald*, Nanaimo, B.C.

The Province, Victoria, B.C., 1894-1898.

The *Province*, Vancouver, B.C.

The *Victoria Daily Times*, Victoria, B.C.

GOVERNMENT REPORTS

"Railway Statistics of the Dominion of Canada," from the *Report of the Deputy Minister of Railways and Canals, 1895 to 1920*, Printed By Order of Parliament, Ottawa, Queen's and King's Printer, Ottawa.

NOTES

a. The research materials used in the preparation of this book are being copied by the Saanich Pioneers' Society and will be available for scrutiny by interested parties or other researchers.

b. The right to copy all reference materials is also offered to the Sidney Museum and any other historical or heritage group that may find them to be useful.

c. The majority of research work for this book was done over a period of more than 2 years in the Provincial Archives and the Provincial Library at Victoria.

d. Map information was obtained from the Legal Surveys Branch and the Archives Map Collection at Victoria.

e. Many legal papers and contracts used as sources of information were obtained from the files of the Solicitor for Victoria in the City Archives. Other information will be found in the records of the City Engineer in the same archives.

f. Much information about the physical layout of the line in later years was obtained in interviews with the late Walter Bate, the only surviving Victoria and Sidney Railway employee at that time.

g. The abandoned grade of the Victoria and Sidney Railway is accessible as a walking and bicycling path in the area of Elk and Beaver Lakes and the author made several visits to sites in the area to verify map and construction specification information.

Photo Credits

(Placement code: T - top; B - bottom; LT - left top; RB - right bottom, etc.)

Author's photos, 161 ... **Boam**, 179 ... **Tom Bown Collection, courtesy of Robert Turner**, 102 (Maynard photo) ... **B.C. Railway Historical Association**, 21, 130 ... **G. Currie Collection**, 143 ... **Delta Museum and Archives**, 90, 103, 104 ... **Norman Gidney Collection**, Appendix F ... **Gosnell**, 16, 20, 36-37 ... **Great Northern Photo**, 32, 146 ... **Howay**, 22 ... **Oscar Jacobson Collection from D. Wilkie**, 184 ... **Allan Klenman Collection**, 150 ... **A.J. Lacoursiere photos**, 62, 162, 172, 186 ... **Colin McKenzie photo**, 207 ... **Gavin Mouat Collection**, 125 ... **Collection of Fred Musclow**, 156 ... **Don and Wendy Norris**, 5 ... **R. Phillips photos**, 192, 208 ... **Provincial Archives of B.C.**, 14 (32104), 16-B (2627), 23-B (56601), 25 (95943), 35 (57185), 40-41, 46 (9392), 56 , 61 (92066), 71-T (96129), 71-B (80799), 73, 78 (49456), 82-T (57314), 82-B (80687), 83 (80688), 84-85 (822), 99-B (320), 111, 117 (68876), 122 (61627), 132 (96131) 158 (61840), 165 (27262), 184-BL, 195 (61844) , 200 (44770)... **Collection of Mrs. C. Rivers**, 153 (Associated Screen Gems photo) ... **G.W. Rogers Collection, courtesy Mrs. Griffin**, 126 ... **Freda Rook Collection**, 120 (W. McMillan photo), 145 ... **C. Rudolph Collection, courtesy F. DeGrouchy**, 148 ... **Saanich Municipal Archives**, 180 ... **Sacred Heart Pastoral Centre Archives**, 68-69 ... **Saanich Pioneers' Society**, 18, 23-TL, 23-TR, 24, 28 (Mrs. O. Coleman), 42, 87, 204-T, 204-B ... **Sidney Museum**, 201 ... **Photo courtesy of Robert Turner**, 176 ... **Victoria City Archives**, 65, 115, 135 (courtesy Jim Gilbert) ... **Victoria** *Daily Colonist*, 88 ... **Victoria** *Daily Times*, 93 ... **Elwood White photos**, 124 ... **H. Whiteoak photo**, 168 ... **David Wilkie Collection**, 129, 170, 173 and 183 (A.J.A. Lacoursiere photos), 174, 189-T, 189-B, 190, 198, 199, ... **Mr. E. Zimmerman Collection**, 137.

Note: Provincial Archive (PABC) photos are followed by catalogue numbers in brackets.

Index

Photographs or illustrations are shown in italics. Information in Appendices is not included.